Searching for Family and Community History in Wales

*Rheinallt Llwyd
and D. Huw Owen (eds.)*

First published in 2014

© the individual authors

© Gwasg Carreg Gwalch 2014

Published with the financial support
of the Welsh Books Council

ISBN: 978–1–84524–466–5

Cover design: Elgan Griffiths

Published by Gwasg Carreg Gwalch,
12 Iard yr Orsaf, Llanrwst, Wales LL26 0EH

Tel: 01758 750432
email: books@carreg-gwalch.com
internet: www.carreg-gwalch.com

Contents

Preface

Local history courses, in both Welsh and in English, had been taught over an extended period of time by the two editors who came to realise, independently of each other, the need for an introductory volume in the Welsh language for active community and family historians within Wales. For those students pursuing English-language courses, reference could be made to a large number of valuable and attractively-produced guides which related to Wales as well as England: this was true, despite the title, of W. B. Stephens's *Sources for English Local History* (1981). Significant developments for studies in a Welsh context were the publication of two volumes edited by John and Sheila Rowlands, namely *Welsh Family History: A Guide to Research* (1993) and *Second Stages in Researching Welsh Ancestry* (1999) [A recent publication in this field was Bruce Durie's *Welsh Genealogy* (2012)].

The intention to rectify the lack of provision for the increasing number of Welsh-language community historians and genealogists was responsible for the publication of *Olrhain Hanes Bro a Theulu* (2009) [Tracing the History of Community and Family], edited by the editors of the present volume, and containing nineteen chapters written by acknowledged authorities in their respective fields of study. A favourable response was elicited, and the receipt of numerous requests to make the contents available to a wider English-language readership explains the appearance of this volume. Six of the chapters were originally written in English and translated by the editors, but their authors, together with the other contributors, have prepared revised versions of their work for this publication. An innovation in the present volume is the chapter on the National Library of Wales by Beryl Evans, Research Services Manager at the National Library. She has also prepared the chapter on the Census; it is with sadness that we refer to the death on 14 March 2011 of Hafina Clwyd, the author of the corresponding chapter in the Welsh-language volume.

A feature of some of the attractively-produced and remarkably-comprehensive English-language volumes published on this subject, such as David Hey's *Journeys in Family History* (2004), was the employment of a team of researchers to assist the author. Unfortunately we were not blessed with similar resources!

The two of us soon realised the extent and magnitude of our task, but at the same time we appreciated the specialist knowledge of our contributors, and their mastery of the relevant sources. They were granted complete freedom to discuss their subjects, and our role was to attempt the standardisation of references, etc. The contributors provided relevant references, and in some instances, the inclusion of Welsh-language entries may be explained by the nature of the subject being discussed and the absence of corresponding English-language sources. The inevitable consequence of examining themes that are often inter-related was the apparent tendency for one chapter to infringe on another. However, the provision of a brief index compiled by Mary Owen will hopefully assist the reader to locate various references to the same subject. Also, whilst we were aware that in the context of community and family history studies some important topics have not been given sufficient attention, such as educational sources and paupers' documents, a limit to our coverage had to be set! We are extremely grateful to all the contributors for their patience and tolerance!

Numerous references have been included to current websites, yet we are aware that these may well be subject to sudden changes and we would therefore advise readers to check the possible website of a specific institution.

We wish to express our appreciation to a number of institutions for allowing us to copy and reproduce materials which are in their custody, and for allowing us to publish them on very generous terms. We wish to sincerely thank The National Archives and *findmypast.co.uk*; the National Library of Wales; the Royal Commission on the Ancient and Historical Monuments of Wales; St. Fagans: National History Museum; Carmarthenshire Archives Services; Ceredigion Archives; and Glamorgan Archives. In addition to the support and guidance of the members of staff of the institutions named above we also wish to especially thank the following for the assistance provided by them in many ways: Iwan ap Dafydd; John E. Davies, Gerallt Nash, Helen Palmer, Richard Suggett and Beth Thomas.

We were also able to reproduce a number of photographs from the collection of Gwasg Carreg Gwalch. Dr. Michael Powell Siddons allowed us to reproduce the photographs of the heraldic genealogical roll of John Hughes, parson of Llanwrin, by Rhys Cain. Dr. Evan L. James is the owner of the photographs of the gravestones of Moelona in the Capel Hawen graveyard and of the Rev. Peter Joseph and Joseph Joseph in the Llwynrhydowen burial ground; and William Troughton those of the crew of the steamer *Glanhafren*, salmon fishing, Tresaith, Tal-y-llyn lake, the Aberystwyth promenade and the Lisburne Arms, Pontrhydygroes, c.1910. Tegwyn Jones has kindly allowed us to copy the ballads whose illustrations accompany Chapter 18.

We also wish to express our appreciation to Elgan Griffiths for his technical expertise in copying many visual items and for designing the cover of the volume. Gwasg Carreg Gwalch has supported the venture from the outset. We wish to thank Myrddin ap Dafydd and his staff for all the work undertaken by them, and we especially appreciate the editorial duties performed with thoroughness and efficiency by Jen Llywelyn. As co-editors we have sought to ensure that all the bibliographical details and website references are accurate, but we are aware that some of the latter may well have changed by the time that the volume is published. We are also aware that the two of us are responsible for any errors which remain.

Rheinallt Llwyd/D. Huw Owen

List of Abbreviations

BBCS	*Bulletin of the Board of Celtic Studies*
DWH	*The Development of Welsh Heraldry*
GCH	*Glamorgan County History*
JHSChW	*Journal of the Historical Society of the Church in Wales*
JHSPCW	*Journal of the Historical Society of the Presbyterian Church of Wales*
JWEH	*Journal of Welsh Ecclesiastical History*
JWRH	*Journal of Welsh Religious History*
NLW	National Library of Wales
NLWJ	*National Library of Wales Journal*
NMRW	National Monuments Record of Wales
ODNB	Oxford Dictionary of National Biography
PCC	Prerogative Court of the Archbishop of Canterbury
PCY	Prerogative Court of the Archbishop of York
RCAHMW	Royal Commission on the Ancient and Historical Monuments of Wales
RCLWM	Royal Commission on Land in Wales and Monmouthshire
T Caerns HS	*Transactions of the Caernarfonshire Historical Society*
TAAS	*Transactions of the Anglesey Antiquarian Society*
Trans. Cymmr.	*Transactions of the Honourable Society of Cymmrodorion*
TWBHS	*Transactions of the Welsh Baptist Historical Society*
WG	*Welsh Genealogies*
WJRH	*Welsh Journal of Religious History*

1. Family and Community History in Wales

D. Huw Owen

The significantly increased interest in family and community history studies during recent years is reflected in the popularity of relevant publications, including magazines such as *Your Family History Magazine*, and the *Family Tree Magazine*; television programmes such as *Who do you think you are?*; the '*Who Do You Think You Are? Live Family History Road Show*' held annually at Olympia, London; and websites such as *Ancestry.co.uk* and *findmypast.co.uk*.

Attempts to explain this trend have referred to the need to discover roots and establish a measure of stability in communities that have experienced exceptional fluctuations caused by cataclysmic social, demographic and technological developments. Wales has not been an exception to these exciting trends, and many newcomers, as well as native Welsh people, have become fully involved in local and family history societies. At the same time there have been expressed two long-standing literary and historiographical traditions, extending over many centuries, from an early date to the present day, of praising a specific locality and tracing the genealogy and family background of an individual.

An intense attachment and allegiance to one's family and locality reflected social and political conditions in early medieval Wales. The kindred grouping occupied a crucial element in Welsh law, and Gerald of Wales, in the late twelfth century, emphasised the importance to the ordinary individual of a knowledge of one's family background. The significance of genealogy and of heraldry in medieval and early modern Wales is discussed by Michael Powell Siddons in Chapter 4, and he refers to the important publications in these fields by himself and P. C. Bartrum.[1]

Detailed descriptions of the localities visited by Gerald of Wales during his tour of 1188 were presented in his volumes, *Itinerarium Kambriae* (History of the Journey through Wales) and *Descriptio Kambriae* (Description of Wales).[2] John Leland travelled extensively throughout the country following his appointment as Royal Antiquary and the commission granted to him in 1533 to inspect the antiquities of Wales and England.[3] A number of significant antiquarian works were produced during the second half of the sixteenth century, and in Wales *Morganiae Archaiographia, A Book of the Antiquities of Glamorganshire*, compiled by Rice Merrick (*c.*1520–1586/7) during the period 1578–1584, was influenced both by contemporary antiquarian scholars and also by the Welsh bardic tradition, with hospitality provided for itinerant poets at Merrick's home, Cottrell, in the parish of St Nicholas, Glamorgan.[4] Gruffudd Hiraethog (d. 1564) and Lewys Dwnn (fl. 1568–1616), both of whom were professionally trained bards, served as deputy heralds appointed by the king of arms, visiting all parts of Wales.

Rhys Merrick,
A Booke of Glamorganshire
Antiquities *(1578)*

By this time the study of genealogy and of the local community was of increasing interest to antiquarian scholars in Wales as in England. A network of contacts linked together Lewys Dwnn with George Owen of Henllys (1552–1613), whose *The Description of Penbrokshire* (1603) appeared a year after his map of Pembrokeshire, which was published by his friend William Camden in the 1607 edition of *Britannia*.[5] The English translation of *Britannia* by Philemon Holland in 1610 influenced Sir John Wynn of Gwydir near Llanrwst (1553–1627), the scholar, bardic patron and author of *The History of the Gwydir Family and Memoirs*, published in 1770.[6] Camden's *Britannia* also motivated Edward Lhuyd, of Llanforda, Oswestry (1660–1709), who contributed sections on Wales to Edmund Gibson's new translation and edition, published in 1695. In 1697 he distributed 4,000 copies of his 'Parochial Queries', containing questions on antiquities, place-names, customs, and natural history, and he toured Wales systematically in the following three years. His manuscripts illustrate his wide-ranging antiquarian, archaeological, philological, and scientific interests.[7]

Edward Lhuyd, c.1660–1709

Camden's influence continued into the second half of the eighteenth century, with Thomas Pennant (1726–98), born at Downing in the parish of Whitford, Clwyd, contributing to Richard Gough's translation and edition of *Britannia* (1789). Pennant, who was mainly interested in antiquarianism, geology, and natural history, was the the author of *Tours in Wales* (1784) and *History of the Parishes of Whitford and Holywell* (1796).[8] Pennant concentrated on north Wales, but contemporary information on south Wales was provided by Benjamin Heath Malkin in his *The Scenery, Antiquities and Biography of South Wales* (1804).[9]

In the early nineteenth century a number of county history volumes were published, including those of Brecknockshire by Theophilus Jones; Ceredigion, by Samuel Rush Meyrick, and Pembrokeshire by Richard

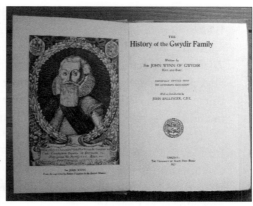

Sir John Wynn,
The History of the Gwydir Family *(1770)*

Gwydir Castle, Llanrwst

Fenton.[10] Whilst living in London, Fenton was a member of influential literary and cultural societies. One of these was the Gwyneddigion, and other prominent members included the lexicographer William Owen Pughe (1759–1835)[11] and the poet and antiquarian Edward Williams, 'Iolo Morganwg' (1747–1826), whose diverse interests and activities have been examined in a series of publications prepared by the University of Wales Centre for Advanced Welsh and Celtic Studies.[12] Another London-based cultural and patriotic society was the Honourable Society of Cymmrodorion, founded in 1751, revived in 1820, and again in 1873, and which continues to be active today. The society has promoted and published scholarly works, including significant studies in genealogy and local history, and the *Dictionary of Welsh Biography* (1959, 2001), providing information on the lives of eminent Welsh people who died before 1970.[13] The society's *Transactions* has continued to appear regularly since 1893, and it has also published the journal *Y Cymmrodor* from 1877 to 1951, and thirteen volumes in the *Cymmrodorion Record Series* (1899–1936), including George Owen's volume on Pembrokeshire.[14]

The study of family and community history in Wales also benefited from record publishing ventures in England, such as the *Record Commission* series, the *Rolls Series*, and the publications of the Historical Manuscripts Commission. Material relating to Wales in repositories in England, especially the British Library and The National Archives, formed in 2003 by the amalgamation of the Public Record

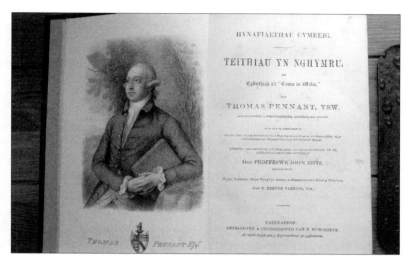

Title page of Thomas Pennant, Teithiau yng Nghymru *(1884)*
[Welsh translation of Tours in Wales *(1784)]*

Office and the Historical Manuscripts Commission, explains the importance to Welsh scholars of these collections and associated finding-aids and publications.[15]

The earliest scholarly society in Wales, and one which continues to flourish, is the Cambrian Archaeological Association, founded in 1846 for the study and the preservation of the antiquities of Wales. Its journal, *Archaeologia Cambrensis*, contains material on genealogy, heraldry, toponomy, folklore, and literature; reports on the society's excavations; and a review of periodical publications in the preceding year. Indexes have been published for the periods 1846–1900 (1964), 1901–1960 (1976), 1961–1980 (2004), and 1981–2000 (2008). Special publications include the proceedings of a conference held at Lampeter in 1985, and a collection of twenty-five essays in honour of Frances Lynch, published in 2012.[16] Each one of the historic counties of Wales has a county history society, of which the oldest is The Powysland Club, which has published the journal *The Montgomeryshire Collections* since 1868, and also a number of other publications, including a county atlas in 1999.[17] Other local historical journals established in the nineteenth century and containing material of Welsh interest include the *Journal of the Chester and North Wales Archaeological and Historic Society* (1849), the *Transactions of the Woolhope Naturalists'*

Field Club (1851), the *Report and Transactions of the Cardiff Naturalists' Society* (1867), and the *Transactions of the Caradoc and Severn Valley Field Club* (1893). Within Wales, county history societies, producing journals which are normally published annually, were established in Carmarthenshire (1905), Cardiganshire (1909–39, 1950), Anglesey (1911), Flintshire (1911, 1951), Brecknock (1928–9), Radnorshire (1931), Caernarfonshire (1939), Merioneth (1950), Denbighshire (1952), Monmouthshire (1954), Glamorgan (1957), and Pembrokeshire (1959). Some anniversaries have been celebrated by special issues. Terrence James' outline of the history of the Carmarthenshire Antiquarian History Society was one of several commemorative contributions in the centennial year issue of *The Carmarthenshire Antiquary* in 2005; the golden jubilee issue of *Morgannwg* in the following year included Gwynedd O. Pierce's survey of the early years of the Glamorgan County History; and in 2009 Geraint H. Jenkins focused attention on the founders of the Ceredigion Historical Society in the centenary year issue of Ceredigion.[18] 2011 witnessed the publication of the *Centenary Transactions of the Anglesey Antiquarian Society and Field Club*, and T. W. Pritchard's history of the Flintshire Historical Society published by Bridge Books, Wrexham on behalf of the Society; and the 100th issue of *The Montgomeryshire Collections* was published in 2012. Other journals produced by well-established local societies include the *Transactions of the Neath Antiquarian Society* (from 1930),[19] and the journal *Morgannwg* regularly contains details of publications produced by local societies within Glamorgan, including the Gower Society, Kenfig Society, and the local history societies in Caerphilly, the Cynon Valley, Gelligaer, Llantrisant, Llantwit Major, the Llynfi Valley, Merthyr Tydfil and Port Talbot.[20]

The various proceedings of these societies include scholarly articles examining various aspects of local history over an extended period of time. These are often accompanied by illustrative material which, in some instances, is presented in colour. The journal *Ceredigion* has been invariably presented with a colour illustration on its cover since the reproduction in 1993 of Alfred Worthington's *Aberystwyth Harbour*.[21] A series of illustrations presented with Pamela Redwood's study in *Brycheiniog* of houses in rural Breconshire in the period 1600–1800 includes fascinating reproductions of photographs taken in 1964 of two longhouses, one in Llangadog and the other in Cwmdu, and also photographs taken in 1997 of the former converted into holiday accommodation for a youth club and the latter a derelict ruin.[22] Attractive colour photographs also accompanied J. R. L. Allen's analysis in *The Monmouthshire Antiquary* of the defences of Venta Silurum (Caerwent), and Brian Poole's discussion in *The Montgomeryshire Collections* on industrial activities and buildings in the county.[23]

The historical societies of the main churches of Wales publish journals, and these promote an awareness of records which are frequently of considerable relevance for family and local historians. The transactions of the historical society of the Welsh Baptists [JWBHS] have been published since 1906, and the corresponding publications of other religious historical societies include those of the Presbyterian Church of Wales [JHSPCW] (1916), the Welsh Independents [*Y Cofiadur*] (1923), the Methodist Church in Wales [*Bathafarn*] (1946), and the Church of Wales [JHSChW] (1949). More recent developments in this field have been the publication of the *The Welsh Journal of Religious History* [WJRH], whose first volume was published in 2006, *The Journal of Welsh Ecclesiastical History* [JWEH] (1984–1992), and *The Journal of Welsh Religious History* [JWRH] (1993–2005).[24] Also, the Newsletter and information leaflets produced by CAPEL, the Chapels Heritage Society established in 1986 to encourage the study and preservation of the Nonconformist heritage of Wales; and the *Newsletter*, published twice a year by the Welsh Religious Buildings Trust, established in 1999.[25]

An awareness of the threat presented to distinctive features of the landscape and history of Wales was also responsible for the foundation in 1970 of *Llafur*, the Society for the Study of Welsh Labour History, which has fostered research into, and the teaching of, the history of the working class in Wales. The society has published since 1972 an annual volume of transactions, which contains scholarly articles and reports on meetings and activities organised by and involving the society, and a special issue on urban communities in south Wales was published in 2007.[26] The contraction of the coal industry had led to the closure and dispersal of many miners' institute libraries, but since 1973 the South Wales Miners' Library, located in Swansea, has collected a wide range of material, including books from miners' institute libraries, pamphlets and printed ephemera, photographs, tapes, and miners' banners. This

Library, housing part of the South Wales Coalfield Collection, is the main library service for the Department of Adult Continuing Education, Swansea University.

Book reviews appear in most of the county historical journals, and attention is also drawn to publications with which the society has been involved. Volumes published by county historical societies include *A History of Caernarvonshire, 1284–1900* (1968) by the Caernarfonshire Historical Society; A. D. Carr, *Medieval Anglesey* (1982 and in 2011), and W. P. Griffith, *Power Politics and County Government in Wales: Anglesey, 1780–1914* (2006), by the Anglesey Antiquarian Society and Field Club in the *Studies in Anglesey History* series; and *Carmarthenshire Memories of the Twentieth Century*, ed. Eiluned Rees (2002) and *Carmarthenshire and Beyond: Studies in History and Archaeology in Memory of Terry James*, eds. Heather James and Patricia Moore (2009) by the Carmarthenshire Antiquarian Society. Reports are often presented on the work of local museums and record offices, and *Morgannwg* regularly contains a series of archaeological notes, prepared by various groups, including members of the Glamorgan–Gwent Archaeological Trust, followed by reports from the Glamorgan Archives and the West Glamorgan Archive Service. Information is also provided on the membership and activities of the local society, with reports of lectures, meetings, and field excursions arranged during the year.[27]

Indexes to the contents of the journals appear at periodic intervals; thus, a cumulative title index to volumes 1–31 of the *Transactions of the Denbighshire Historical Society* was presented in volume 32 (1983). A comprehensive index compiled by Andrew Green to the *Transactions of the Carmarthenshire Antiquarian Society* from 1905 to 1977 was published by the society in 1981, with a supplement covering the period 1978–87. Detailed indexes have also been published to the *Transactions of the Radnorshire Society* (1984), with a supplement compiled by R. W. D. Fenn and J. B. Sinclair (1987), and individual issues from 2004 until 2009 contained an index. Indexes to the transactions of the Anglesey Antiquarian Society and Field Club and publications of the Flintshire Historical Society were compiled respectively by Dewi O. Jones (1987) and Dennis G. Roberts (1998).

County history societies have also been responsible for publishing record sources which are relevant for family and local historians. The publications of the Flintshire Historical Society Record Series include *Flint Pleas, 1283–5*, ed. J. G. Edwards (1921), and *Flintshire Ministers' Accounts*, ed. D. L. Evans (1929). Several volumes were published in the *West Wales Historical Records* series (1910–29). The tradition established by the *South Wales and Monmouth Record Society Publications* (1932) has been maintained by the South Wales Record Society, established in 1982 to publish editions of historical records relating to the history of south Wales. Publications include *Men at Arms: Musters in Monmouthshire, 1539 and 1601–2*, ed. Tony Hopkins (2009); and *The Swansea Wartime Diary of Laurie Latchford, 1940–41*, eds. Kate Elliot Jones and Wendy Cope (2010).

There are a number of active family-history societies in Wales, with meetings held regularly, and research projects including the transcription of monumental inscriptions in churches and graveyards, the transcription and indexing of parish registers, and the preparation of census indices. The Clwyd Family History Society Resource Centre at Cefn Mawr provides research facilities for members with access to a range of family and local history sources. Its journal *Hel Achau* contains details of activities, lists of publications including parish registers and monumental inscriptions, and various contributions, such as the transcription in the June 2012 issue of a conveyance of tithe rent charges in the Wrexham area in 1860.[28] The Association of Family History Societies of Wales co-operates fully with the Federation of Family History Societies, and the two bodies jointly published *Welsh Family History: A Guide to Research*, ed. John Rowlands et al. (1993). The Federation published John and Sheila Rowlands, *The Surnames of Wales* (1996), and, in conjunction with the Department of Continuing Education, University of Wales, Aberystwyth, *Second Stages in Researching Welsh Ancestry*, eds. John and Sheila Rowlands (1999). The numerous publications of the Federation and the Family History Online website provide valuable information and guidance for Welsh family historians. Similarly, the activities and publications of the British Association for Local History, and, before that, of the Standing Conference for Local History, have assisted Welsh as well as English local historians, as both organizations have sought to encourage the study of local history in Wales and provide necessary services. The quarterly journal *The Local Historian* occasionally publishes articles and book reviews of specific Welsh interest, such as the report on the

'History in the Landscape' residential conference held at Aberystwyth in July 1994; and the survey in 2013 of a number of volumes on Welsh history published by the University of Wales Press.[29]

This journal, and other publications of the BALH and the Historical Association, including the journal *History*, have succeeded in drawing attention to research work undertaken in other localities and also to the availability and value of source-material. Other journals, whose scope is not confined to Wales but which at times contain material of specific Welsh interest, include *The Agricultural History Review, Antiquity, The Archaeological Journal, Folk Life: Journal of Ethnological Studies* and *History Workshop Journal*, and reference has already been made to the popularity of magazines such as *Your Family History Magazine* and the *Family Tree Magazine* which concentrate on family history. The Socialist History Society's *Occasional Papers* published in 2005 featured local history studies in Wales.[30] The involvement of Welsh historians in other co-operative ventures, for instance *The Agrarian History of England and Wales*[31] has also proved fruitful. These volumes were published by the Cambridge University Press, whose other publications include D. Walker's *Medieval Wales* (1990), and Geraint H. Jenkins' *A Concise History of Wales* (2007). The major publications of the Oxford University Press, which again facilitate the work of Welsh family and local historians, include volumes on medieval Welsh history by Professors William Rees and Rees Davies, and the Press has also co-operated with the University of Wales Press to publish the six volumes presenting the authoritative history of Wales.[32]

The University of Wales has made an immense contribution to scholarship in Wales, and has promoted the study of family and local history in many ways. The University of Wales Press, established in 1922, has published a large number of significant monographs and texts, and also volumes in *The Histories of Wales* series,[33] and the *Studies in Welsh History* series of monographs, including studies of quarrymen in north Wales, judicial developments in Denbighshire, and urban history in Swansea.[34] *Settlement and Society in Wales*, ed. D. Huw Owen (1989), a collection of essays examining various aspects of the development of the landscape, settlement patterns, and social framework of Wales, contains Glanmor Williams' survey of the long and honourable tradition of local history studies in Wales. The

University's Board of Celtic Studies has been responsible for several important series of publications, with the History and Law Committee publishing major groups of historical records, including the Merioneth Lay Subsidy Roll 1292–3, and the Religious Census of 1851.[35] The biennial journal *Welsh History Review* has been published since 1960 and includes, every year, a list of periodical articles relating to Welsh history in a preceding year, and also, occasionally, lists of postgraduate theses on Welsh history, and of major accessions to repositories in Wales relating to Welsh history. *The Bulletin of the Board of Celtic Studies* was published from 1921 until 1993, with an index, compiled by Simon Rodway, in 2003. In 1993 the Bulletin was amalgamated with *Studia Celtica*, which had appeared since 1996. The Social Studies Committee published in 1988 the National Atlas of Wales.[36]

The University of Wales Press has been closely involved in the publication of official county histories, which have also been supported by local authorities. The publication in 1988 of the sixth volume of the Glamorgan County History completed an enterprise launched in 1930 to publish a six-volume history of the county.[37] Joseph Bradney had published his four-volume *A History of Monmouthshire* in the period 1904–33, and four volumes in the proposed five-volume *Gwent County History* have been published.[38] Two volumes of the history of Merioneth were published in 1967 and 2001; three volumes of the Pembrokeshire County History in 1987, 1993 and 2003; and two volumes of the Cardiganshire County History in 1998 and 2001.[39] J . E. Lloyd's *A History of Carmarthenshire* had appeared in two volumes in 1935 and 1939, and A. H. Dodd was the author of *A History of Caernarfonshire,1284–1900* (1968).

Local and family history featured prominently in the subjects studied by classes organised by Departments of Extra-Mural Studies or Departments of Continuing Education of the constituent colleges of the University of Wales.[40] The Workers' Educational Association, the voluntary organization designated as a provider of adult education, effectively promoted the study of local history in many areas, and four lectures delivered under the auspices of the WEA in Merthyr Tudful were published by the University of Wales Press in 1966.[41] Also, an extremely active WEA branch at Llanelli, where classes on a wide range of subjects, including local history, have been organised since 1914, has published annually since 1986 *Amrywiaeth Llanelli Miscellany*, and also the volume *Footprints of Faith*, a series of lectures on 'The Anglican Church and Nonconformity in Llanelli' delivered to classes organised by the WEA in 1987–8.[42]

Local authorities have supported ambitious ventures to publish volumes on local history. Carmarthenshire County Council published, in 2002, R. S. Craig, R. Protheroe Jones, and M. V. Symons, *The Industrial and Maritime History of Llanelli and Burry Port, 1750–2000*, and in 2009 Huw Edwards, *Capeli Llanelli, Our Rich Heritage*. Studies of towns and cities include A. H. Dodd, *A History of Wrexham* (1957), W. Rees, *Cardiff: A History of the City* (1969), Ieuan Gwynedd Jones, *Aberystwyth 1277–1977* (1977) and *Swansea, An Illustrated History*, ed. Glanmor Williams (1990). The *Glamorgan Historian* series, vols. 1–12 (1963–81), together with four other volumes on Glamorgan (1959–62) and a number of publications including collections of photographs illustrating various towns and districts, represent the remarkable contribution of an individual, Stewart Williams, to the historiography of local studies in Wales. Other publishing ventures which illustrate individual initiative include *Neath and District, a Symposium*, ed. Elis Jenkins (1974); D. B. James' two volumes, *Myddfai: Its Land and Peoples* (1991) and *Ceredigion: Its Natural History* (2001), and W. R. B. Robinson, *Early Tudor Gwent, 1485–1547* (2002).

A number of institutions, such as the National Library of Wales and National Museum Wales, both of which were founded by royal charters in 1907, have also proved to be of critical importance on account of their extensive and valuable collections and associated publications. The National Library of Wales, located at Aberystwyth, has collected since its establishment a wide range of manuscript, archive, printed, cartographic, visual, sound and moving image material relating to Wales and the Celtic countries.[43] One of the six legal deposit libraries in the United Kingdom and Ireland, its right to practically all the publications of the British Isles has by now been extended to non-print and electronic publications. This provision is extremely valuable for community and family historians, especially in relation to the various printed, archive, cartographic and visual materials discussed in this volume,[44] and also relevant items in the National Screen and Sound Archive of Wales, including sound and video recordings, films, and radio and television programmes relating to Wales, with the Library being a designated archive for off-air recordings.

Amgueddfa Cymru–The Museum of Wales consists of the National Museum Cardiff; St Fagans National History Museum; Big Pit: National Coal Museum; National Waterfront Museum (Swansea); National Roman Legion Museum (Caerleon); the National Wool Museum (Drefach Felindre); and the National Slate Museum (Llanberis). Artefacts excavated in various areas of Wales, forming the archaeological collections of Wales, are displayed at the National Museum, Cardiff. An extensive collection of sound recordings illustrating the oral history, traditions and dialects of Wales is housed at St Fagans: National History Museum. A row of terrace houses originally erected at Rhyd-y-Car, Merthyr Tydfil, in around 1800 was re-erected at St Fagans in 1988, and four slateworkers' houses, 1-4 Fron Haul, moved from Tanygrisiau near Blaenau Ffestiniog, were opened at the National Slate Museum in 1999. These houses were adapted to illustrate different periods in the history of these industrial communities.[45]

The Royal Commission on the Ancient and Historical Monuments for Wales was established in 1908 to make an inventory of the ancient and historical monuments of Wales and Monmouthshire.[46] It has published, since 1911, inventories covering a number of the historic Welsh counties, including several volumes on Caernarfonshire (1956, 1960, and 1964) and Glamorgan (1976, 1981, 1982, 1988, and 1991). These handsome volumes contain an abundance of illustrative material with colour and monochrome plates and sequences of line-drawings, plans, and sections explaining and expanding upon the detailed descriptions of distinctive internal features, and of the external appearance, of a wide range of buildings and settlements, including hill forts, castles, platform houses, monastic granges, deserted villages, gentry houses, farmhouses, and cottages.[47] It is now considered that the function of inventories may best be fulfilled by electronic resources, accessible through *Coflein*. By a Royal Warrant of 1992 the Commission was empowered to survey, record, publish, and maintain a database of ancient and historical sites, structures, and landscapes in Wales. In 1964 the records of the Royal Commission were amalgamated with the Welsh section of the National Buildings Record to form the National Monuments Record of Wales, which is also based in Aberystwyth. The NMR seeks to collect, maintain, and make available, by means of *Coflein*, a free public online database, information about archaeological sites and buildings of all periods, with catalogue information about its

23

archive collections; and extensive collections have been assembled of photographs, drawings, and surveys, together with documents, maps, databases, and a small library.[48]

Cadw (Welsh Historic Monuments), the official guardian of the built heritage of Wales, was established in 1984 with a statutory responsibility for protecting, conserving, and presenting the ancient monuments and historic buildings of Wales. Revised guides to Welsh historical sites have been published, and these attractive, informative, and popular publications have numerous illustrations which effectively depict the architectural detail presented in the text. Other volumes that successfully interpret the heritage of Wales include Elizabeth Whittle, *The Historic Gardens of Wales* (1992). Sian Rees, *Dyfed* (1992) and Elizabeth Whittle, *Glamorgan and Gwent* (1992) launched a series of regional guides. Conferences are organised, and the papers presented to the third Cadw Archaeological Conference held at Cardiff in 1986 were later published.[49] Four archaeological trusts were established in Wales to cover the former counties of Clwyd-Powys, Glamorgan-Gwent, Gwynedd, and Dyfed; and help protect, record and interpret all aspects of the historic landscape.[50]

Archivists were appointed in Monmouthshire in 1938 and in Glamorgan in 1939, but most of the county record offices were established after the Second World War, as in Caernarfonshire (1948), Flintshire (1951), Merioneth (1952), and Carmarthenshire (1959). An archive service was established in Powys in 1984, and in 1992 the West Glamorgan Record Office was founded, with the Glamorgan Archive Service thereby serving the counties of Mid and South Glamorgan. The A. N. Palmer Local Studies and Archive Centre in Wrexham houses the main Local Studies Collection transferred from Wrexham Library, together with the existing Archives Service. Record offices at Llangefni, Aberystwyth, Ruthin and Haverfordwest serve respectively Anglesey, Ceredigion, Denbighshire and Pembrokeshire. The collections held in county record offices include the quarter sessions records, covering all aspects of local administration before the creation of county councils in 1888. The earliest series are those of Caernarfonshire, which survive from 1541, and their value was emphasised in two publications.[51] These records include land tax assessments, enclosure awards, poll books, and electoral registers (after 1832). Other records which are frequently consulted include rate books, parish and Nonconformist registers, family and estate papers, a wide range of educational, industrial, and business records, and, especially in the Gwynedd Archives Service, a large collection of maritime records.[52]

Record offices have been responsible for a wide range of publications in addition to the detailed annual reports. These include Donald Moore, *The Earliest Views of Glamorgan* (1978) and *A Catalogue of Glamorgan Estate Maps*, compiled by Hilary M. Thomas (1992), both of which were published by the Glamorgan Archives Service. The series 'Studies in Swansea's History', includes R. T. Price, *Little Ireland, Aspects of the Irish and Greenhill, Swansea* (1992). Volumes published by the Gwynedd Archives and Museum Service include M. Elis-Williams, *Bangor, Port of Beaumaris* (1988) and Eric Jones and David Gwyn, *Dolgarrog, An Industrial History*, (1989); and the journal *Cymru a'r Môr/Maritime Wales*, has been published since 1976. The Friends of the Clwyd Archives are responsible for the *Clwyd Historian: Hanes Bro Clwyd*, which was first published in 1977.

Archival material, together with maps, newspapers, photographs, and audio-visual material, are held in some of the public and academic libraries of Wales. The oldest public libraries in Cardiff and Swansea were established respectively in 1862 and 1870 and both institutions have over the years collected a wide range of material. A number of public libraries have supported publishing ventures. The Local History Research Group, based at the Llanelli Public Library, published a series of monographs, including M. V. Symons, *Coal Mining in the Llanelli Area, i. 16th Century to 1829* (1979), and D. Q. Bowen, *The Llanelli Landscape* (1980). Facsimile editions of works published by library authorities include *William Spurrell, Carmarthen and its Neighbourhood* (1879, reprinted by the Dyfed County Council Cultural Services Department, 1995); and John Lewis, *The Swansea Guide* (1851, reprinted by the West Glamorgan County Council Library and Information Service in 1989. The Swansea Central Library (City and County of Swansea Library Service) established the Cambrian Index Online project which provides researchers with speedy access to the information contained in *The Cambrian*, the first newspaper to be published in Wales, at Swansea in 1804.

University libraries also contain important collections, such as those relating to north Wales estates, mines, and quarries, housed at Bangor University. Swansea University archive collections are housed at the

Richard Burton Archives, officially launched at the university in April 2010. The material held here includes political and trade union records associated with the copper, tinplate, coal and steel industries, family records and genealogical material previously held in the Royal Institution of South Wales.[53] The Royal Institution, founded in 1834, continues to operate as a voluntary learned society. It publishes *The Swansea History Journal, Minerva*, and acts as the Friends Group of Swansea Museum which, completed in 1841, and administered by the Museum Services of the City and County of Swansea, is the oldest public museum in Wales. A number of museums effectively interpret the localities in which they are sited. Specialised museums concerned with specific subjects include the Gwent Rural Life Museum, Usk; the Lloyd George Museum, Llanystumdwy; and the Robert Owen Memorial Museum, Newtown. J. Geraint Jenkins, *Exploring Museums, Wales* (1990), a Museums Association Guide, described the collections and facilities of 131 museums and galleries in Wales.

Publishing firms operating within Wales have been responsible over an extended period of time for a number of significant volumes on local history in both the English and Welsh languages,[54] and so also have various local groups and historical societies.[55] There is an important tradition of Welsh-language publications in this field, and notable examples include the *Crwydro* series featuring the various Welsh counties with the first volume, T. I. Ellis, *Crwydro Ceredigion*, published in 1952. An English translation of Ffrancis Payne's *Crwydro Sir Faesyfed* was published in two issues of the *Transactions of the Radnorshire Society*.[56] Each volume in the *Cyfres y Cymoedd* ('Valleys' Series, 1993–2003), contained chapters on the cultural heritage of South Wales valley communities; the *Cyfres Broydd Cymru* ('Welsh Regions' Series), concentrated on specific localities, including those where the National Eisteddfod had been held; and the *Bro a Bywyd* series provided illustrative material relating to the lives of prominent Welsh literary figures.

Relevant bibliographical data is available in *A Bibliography of the History of Wales* (1962), with supplements for the period 1959–71 in the *Bulletin of the Board of Celtic Studies* (1963, 1966, 1969, and 1972), and in *A Bibliography of the History of Wales*, ed. Philip Henry Jones (microfiche, 1988). The National Library of Wales was responsible for the compilation of *Llyfryddiaeth Cymru/Bibliography of Wales*

(1985–6, 1987–8, 1989–90), and the various methods provided by the Library to facilitate access to its collections are outlined on the Library's website (*www.llgc.org.uk*) with the Family History and Digital Mirror sections especially valuable. The community and family historian in Wales will also undoubtedly benefit from the information provided by the websites and publications of the other national institutions, and the various societies discussed above.

Welsh family and local historians have also benefited from volumes published in England. A number offer guidance for local and family historians,[57] whilst others concentrate on specific localities.[58] The Chalford Publishing Company Ltd, Stroud co-operated with Welsh record offices to publish volumes comprising photographic collections of specific locations in its *Archive Photographs Series*, and examples include *Cymoedd y Gwendraeth Valleys*, compiled by the Economic and Leisure Department (Cultural Services), Carmarthenshire County Council (1977); and *Sir Y Fflint/Flintshire*, compiled by the Flintshire Record Office (1996). The collection of photographs of Llandudno compiled by Christopher Draper and John Lawson-Reay, *Llandudno through Time*, was published by Amberley Publishing in 2010; John Davies, *Hanes Cymru* (1990) and an English translation, *A History of Wales* (1993), a comprehensive one-volume history of Wales from the earliest period to the late 1950s, were published by Allan Lane: the Penguin Press; and Philip Jenkins' *A History of Modern Wales, 1536–1990* was published by Longman in 1997. Seven volumes have been published in Penguin's *The Buildings of Wales* series.[59]

NOTES

1   See pp.78–80
2   Gerald of Wales, *The Journey Through Wales and The Description of Wales*, trans. with introduction, Lewis Thorpe (2004)
3   *The Itinerary in Wales of John Leland in or about the years 1536–1539*, ed. Lucy Toulmin Smith (1906); Derek Williams, *An Epic Tudor Journey, John Leland's Itinerary of Northern Wales* (2008)
4   Rice Merrick, *Morganiae Archaiographia, A Book of the Antiquities of Glamorganshire*, ed. Brian Ll. James (South Wales Record Society, 1983)
5   George Owen, *The Description of Penbrokeshire*, ed. Dillwyn Miles (1994); *Camden's Wales*, trans. Edward Lhuyd, introduction by Gwyn Walters (1984); see also p.198
6   Sir John Wynn, *History of the Gwydir Family and memoirs*, ed. J. Gwynfor Jones (1990)
7   Brynley F. Roberts, *Edward Lhuyd, the Making of a Scientist* (1980); Glyn

Daniel, 'Edward Lhuyd, antiquary and archaeologist', *Welsh History Review*, iii, 4 (1967), 345–357

8   Thomas Pennant, *History of the parishes of Whiteford and Holywell* (1796), reprinted by the Clywyd County Council Library and Museum Service in 1988; a version of his *Tours in Wales* (1784), abridged by David Kirk, was published by Gwasg Carreg Gwalch in 1998

9   Benjamin Heath Malkin, *The Scenery, Antiquities and Biography of South Wales* (1804)

10 Theophilus Jones, *History of the County of Brecknock* (2 vol., 1805, 1809); Samuel Rush Meyrick, *History and Antiquities of the County of Cardigan* (1808); Richard Fenton, *A Historical Tour through Pembrokeshire* (1811)

11 Glenda Carr, *William Owen Pughe* (1983 and 1993)

12 One of these publications was *A rattleskull genius*, ed. Geraint H. Jenkins (2005)

13 *Dictionary of Welsh Biography* (1959, 2001); the online version, *Biography Online*, was launched by the National Library of Wales in 2004

14 George Owen, *The Description of Penbrokshire,* ed. Henry Owen (4 vols., Cymmrodorion Record Series, 1902–1936)

15 Stella Coldwell, *The National Archives* (2006); David Hey, 'The Antiquarian Tradition', *The Oxford Companion to Family and Local History*, ed. David Hey (2008), 66; ibid., 293–6; 428, 509

16 *Welsh Archaeological Heritage*, eds. Donald Moore and David Austin (1986).

17 *The Historical Atlas of Montgomeryshire*, ed. David Jenkins (1999)

18 Terrence James, 'Hanes Byr/A Brief History', *The Carmarthenshire Antiquary*, XLI (2005), 7-12; Gwynedd O. Pierce, 'The Glamorgan History Society and Morgannwg: The Early Years', *Morgannwg*, L (2006), 7–42; Geraint H. Jenkins, 'Our Founding Fathers and Mothers: The Cardiganshire Antiquarians', *Ceredigion* XVI (2009), 133–169

19 In 2009 the Society published *The Neath Antiquarian*, vol. 1, ed. Keith Tucker (2009), comprising ten illustrated chapters by local historians of the Neath area.

20 *Morgannwg*, LIII (2009), 165-9; LIV (2010), 233, 237-9, 242-5; LV (2011), 140-2, 151-2, 177-8, 187-190

21 *Ceredigion*, XII, 1 (1993), front cover

22 Pamela Redwood, 'Houses and History in Rural Breconshire, 1600–1800', *Brycheiniog, XLIII (2012), 50, 51*

23 J. R. L. Allen, 'The defences of Venta Silurium (Caerwent), A new analysis of the building programme', *The Monmouthshire Antiquary, The Proceedings of the Monmouthshire Antiquarian Society*, XXVIII (2012), 19, 22, 25, 30; Brian Poole, 'Industry and the industrial buildings of Montgomeryshire', *The Montgomeryshire Collections*, 100 (2012), 340–1, 343, 347–353

24 See also pp.82–3, 87

25 D. Huw Owen, *The Chapels of Wales* (2012), 18–20

26 *Urban Communities in Modern South Wales*, eds. Neil Evans, Ursula Masson and Steven Thompson (Llafur Special Issue, 2007)

27 *Morgannwg*, LV (2011) 1–4, 88–131

28 *Hel Achau, Journal of the Clwyd Family History Society*, 113 (June 2012), 17–26

29 D. Huw Owen, 'History in the Landscape', *The Local Historian*, 25, 2 (1995), 109–115; Maggie Escott, 'Review article: perspectives on the history of Wales', *ibid.*, 43.1 (February 2013), 70–74

30 Lionel Munby, D. Huw Owen, James Scannell, *Local history since 1945: England, Wales and Ireland*, Socialist History Society, Occasional Papers, No 21 (2005)

31 *The Agrarian History of England and Wales* was published in eleven volumes from 1967 to 2000, and the periods covered extended chronologically from Prehistory [vo. I.i] to 1939 [vol. viii]

32 William Rees, *South Wales and the March, 1284–1415* (1924); R. R. Davies, *Lordship and Society in the March of Wales* (1978); K. O. Morgan, *Rebirth of a Nation, Wales 1880–1980* (1981); R. R. Davies, *Conquest, Coexistence and Change, Wales 1066–1485* (1987); Glanmor Williams, *Recovery, Reorientation and Reformation, Wales c.1415–1642* (1987); Geraint H. Jenkins, *The Foundations of Modern Wales, Wales 1642–1780* (1987); T. M. Charles-Edwards, *Wales and the Britons, 350–1064* (2013)

33 Volumes in this series include Roger Turvey, *Pembrokeshire, The Concise History* (2007)

34 R. Merfyn Jones, *North Wales Quarrymen* (1999); Sharon Howard, *Law and Disorder in early-modern Wales: crime and authority in the Denbighshire courts, c. 1660–1730* (2008); Louise Miskell, *Intelligent town: an urban history of Swansea, 1780–1855* (2012)

35 *The Merioneth Lay Subsidy Roll 1292–3*, ed. K. Williams-Jones (1976); *The Religious Census of 1851, i: South Wales*, eds. Ieuan Gwynedd Jones and David Williams (1976), *ii North Wales*, ed. Ieuan Gwynedd Jones (1981)

36 *The National Atlas of Wales*, ed. Harold Carter (1988)

37 *Glamorgan County History, 6, Glamorgan Society 1780–1980*, ed. Prys Morgan (1988)

38 *The Gwent County History*, 1: *Gwent in prehistory and early history*, eds. Miranda Aldhouse-Green and Ray Howell (2004); 2: *The age of the Marcher Lords, c.1070–1536*, eds. Ralph A. Griffiths, Tony Hopkins and Ray Howell (2008); 3. *The Making of Monmouthshire*, eds. Madeleine Grey and Prys Morgan (2009); 4, *Industrial Monmouthshire, 1780–1914*, eds. Chris Williams and Sian Rhiannon Williams (2011)

39 *History of Merioneth*, 1, E. G. Bowen and C. A. Gresham (eds.) (1967); II, J. Beverley Smith and Llinos Beverley Smith (eds.) (2001); *Pembrokeshire County History*, III, ed.B. E. Howells (1987); IV, ed. David W. Howell (1993) and II *Medieval Pembrokeshire*, ed. R. F. Walker (2002); *Cardiganshire County History*, 3, eds. Geraint H. Henkins and Ieuan Gwynedd Jones (1998); and I, eds. J. I. Davies and D. P. Kirby (2001)

40 Details of university diploma and MA dissertations relating to Glamorgan presented at Cardiff and Swansea were published in *Morgannwg*, XXXV (1991), 79–84; a number of these dissertations formed the basis for later publications

41 *Merthyr Politics: the Making of a Working-class Tradition*, ed. Glanmor Williams (1966)

42 *Footprints of Faith*, ed. John Edwards (1991)

43 The history of the National Library has been outlined in W. Ll. Davies, *The National Library of Wales: a survey of its history, contents and its activities* (1937); and David Jenkins, *A refuge in peace and war* (2002)

44 See pp.43–48, 57–67

45 Publications by members of the staff of the museum include I. C. Peate, *The Welsh House* (1946), J. Geraint Jenkins, *The Welsh Woollen Industry* (1969), Eurwyn Wiliam, *Farm Buildings of North-east Wales, 1550–1900* (1982); Gerallt D. Nash, *Workmen's Halls and Institutions: Oakdale Workmen's Institute* (1995), and Beth Thomas, *Cytiau chwain a phalasau breuddwydion/ Fleapits and picture palaces* (1997)

46 A fascinating account of its development and activities was provided in the volume *Hidden Histories: Discovering the Heritage of Wales*, eds. Peter Wakelin and Ralph A. Griffiths (2008)

47 Other relevant publications include P. Smith, *The Houses of the Welsh Countryside* (1975, 2nd edn., 1988); Stephen Hughes, *Copperopolis, Landscapes of the Early Industrial Period in Swansea* (2000, repr. 2005); Richard Suggett,

Houses and History in the March of Wales, Radnorshire 1400–1800 (2005), and Eurwyn Wiliam, *The Welsh Cottage: Building Traditions of the Rural Poor, 1750–1900* (2010)

48 Examples of these guides include Arnold Taylor, *Caernarfon Castle* (2004), Peter Wakelin, *Blaenavon Ironworks* (2006), and D. H. Evans, *Valle Crucis Abbey* (2007)

49 *The Welsh Industrial Heritage: a Review*, ed. C. Stephen Briggs (1992) [CBA Research Report no. 79]

50 Publications which result directly from the work of the trusts include G. G. T. James, *Carmarthen: an Archaeological and Topographical Survey* (1980) and D. M. Robinson, *South Glamorgan's Heritage* (1985)

51 *Calendar of the Caernarvonshire Quarter Sessions Records*, i: 1541–58, ed. W. Ogwen Williams (1956), and *Denbighshire Quarter Sessions Records*, ed. A. G. Veysey (1991)

52 Published guides to county record offices include W. Ogwen Williams, *Guide to the Caernarvonshire Record Office* (1952), A. G. Veysey, *Guide to the Flintshire Record Office* (1974), and Kim Collis, *The West Glamorgan Archive Service: A guide to the collections* (1998)

53 See also the reference to the South Wales Miners' Library, pp.17–18

54 The volumes published include W. J. Lewis, *Born on a Perilous Rock* (1980, Cambrian News, Aberystwyth); Brinley Richards, *History of the Llynfi Valley* (1982, D. Brown & Sons, Cowbridge); Roy Thorne, *Penarth – A History* (1982, The Starling Press, Risca); Malcolm Seaborne, *Schools in Wales 1500–1900* (1992, Gee and Son); Lewis Lloyd, *The Port of Caernarfon, 1793–1900* (1989, Gwasg Pantycelyn); J. B. Sinclair and R. W. D. Fenn, *Marching to Zion, Radnorshire Chapels* (1990, Cadoc Books); Sally Roberts-Jones, *The History of Port Talbot* (1991, Goldleaf Publishing, Port Talbot); Philip Riden and Keith Edwards, *Families and Farms in Lisvane, 1850–1950* (1993, Merton Priory Press, Cardiff); Caroline Charles-Jones (ed.), *The Francis Jones Treasury of Historic Pembrokeshire* by Francis Jones (1998, Brawdy Books); Gwynedd O. Pierce, *Place Names in Glamorgan* (2002, Merton Press); Gerald Morgan, *Ceredigion, a Wealth of History* (2005, Gomer Press, Llandysul); T. W. Pritchard, *The Making of Buckley and District* (2006, Bridge Books, Wrexham); Ceiriog Gwynne Evans, *Once Upon a time in Goginan* (2009, Y Lolfa); Gwen Awbery, *Tracing Family History in Wales: how to read the inscriptions on Welsh gravestones* (2010, Llygad Gwalch)

55 Examples of volumes published by local groups include T. Arber-Cooke, *Pages from the History of Llandovery* (1975, Llandovery Civic Trust Association); E. G. Bowen, *A History of Llanbadarn Fawr* (1979, Ysgol Cwmpadarn Centenary Celebrations Joint Committee, Llanbadarn Fawr); Keith Kissack, *Medieval Monmouth*, (1974), *Victorian Monmouth* (1986) and *The building of Monmouth* (1989, The Monmouth Historical and Educational Trust); *Abergavenny in the Twentieth Century* (1992, Abergavenny Civic Society); *Bridgend 900*, ed. David J. Pearce (1993, Bridgend and District Local History Society); David Wyn Davies, *A Pictorial history of Machynlleth Mewn Hen Luniau* (1996, Machynlleth and District Civic Society); and those by historical societies include *Llanbrynmair yr ugeinfed ganrif/Llanbrynmair in the twentieth century* ed. Marian Rees (2005, Llanbrynmair Local History Society), and *Cofio'r Cefn/Cefn Remembered*, ed. Meurig Owen (2007, Cefn Meriadog Historical Society)

56 Dai Hawkins ('Dafydd y Garth', 'Exploring Radnorshire', *Transactions of the Radnorshire Society*, LXXVIII (2008) and LXXIX (2009)

57 These include W. B. Stephens, *Sources for English Local History* (Cambridge University Press, 1981); W. G. Hoskins, *Local history in England* (Longman, 1985); Philip Riden, *Record sources for local history* (1987, Batsford); Jean Cole

and Joan Titford, *Tracing your family tree* (2003, Countryside Books); Amanda Bevan, *Tracing your ancestors in the Public Record Office* (2002, Public Record Office); Mark Herber, *Ancestral Trails, The Complete Guide to British Genealogy and Family History* (2008, The History Press, in association with the Society of Genealogists); *The Family and Local History Handbook*, 12th ed. Robert Blatchford and Elizabeth Blatchford (2009, Robert Blatchford Publishing); *New directions in local history since Hoskins*, ed. Christopher Dyer, Andrew Hopper, Evelyn Lord and Nigel Tringham (2011, University of Hertfordshire Press); Bruce Durie, *Welsh Genealogy* (2012, The History Press); see also p.42 for the volumes by Nick Barratt, David Dymond and David Hey.

58 Examples of volumes published in England include Ian Soulsby, *The Towns of Medieval Wales* (1983, Phillimore); Gareth Evans, *Dunvant, Portrait of a Community* (1992, Stowefield Publications, Stafford); M.R.C.Price, *The Llanelly and Mynydd Mawr Railway* (1992, The Oakwood Press, Headington, Oxford); and Sue Passmore, *Llanllwchaearn, A Parish History* (2010, Grosvenor House Publishing, Guildford)

59 *The Buildings of Wales*: R. Haslam, *Powys* (1979); E. Hubbard, *Clwyd* (1994); John Newman, *Glamorgan* (1995); and *Gwent/Monmouthshire* (2002); Thomas Lloyd, Julian Orbach and Robert Scourfield, *Pembrokeshire* (2004) and *Carmarthenshire and Ceredigion* (2006); Richard Haslam, Julian Orbach & Adam Voelker, *Gwynedd: Anglesey, Caernarvonshire and Merioneth* (2009); Robert Scourfield, Richard Haslam, *Powys* (2013)

2. Printed Sources

Rheinallt Llwyd

For those researching aspects of community and family history there is a wide range of primary and secondary sources at their disposal, and some of these major sources are discussed in detail in this volume. This chapter will briefly discuss some of the most important printed sources that are often invaluable for researchers. Despite rapid and revolutionary developments in electronic and digital technologies, there are certain traditionally printed sources of information that are still of considerable importance to both community and family historians. Indeed, the core of local studies collections in most libraries will consist of printed books and pamphlets and will include both current and older materials.

Government publications – at both national and local level
A substantial number of central government publications will be of interest to community historians, especially parliamentary papers and Acts of Parliament. Also Parliamentary Reports of Select Committees and Royal Commissions, covering numerous topics will often relate to specific local communities. In addition to those general acts of parliament that apply to everybody, everywhere, there are many other more local and private acts of parliament relating to topics such as land enclosures, the building of roads and bridges, and the development of canals and railways in specific areas. Other important sources are reports emanating from parliamentary inquiries into particular topics

and in many such reports will be found a list of witnesses who gave evidence. Two famous reports on different topics providing a wealth of information relating to Wales are the *Report of the Commissioners of Inquiry into the State of Education in Wales* (1847) which became famously known as the Blue Books, and the detailed report made by the Royal Commission on Land in Wales which investigated land tenure in the country at the end of the nineteenth century, the *Report of the Royal Commisson on Land in Wales and Monmouthshire* (1896). A by-product of that enquiry, and equally valuable, were the *Minutes of Evidence taken before the Royal Commission on Land in Wales and Monmouthshire; with appendix of documents*, published in five volumes (1894–96).

Poll Books go back as far as 1696 when it became necessary for those organising county elections to list how each elector had voted. Soon afterwards such lists were commercially published and although there are variations in presentation in different parts of the country, all poll books will list electors and how they voted, with many also providing addresses and occupations of electors. For a long time, of course, only men who had certain property qualifications were entitled to vote, but such lists can obviously be useful for family historians. Following the Reform Act of 1832 it became necessary for local authorities to produce annual Electoral Lists and again one has to bear in mind that only men had a right to vote (based on property qualifications) until 1918 and that no full list of women voters exists before 1928 when all women over twenty-one years of age were given the right to vote. Other lists of value to both community and family historians are Lists of Freeholders which provide information on the higher strata of society but information contained in various publications relating to Census Returns are more inclusive and these are discussed in detail in Chapter 10.

A comprehensive account will also be given in Chapter 9 of those sources produced at local government level and many of these will be available in printed form such as the minutes of committees and sub-committees. The reports of local government officers can also be of enormous value, such as the reports of local medical officers following the outbreak of contagious diseases or as a result of fatal accidents in a particular area. Local authorities still produce detailed reports on the activities of their main departments, although there is an increasing tendency, nowadays, for these minutes to be created and communicated

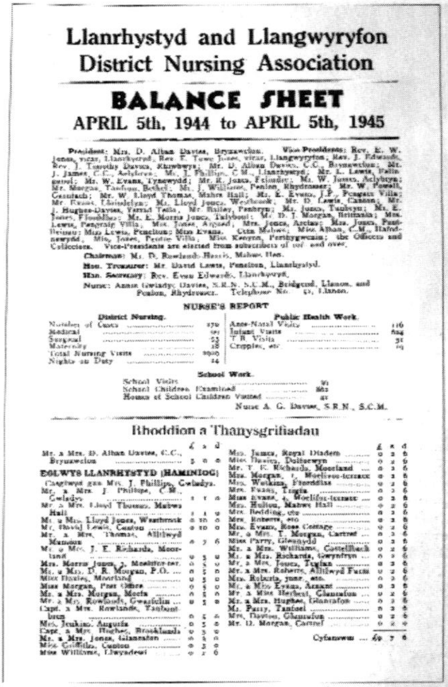

Llanrhystyd and Llangwyryfon District Nursing Association

BALANCE SHEET
APRIL 5th, 1944 to APRIL 5th, 1945

[balance sheet details largely illegible — list of Presidents, Vice-Presidents, officers, Nurse's Report on District Nursing, Public Health Work, School Work, and a list of subscriptions under "Rhoddion a Thanysgrifiadau"]

Balance Sheet, Llanrhystud and Llangwyryfon District Nursing Association, 1944–5

electronically. All local authorities will by now have well-developed websites where information is often revised on a daily basis. There is, however, a danger that a lot of such information can be lost unless it is systematically archived on a regular basis.

For the community historian another valuable source of information will be found in materials published and distributed on behalf of local businesses and industries, societies and institutions in the form of annual reports, reviews, policy documents and development plans, school and college prospectuses, the reports of chapels and churches and numerous catalogues and other miscellaneous commercial literature of all sorts. Many local authorities also produce guides which contain information relating to services and events and personalities. These are often regularly revised and it is interesting to compare different versions over a period of time.

Topographical works and guidebooks

Before local authorities began publishing guidebooks aimed at attracting tourists there was, in Wales as elsewhere, a tradition of publishing topographical guides, especially from 1770 onwards. For example, between 1770 and 1850, some eighty guidebooks and tour diaries relating to different parts of Wales were published and we know that others have survived in manuscript form, many of which can be located in record offices and libraries. A substantial number are located at Cardiff Central Library, for example.[1] Although the visits of these

THE NEW

ABERYSTWYTH GUIDE

TO THE

WATERS, BATHING HOUSES, PUBLIC WALKS, AND AMUSEMENTS;

Including Historical Notices and general Information,

CONNECTED WITH

THE TOWN, CASTLE RUINS, RIVERS, HAVOD, THE DEVIL'S BRIDGE,

And all Places of Note or Interest adjacent.

———

EMBELLISHED WITH A MAP AND TWO VIEWS.

———

BY T. J. LLEWELYN PRICHARD,

Author of "Welsh Minstrelsy," &c.

———

Away, ye gay landscapes! ye gardens of roses!
  In you let the minions of luxury rove;
Give me the rocks where the snow-flake reposes,
  Though still they are sacred to freedom and love:
England! thy beauties are tame and domestic,
  To one who has roved on the mountains afar;
Oh! for the crags that are wild and majestic,
  The cat'racts of Cymru and Alpine heights rare!

BYRON.—adapted.

———

ABERYSTWYTH:

Printed for and Sold by Lewis Jones, Bookseller,
and Sold at Cranston's Library;

SOLD ALSO, IN LONDON, BATH, CHELTENHAM, SHREWSBURY, BIRMINGHAM, WORCESTER, HEREFORD, BALA, AND CARMARTHEN.

———

1824.

The New Aberystwyth Guide (1824)

Guide to the Dolgellau area (1904)

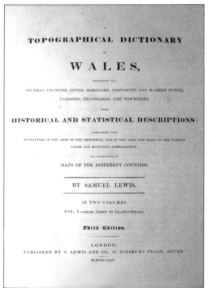

Samuel Lewis, A Topographical Dictionary of Wales (1833)

travellers were usually fairly brief the best ones provide valuable observations on local customs, events and personalities. A prime example is Thomas Pennant's *Tours in Wales* (1778, 1781), which is still a valuable source for community historians researching the northern counties of Wales. The tradition of publishing guidebooks to various areas of Wales is still a thriving business with publishers such as Gwasg Carreg Gwalch prominent in the field. By the end of the eighteenth century the topographical dictionary had also become popular and the best example we have is Samuel Lewis, *A Topographical Dictionary of Wales* (1833, 1844, 1849) produced in two volumes and including an atlas. It offers a brief historical description of every village and town in addition to information on the civil and religious organisation within a particular area.

Directories

Directories providing information about trade and industry and listing prominent individuals with their addresses and occupations first appeared in London in 1677, and by the end of the eighteenth century had become popular as the industrial revolution progressed. The first directories were on a national level but with urban changes and population growth during the nineteenth century the tendency was to produce regional

Notes on Dinas Mawddwy and Mallwyd
in Pigot & Co.'s Directory (1835)

and then county directories. *Kelly*, which became the largest publisher in the field, ventured to produce directories on large towns and cities, and by the 1830s it was possible to obtain information in directories on even the most rural and inaccessible areas of Wales. A great deal of background information is provided on each parish in addition to information about prominent and influential individuals and their occupations within the community. Directories can be of particular value to family historians, since so many individuals are named. They also provide us with information relating to the growth of towns and villages and the condition of individual trades and businesses. However, as with all reference sources they must be used with care.

Biographical sources
Biographical information can be of immense importance to both family and community historians, and *The Dictionary of Welsh Biography down to 1940* (1959) and its various supplements will often be the obvious starting point.[2] For those interested in gentry families there are other famous and long-established sources, in various editions, such as *Kelly's Handbook, Burke's Landed Gentry, Walford's County Families*. Various editions of *Who's Who* not forgetting *Who's Who in*

Wales (1937), can also be a good starting point. The *Alumni Oxonienses 1500-1886* and *Alumni Cantabrigienses 1261-1900* provide details about former students of Oxford and Cambridge. Other valuable sources which provide information relating to individuals who pursued careers in the Church of England will be found in *Crockford's Clerical Directory*, first published in 1858, and in Foster's *Index Ecclesiasticus*, which covers the earlier decades of the nineteenth century. And we should not forget the annual publications of various Nonconformist denominations in Wales, which provide a wealth of biographical information on ministers of religion.The nineteenth century was also noted for the hundreds of biographies (*cofiannau*) of Welsh Nonconformist ministers that were published and some of the better ones will often include a great deal of local information that is not to be found anywhere else.

Family historians should also be aware of Lewis Dwnn's *The Heraldic Visitations of Wales and Part of the Marches* that was recently re-published in 2005 by Bridge Books. It was that press which also published a facsimile copy of the important work by J. E. Griffith, *Pedigrees of Anglesey and Caernarvonshire Families*, first published in 1914. T. Ceiri Griffith has published a number of Welsh language texts which provide detailed information on the genealogy of families connected with Caernarfonshire, Merioneth and Montgomeryshire. One should also be aware of the comprehensive index of some 40,000 cards relating to Welsh individuals produced by W. W. Price (1873–1967), Aberdare, which is now located at the National Library of Wales.

Sales Catalogues

Sales catalogues, especially of landed estates in Wales are a source of which every community historian, and sometimes family historians also, should be aware. They will often contain maps and plans as well as outline history of estates with a detailed list of owners and tenants, and sometimes photographs of houses and buildings that have long disappeared. Lists of items sold at auctions can be valuable, especially if prices have been noted. Equally valuable, where they have been kept and archived, are more recent collections of literature produced by individual estate agents since they will provide the community historian with a guide to the state of the housing market in various localities.

Ephemera

Ephemera has been defined by the Ephemera Society as 'the minor transient documents of everyday life', and although impermanent and short-lived in nature can often be valuable to both community and family historians as they try to re-create conditions under which people lived in the past. Normally divided into the two main categories of historical and contemporary ephemera, they will include items such as posters, tickets, bills and receipts, timetables, leaflets, political and election literature, trade literature, and all the materials that are produced for advertisements and propaganda purposes. Ephemeral materials will often offer a different perspective to more formal and traditional sources and add visual significance to events and occurrences. On occasions materials of an ephemeral nature, such as advertisement posters, may be the only evidence that have survived of a particular event. Therefore, they often supplement and complement more traditional and established sources in addition to providing an alternative account of everyday life.

Local Literature

There are numerous references in Chapter 1 to books that deal with the history of specific villages, parishes and counties in Wales, and the tradition of publishing materials on particular localities is a long and honourable one. In addition to scholarly works, any community historian should also be aware of fictional works such as novels and short stories, plays and poetry which have local contexts. Autobiographies are often particularly valuable because they portray ways of life which have long disappeared and will often contain details which are rarely found in any other sources.The value of ballads and other forms of folk verse will be discussed in Chapter 18 for they again will often contain unique local information not to be found anywhere else. Welsh Ballads Online is now an invaluable service offered by the National Library of Wales through the website (*http://www.llgc. org.uk/baledi*).

Newspapers and periodicals

Experienced community and family historians will know how valuable local newspapers and periodicals can be for their researches. Indeed one observer claimed that 'local newspapers ... are the most important

THE DEMETIAN MIRROR;
or,
Aberystwith Reporter, & Visitants' Informant,
FORMING A
RECORD OF LOCAL EVENTS, AND CHANNEL OF GENERAL INFORMATION.

The Demetian Mirror *(1840),*
a weekly newspaper published
every Saturday by J Cox in his
library at Aberystwyth

published primary source for the historian'.[3] Although once read they will usually be discarded, if there is a need to research historical topics they can be invaluable since they better reflect trends in society than almost any other source. The wealth of information they contain, ranging from announcements of births, marriages and deaths, obituaries, advertisements of businesses and sales, and quite often more substantial articles, will often be unsurpassed. Until recently, however, despite the vast amount of local information contained in newspapers and periodicals they were often inaccessible to most ordinary users because of problems relating to storage and handling and the lack of any index to their contents. Nowadays, developments in digital technology has transformed the situation and the launch of Welsh Newspapers Online,[4] further discussed in Chapter 3, has been a major landmark. With the earlier launch of Welsh Journals Online (*welshjournals.llgc.org.uk*), community and family historians in Wales now have at their disposal a vast amount of printed literature.

Ever since the first appearance of Welsh almanacs at the end of the seventeenth century the custom of reporting present events and announcing future activities gained popularity and eventually led to the growth of the periodical and newspaper industry in Wales. The *Cambrian*, the first newspaper to be published in Wales, appeared in Swansea in 1804 and was followed by the *North Wales Gazette* published at Bangor in 1808. The first Welsh-language weekly, *Seren Gomer*, also appeared at Swansea, in 1814.

In addition to what is now available online, the following printed sources, compiled by Dr Huw Walters, provide invaluable background information for those using newspapers and periodicals for their researches: *The Welsh Periodical Press, 1735–1900* (1987); *A Bibliography of Welsh Periodicals, 1735–1850* (1993); *A Bibliography of Welsh Periodicals, 1851–1900* (2003). The National Library of Wales also offers a comprehensive list of Welsh language community newspapers (*papurau bro*), an interesting phenomenon which developed from the beginning of the 1970s, and another valuable source for both community and family historians. Mention must also be made of Newsplan Wales which formed part of a co-operative programme covering all the regions of the United Kingdom and Ireland with the aim of preserving local newspapers and making them available for potential users. Further details about this important project will be found at *hhp://www.newsplancymru.info/*

Research Theses and Dissertations
There are examples, over a number of years, of students at various colleges and universities undertaking research at both undergraduate and post-graduate level, into aspects of community history in Wales, and many such dissertations and theses have been safeguarded in the libraries of individual institutions. Often they will be an important source and can be located by checking the library catalogues of higher education establishments in Wales.

General reference works
Although there is ample evidence that community and family history subjects are popular topics in Wales, as elsewhere, there are surprisingly few general books which deal with these specifically in the Welsh context. Notable examples are the two volumes edited by John and Sheila Rowlands, namely *Welsh Family History: a Guide to Research* (2nd edn,1998) and *Second Stages in Researching Welsh Ancestry* (1999). More recently has been the publication of Bruce Durie, *Welsh Genealogy* (2012). In England, on the other hand there are dozens of texts that provide an introduction to sources for both family and community historians. For community historians in particular, W. E. Tate, *The Parish Chest* (3rd edn, 1983) is still valuable although it was first published as long ago as 1946. The following also offer detailed guidance for those researching their communities: Philip Riden, *Record*

Sources for Local History (1987); Kate Tiller, *English Local History: an Introduction* (2nd edn, 2001); John Richardson, *The Local Historian's Encyclopedia* (3rd edn, 2003); Paul Carter and Kate Thompson, *Sources for Local Historians* (2005). And of special interest is David Hey (ed), *The Oxford Companion to Family and Local History* (2nd edn, 2008) which includes a number of extended articles on various topics and special themes including a chapter on 'Welsh Local and Family History'.[5]

There are also a number of important general texts which deal specifically with family history with the most notable being the following: David Hey, *Journeys in Family History* (2004); Reader's Digest, *Explore your Family's Past: Trace your Roots and Create a Family Tree* (3rd edn, 2011); Nick Barratt, *Who do you Think you Are? Encyclopedia of Genealogy* (2008) and Reader's Digest, *How to Trace your Family History on the Internet* (2008). In each of these volumes there are numerous references to sources, printed and electronic, and detailed guidance on how to construct family trees. To those that wish to publish the fruits of their researches David Dymond, *Researching and Writing History: a Practical Guide for Local Historians* (1999) is still particularly useful.

NOTES

[1] Robin Gard, *The Observant Traveller: Diaries of Travel in England, Wales and Scotland in the County Record Offices of England and Wales* (1989)
[2] The Welsh Biography Online will be found at
     http://yba.llgc.org.uk/en/index/html
[3] John Tosh, *The Pursuit of History* (1993)
[4] Available at *welshnewspapers.llgc.org.uk*
[5] D. Huw Owen, 'Welsh Local and Family History' in David Hey (ed.), *The Oxford Companion to Family and Local History (2nd edn., 2008)*, 90–100

3. The National Library of Wales, Aberystwyth: How to get Started

Beryl Evans

Tracing your Welsh ancestors is not much different to tracing English ancestors, other than that you may occasionally come across some information in the Welsh language. Do not be disheartened, as there are always staff available at the National Library of Wales who can advise you further. (Very few of the documents are completely in Welsh.)

Since the Acts of Union in 1536 and 1542, Wales has been an administrative region of England with the same format for parish registers, census returns, civil registration and other records. Family history has always played an important part of life in Wales, so much so that under the ancient Laws of Hywel Dda it was a legal requirement to be able to recite several generations of kinship. It is very fitting therefore that the National Library of Wales is deemed to be the main centre in Wales to research family history.

The campaign to establish a national library for Wales started in 1873 when a committee was formed to collect Welsh material and house it at the University College in Aberystwyth. The location of the Library in Aberystwyth was partly determined because a collection was already available at the College. Sir John Williams, physician to Queen Victoria and an avid book and manuscript collector, had also said he would present his collection to the library if it were established in Aberystwyth.

External view of the National Library of Wales
With the permission of the National Library of Wales

When the Library was established by Royal Charter on 19 March 1907, Sir John was named as the first President.

The main aim of this chapter is to give an overview of some of the main sources and facilities available at the Library for family historians (all free of charge), but it is by no means an exhaustive list of what is available. To make the best use of your time during a visit to the Library some preparation needs to be done beforehand. Gather together as much information as possible relating to family members, working backwards from yourself. Talk to members of the family – take notes and/or record information; search for various items of documentary evidence – certificates, photographs, diaries, letters, reports, funeral leaflets, newspaper cuttings etc that can give you clues. Once gathered and organised, this information can be used to trace your family tree back even further.

The next step is to decide which branch of your tree you are going to research and make a list of sources to be consulted. This can be done by using information from the Library website (*www.llgc.org.uk*) or if you cannot find the necessary details or are unable to visit in person you may wish to use the Enquiries Service (*www.llgc.org.uk/enquiries*).

The Enquiries Service can be contacted in several ways – by completing the online enquiry form at the above address; by email (*enquiry@llgc.org.uk*); by telephone 01970 632 933, or by writing to the Enquiries Service, The National Library of Wales, Aberystwyth, Ceredigion, SY23 3BU. There is also an instant chat service all day on Tuesday and Thursday if you need a quick reply to any questions; this is available through the website.

For those visiting in person a readers' ticket is essential. You will find further information and registration online (*www.llgc.org.uk/readersticket*). It is also quick and easy to obtain if you come to the Library and go to Reception, by the main door.

There are two main reading rooms at the National Library of Wales: the North Reading Room where all printed books and original newspapers can be viewed, whilst original archives, manuscripts, maps, pictures, photographs and microform collections can be consulted in the South Reading Room.

The North Reading Room
With the permission of the
National Library of Wales

The Library offers a number of Information Sessions in order for users to make the best use of the facilities and time whilst at the Library. These are 30-minute sessions with a dedicated member of staff based on individual needs. A session can be booked online (*www.llgc. org.uk/surgeries*).

The current sessions being offered are:

- Welcome Session
- Family and Local History
- Electronic Resources
- Maps, Photographs and Property History
- National Screen and Sound Archive of Wales

The South Reading Room
With the permission of the National Library of Wales

Civil Registration

As family historians most of you will be familiar with civil registration records – birth, marriage and death certificates – that have been in use from 1837. I shall not say much about them here except that the Library does not hold or issue any certificates. We hold only microfiche and online indexes which are available to search free of charge. Any requests for copies of certificates should be made to the local registry office or General Register Office. However, it is not commonly known that the Library holds microfiche indexes for the following, covering various dates: Air Births and Deaths; Army Births, Marriages and Deaths; Births, Marriages and Deaths Abroad, War Deaths, High Commission Births, Marriages and Deaths, Marine Births and Deaths and Regimental and Consular Births.

Census Records

The census, taken every ten years since 1801, is one of the most useful resources for a family historian. Only the census returns since 1841 hold any information of genealogical value and these cover the whole of Wales. Earlier returns contained only statistics and have not generally

46

survived. A separate chapter will deal with the census returns in greater detail, so I shall give details of what is available at the Library. Due to an Act of Parliament census information is closed for 100 years to protect individuals' confidentiality, so the 1911 census is the latest census available.

Before the introduction of commercial family history sites, census returns were made available on microfilm or microfiche. This format is available for the returns from 1841 to 1901 at the Library, but when the 1911 returns were released, they were available only online. At present all census returns from 1841 to 1911 can be accessed free of charge within the National Library of Wales building through the commercial sites of Findmypast and Ancestry Library, along with many other family history related datasets. You can access these sites at home, of course, but they will require payment.

In addition, many of the census returns in Wales have been transcribed and indexed by enthusiastic individuals or by family history societies. Copies of these are available at the Library for the readers to use. Details of holdings can be found by searching the Library catalogue online (*http://cat.llgc.org.uk*).

Marriage Bonds

Before marrying in a parish church you had to make sure there was no impediment to the marriage. This was usually done by publishing banns (declaring the intention to marry) on three successive Sundays prior to the ceremony. If the bride and groom were of different parishes the banns had to be published in both parish churches. Those that could afford to, and wished to avoid the publicity and delay, could marry by licence. This was granted by the Church. The bridegroom would appear before a surrogate and swear on oath that he knew of no impediment to the marriage. The oath is recorded in a document known as an affidavit or an allegation.

Before 1823, the bridegroom and another witness, usually a friend or relative, would also enter into a bond, a document obliging them to pay a sum of money. These are known as the marriage bonds. If an impediment to the marriage should come to light, then they both would forfeit the considerable sum of money noted in the bond. Under normal circumstances the sum of money would not be paid.

Other documents that can be found with the bonds and affidavits are baptism certificates, letters of consent or orders to issue a licence. The

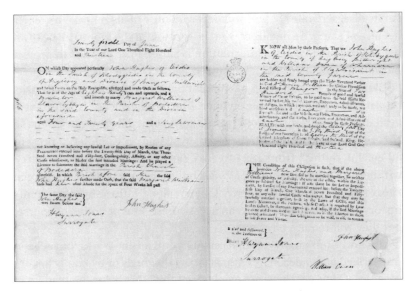

Marriage bond, John Hughes, Ceidio,
parish of Rhodogeidio, Anglesey (1813) (NLW B46/112)
With the permission of the National Library of Wales

licences themselves are rarely found as there was no obligation on the clergy or married couple to keep the licence once the marriage was solemnised.

If a marriage took place in Wales by licence the surviving bond or affidavit is likely to be amongst the records held at the National Library of Wales. The Library has indexed documents relating to about 90,000 marriages which took place in Wales between 1616 and 1837. The index is available to search through the Library's full catalogue (*http://cat.llgc.org.uk*).

The covering dates for each diocese are as follows: Bangor 1757-1931 (four documents 1691-96); Llandaff 1733–1941 (a few 1665–1708); St Asaph 1690–1938 (a few 1616–89) and St David's 1661–1867 (with two documents 1616–1621). Only the pre-1837 documents have been indexed at present, however; later documents can be found if a diocese and approximate date of marriage is known.

Parish Registers and Bishops' Transcripts

In order to trace your family before the beginning of civil registration

48

Tre'r Ceiri hillfort (Caernarfonshire) from the west, showing the fine stone fort sited on the rocky summit.
© Crown copyright: RCAHMW

Heraldic genealogical roll of John Hughes, incumbent of Llanwrin
[Montgomeryshire] by Rhys Cain (NLW, WPR 22)
With the permission of Dr. Michael Powell Siddons
and the National Library of Wales

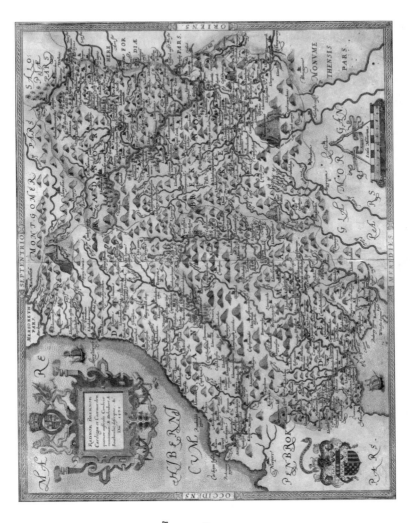

Christopher Saxton,
Radnor, Breknok,
Cardigan et Caermarden
(1579)
By permission of the
Carmarthenshire Archive
Services

51

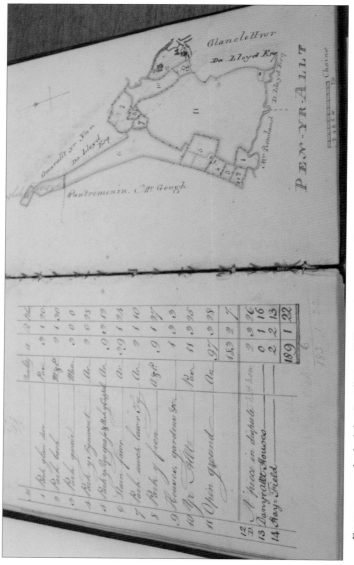

Estate map and schedule, Castell Howell Estate, the property of David Lloyd, Esq. by Charles Hassall, 1795
With the permission of Ceredigion Archives

Ordnance Survey map, 1: 2500, 1st ed. (1881)
Note the river Wye and the town and castle of Chepstow

53

Julius Caesar Ibbetson, The Entrance to Llangollen, *1792*
with the permission of The National Library of Wales

Hugh Hughes, Coracle Makers *(1842)*
with the permission of The National Library of Wales

Port Talbot Steelworks
© Crown Copyright: RCAHMW

in 1837, parish registers are a crucial source for information. Thomas Cromwell ordered in 1538 that every parish should keep a record of every baptism, marriage and burial. The survival of registers varies from parish to parish, but not many have survived from the early period. All original registers are now held at the appropriate county record office, but microfilm copies of over 500 parishes are held at the Library. A joint project between Archives Wales, The Church of Latter Day Saints and the National Library of Wales saw the digitisation of all available parish registers in Wales. These have subsequently been indexed and free access is available at the Library to search and view these online registers through Findmypast. For dates of surviving parish registers see *Cofrestri Plwyf Cymru/Parish Registers of Wales* ed by C. J. Williams and J. Watts-Williams (Aberystwyth: National Library of Wales, 2000).

Also recorded in the book are the surviving dates of bishops' transcripts. These were transcripts of the parish registers made by the incumbent at the end of every year and sent to the bishop of the diocese. Not many have survived pre-1660, but all the original transcripts are held at the National Library of Wales. They are invaluable for filling missing gaps in registers or to verify illegible entries. The transcripts for the dioceses of Bangor and Llandaff are available to view on microfiche, the other dioceses are available in original format.

Many of the parish registers and bishops' transcripts have been transcribed and indexed by various family history societies, many of these publications in various formats are available within the Library's collections to view, a search of the online catalogue (*http://cat.llgc.org.uk*) will show what is available.

Nonconformist Records

Although less comprehensive than Anglican records, Nonconformist records should not be forgotten. As a result of the Civil Registration Act of 1836 many original Nonconformist registers are now housed at The National Archives in Kew. These are available to search online for a fee (*www.bmdregisters.co.uk*). However, microfilm copies of these registers are available at the Library to view free of charge. Some pre-1837 registers were copied locally before being surrendered to the Registrar General; others never found their way to London; a few of these early registers and copies as well as later registers are now held at the Library. Unfortunately, Nonconformist records have not been as safely and conscientiously kept or stored as those of the Anglican Church, so it is unusual to find a register before the nineteenth century. For surviving registers see *Cofrestri Anghydffurfiol Cymru/ Nonconformist Registers of Wales* ed. Dafydd Ifans (Aberystwyth: National Library of Wales, 1994) and also the CAPELI database available in the South Reading Room at the Library.

Other Nonconformist records that will be of value to family historians are the lists of members, contribution books, annual reports – which often record details of births, christenings, marriages, deaths and burials, and denominational periodicals, too, often contain a section for births, marriages, and deaths. Although primarily of value for details of members of the denomination in question, notes on members of other denominations may often appear in the following publications: *Yr Eurgrawn Wesleyaidd* (first published 1809, Wesleyan Methodist); *Seren Gomer* (1818, Baptist); *Y Drysorfa* (1831, Calvinistic Methodist); *Yr Haul* (1835, Anglican Church in Wales); *Y Diwygiwr* (1835, Congregational); *Yr Ymofynydd* (1847, Unitarian). More information can be found under Denominational Magazines on the Library's website (*www.llgc.org.uk/index.php?id=516*) and through the Library's online catalogue (*http://cat.llgc.org.uk*).

Wills and other Probate Records

Wills, which were proved in the Welsh ecclesiastical courts before the introduction of Civil Probate on 11 January 1858, have been deposited in the Library. The old indexes produced by the courts themselves have now been replaced by an online index (*www.llgc.org.uk/probate*). No digital images for wills or administrations are currently available for Hawarden, Brecon or St Asaph pre-1660, but the entries do appear in the online index.

The covering dates of the surviving probate records are:

Bangor:	1635–1858
Brecon:	1543–1858
Chester (Welsh wills):	1557–1858
Hawarden:	1554–1858
Llandaff:	1568–1857
St Asaph:	1565–1857
St David's:	1556–1858

For the period after 1858 the Library has custody of register copy wills from five registries, covering all but one (Montgomeryshire) of the Welsh counties, and a full set of the annual index of all wills and administrations granted in England and Wales, known as the *Calendar of Grants*, from 1858 to 1972.

In addition to the official probate records, some wills and inventories and other papers associated with probate can be found in the consistory court papers filed with the diocesan records of the Church in Wales. Thousands of wills occur in the Library's collections of family, estate and personal papers; some of these may not survive in the official probate records, or may never have been proved, or may have been proved outside Wales. These can be searched through the Library's online catalogue (*http://cat.llgc.org.uk*).

Wills, letters of administration and other probate records provide an invaluable historical source. It must be realised, however, that for most people neither will nor administration ever existed, but it is always worth checking as some of even the poorest people left wills.

Before 12 January 1858, proving wills and granting letters of administration in England and Wales was the responsibility of ecclesiastical courts, each having its own area of jurisdiction.

Which court had jurisdiction in any given case was determined largely by the place of death and the extent and location of the estate of the deceased. Wills were normally proved in the episcopal consistory court (the diocesan or bishop's court). If the estate comprised goods in two or more dioceses within the same province, probate was granted in either of the two provincial courts of the Archbishop of York and the Archbishop of Canterbury. The Prerogative Court of the Archbishop of York (PCY) administered the northern province (the northern dioceses of England which included the southern detachment of Flint), while the Prerogative Court of the Archbishop of Canterbury (PCC) covered the southern province (the southern English dioceses and Wales). If the deceased had held goods in both provinces, probate was undertaken by the PCC, which had over-riding jurisdiction throughout England and Wales.

The right to grant probate was also held by certain church and secular courts called 'peculiars' because they were 'of peculiar or exempt jurisdiction', i.e. outside the authority of the archdeacon or bishop. There was only one peculiar in Wales, that of Hawarden, co. Flint, which had jurisdiction in the parish of Hawarden.

The pre-1858 probate records deposited in this Library comprise those of the episcopal consistory courts of St Asaph, Bangor, St David's, and Llandaff, the consistory court of the archdeaconry of Brecon, the peculiar of Hawarden, and the Welsh wills proved at the episcopal consistory court of Chester. There were no ecclesiastical courts in Wales below the diocesan level. In probate matters, the consistory court of the archdeaconry of Brecon, one of the four archdeaconries of the diocese of St David's, acted as the diocesan court in a local capacity.

The following is a brief summary of the position in Wales. The original wills and administration bonds generally survive from about 1600 except for Bangor, where very few have survived prior to 1635. There are, however, records in original or copy form dating back to the latter half of the sixteenth century, but survivals are few. The earliest surviving volumes of register copy wills are for St Asaph (from 1565) and Brecon (from 1543), both pre-dating the surviving original records. During the Interregnum between monarchs (1649–1660), the local courts ceased to function, with resultant gaps in the Bangor and St Asaph records between 1648 and 1660 and in Brecon and Carmarthen (St. David's diocese) between 1653 and 1660. Despite this, some wills, mainly for Glamorgan, were proved during this period at Llandaff. The records of the court of civil commission which functioned during the Commonwealth are filed at The National Archives with those of the PCC. Probate act books are available for the Welsh courts (except Bangor and Brecon and for the Welsh wills proved at Chester), but surviving series are incomplete.

In 1858, responsibility for probate was transferred from the complex system of church courts to a simpler system of civil probate registries. The search for a post-1858 will becomes a much easier task. Since 12 January 1858, wills and administrations in England and Wales have been proved and granted in either the Principal Registry of the Family Division, (formerly the Principal Probate Registry), First Avenue House, 42-49 High Holborn, London WC1 6NP, or the appropriate district registry. Copies of all wills proved in district registries are held at First Avenue House. Until 1941, the district registries made a second copy of the will which was entered and bound into volumes of register copy wills. It is these volumes of copy wills from the district registries having jurisdiction in Wales which constitute the post-1858 probate records deposited in the Library.

The post-1858 records comprise those from the district registries at St Asaph, Bangor, Carmarthen, Llandaff and Hereford. The exception is Shrewsbury, which covered Montgomeryshire. The following details regarding jurisdictions and record holdings are based on information contained in the typescript schedule of probate records. It should be noted that the jurisdictions reflect the territorial position contemporary with the period of records, i.e. 1858-1941, not the current situation. Territorial jurisdiction was abolished in 1926, and the registries at St Asaph and Hereford were closed in 1928.

Probate Court	Jurisdiction (counties)
St Asaph	Most of Denbigh and Flint; parts of Caernarfon, Merioneth, Montgomery, Salop
Bangor	Bangor, Anglesey; most of Caernarfon; parts of Denbigh, Merioneth, Montgomery
St David's	Cardigan, Carmarthen and Pembroke; part of Glamorgan (deanery of Gower)
Llandaff	Most of Glamorgan and Monmouth
Brecon	Brecon; most of Radnor; parts of Monmouth; Monmouthshire
Hawarden	Parish of Hawarden, co. Flint
Chester	Parts of Flint and Denbigh (one Parish – Holt)
Hereford	(This group has been transferred to the Herefordshire Record Office) Parts of Monmouth, Montgomery and Radnor. This court also had jurisdiction in those parishes which were partly in Shropshire and partly in Montgomery, ie. Alberbury, Mainstone and Worthen

Probate Court	District Registry
St Asaph	Denbigh, Flint and Merioneth
Bangor	Anglesey and Caernarfon
Carmarthen	Cardigan, Carmarthen, Pembroke, and part of Glamorgan (Gower)
Llandaff	Monmouth and Glamorgan (except Gower)
Hereford	Brecon, Radnor and Hereford

The post-1858 records consist of large bound volumes of copy wills spanning the years 1858 to 1941, when registries ceased to copy wills into registers. They cover all the historic counties of Wales (except for

Montgomeryshire), and one English county – Herefordshire. Post-1858 Montgomeryshire wills were proved at the Shrewsbury District Registry whose records are at the Shropshire Record Office.

Contemporary manuscript indexes together with modern card indexes cover most of the records. Deficiencies can be made up by using the printed *Calendar of Grants*, an annual index of all wills and administrations granted in England and Wales since 1858. This index is available at First Avenue House, most District Probate Registries and some local record offices, and for the period 1858–1972 at the Library.

A brief summary of the holdings for each registry is given below:

St Asaph	Register copy wills, 1858–1928. There are no separate MS indexes, but indexes can be found in the volumes for 1860-1 and 1865–1923
Bangor	Register copy wills, 1858–1941. Card index, 1858–1941
Carmarthen	Register copy wills, 1858–1941. MS indexes, 1858–1923. Card index, 1924–1941
Llandaff	Register copy wills, 1858–1940. MS indexes, 1858-1905
Hereford	Register copy wills, 1858–1928. MS indexes, 1858–1928

In general PCC and PCY proved the wills of persons of wealth and substance, while the lower courts dealt mostly with the estates of ordinary people; but this was not always the case. If the will of a person of modest means cannot be found in the records of the local courts a search of the higher courts should not be ruled out, especially in the nineteenth century. PCC also had jurisdiction of the English and Welsh estates of persons who died abroad and at sea. During the Commonwealth, 1653–60, a court of civil commission was established in London which had sole jurisdiction in England and Wales.

The records of PCC are held at The National Archives, Kew. You can search the complete series of PCC wills (1354–1858) through the Discovery catalogue on The National Archives' website. The National Library of Wales holds microfilm copies of the PCC wills from 1354 to 1858 on open access in the South Reading Room.

Tithe Maps and Schedules

Following the Tithe Commutation Act of 1836, tithe maps were drawn for every parish in England and Wales, showing the land included within each parish. These maps were produced during the period 1838 to 1854. The accuracy, scale and size of each map varied from parish to parish as over 200 different surveyors worked on the task in Wales alone.

The maps show farms and dwellings on which tithe was paid. The apportionment schedules are the keys to the maps and give the following information:

Name of landowner and tenant/occupier
Field/plot numbers
Description of land, more often than not the field names
State of cultivation such as arable, pasture or meadow
Area of field/plot in acres
Amount of tithe due

For many parishes, the tithe maps are the only large-scale maps showing the landscape prior to the Industrial Revolution. Copies of the maps and apportionments for the whole of Wales are available in the South Reading Room at The National Library of Wales. More detailed information can be found in *The Tithe Maps of Wales* by Robert Davies (1999). The map collection at the Library includes many more maps which may be of use to the family historian – printed and manuscript maps, farm and estate maps and sale catalogues. The maps collection can be searched through the online catalogue (*http://cat.llgc.org.uk*).

Court of Great Session Records

Legal and administrative archives encompass a great mass of material relating to the administration of areas from the whole of Wales, to parishes, townships, hamlets and manors. They often relate to legal actions before various courts of law, but, even so, information about persons of unimpeachable character, as well as the wrongdoers themselves, is often given.

Transactions concerning land were also conducted before some of these courts, mainly the Great Sessions and Manorial Courts. The Court of Great Sessions in Wales was the most important of these bodies. It came into being with the union of England and Wales and continued from 1543 to its abolition in 1830. These records have been greatly underused by family and local historians in the past, possibly due to their complexity, the physical size of both the collection and documents themselves, and the lack of published information relating to these records. It is one of the most valuable collections held at the National Library and is unique to Wales. I shall not go into too much detail as a separate chapter will cover these records in more depth.

The only class of records from the collection to be indexed in any detail are the crimes, criminals and punishments found in the Gaol Files between 1730 and 1830. The index can be found through the Crime and Punishment database on the website (*www.llgc.org.uk/sesiwn_fawr/index_s.htm*). A search can be made by 'name of accused' and also by 'offence' or a combination of both. Drop-down menus can also be used for other options, or a free text search can be made.

As sometimes no verdict appears in the gaol files, we can turn to the Criminal Register for Wales for possible verdicts. The original register is held at The National Archives, Kew but the Library holds a microfilm copy for the period 1808–1892, which covers cases in the Great Sessions Court until 1830 and then the Assize Courts thereafter.

For anyone interested in gaining more information about the Great Sessions records, Glyn Parry's book *A Guide to the Records of the Courts of Great Sessions* (1995) is an essential tool. It gives a detailed introduction to the various classes of records used by the court.

Manorial records

It has been suggested that manorial records are one of the most important groups of genealogical records after parish registers and wills. The variety of documents within this group is defined by the Manorial Documents Rule of 1959:

> court rolls, surveys, maps, terriers, documents and books of every description relating to boundaries, wastes, customs of a manor

A 'manor', without going into great detail, was a piece of land, varying greatly in size, each one with its own lord. The lord granted land within the manor to tenants in return for rent or services. Each manor also had a manor court over which the lord or his steward would preside, and tenants were jurors. The courts would set out the conditions of tenure, create by-laws, also known as 'customs of the manor', and appoint minor officials within the manor, and in many cases would have jurisdictions over petty offences.

These documents are an important source as they more often than not pre-date existing parish registers and can be useful in listing names of tenants, dates of deaths and names of heirs, and can be particularly useful in tracing successive tenants of a property and relationships between them. Many of the documents produced by the courts were lists of names, such as suitors, jurors, tenants and petty constables. It must be remembered that survival of the records varies greatly in various parts of Wales. The manorial records held by the Library, mainly to be found with the estate records and listed with them, are indexed separately. They are most comprehensive for Montgomeryshire (mainly the Powis Castle and Wynnstay estate records); substantial holdings for Glamorgan and Monmouthshire (mainly the Badminton, Bute, and Tredegar estate records) are all held at the National Library. It must be remembered that in many parts of Wales the manorial system never really took root. This is particularly true of the north Wales counties of Anglesey, Caernarfonshire and Merionethshire.

An index to the manors and manorial records of Wales is available online via the website of the Manorial Documents Register (*www.nationalarchives.gov.uk/mdr/*).

The only comprehensive guide to the records is *Welsh Manors and their Records* by Helen Watt (2000).

Archives
The main non-print collections held at the Library consist of hundreds of collections covering a variety of subjects by many individuals, families, institutions and societies: archives, manuscripts, maps, photographs, screen and sound records. Many of these sources can be useful for the family historian. The estate and family records from many areas of Wales are within our holdings and relate not only to the landed families but also to our ancestors who worked and provided various services to these people over the centuries.

Access to the archives that have been catalogued is available online by searching the Library's catalogue (http://cat.llgc.org.uk) or for archives and manuscripts that have not yet been included in the full catalogue (http://isys.llgc.org.uk/). Free text searches in various combinations can be made for names, places, subjects and dates. Paper copies of the schedules relating to these collections can also be accessed within the South Reading Room at the Library.

Welsh Newspapers

The National Library of Wales since its foundation has collected newspapers published in Wales, and those outside Wales, in Welsh and of Welsh interest. By their very nature they are not intended to last indefinitely as old newspapers become acidic and brittle with time, and present major conservation problems. In the past making high-quality, preservation-standard microfilm of original newspapers has helped conserve original newspapers.

However, with the introduction of digitisation things have moved on considerably and as a result the beta launch of Welsh Newspapers Online (*http://welshnewspapers.llgc.org*) in March 2013 heralds the arrival of over 1 million pages of historical Welsh newspapers on the web. This a free resource from the National Library of Wales that will allow anybody with an interest in the history and people of Wales to browse and search over 100 titles from its rich collection of pre-1910 newspapers.

Digital technology allows the National Library of Wales to radically extend the use and value of this magnificent record of everyday knowledge by converting the primary paper format into digital form and making it freely available for use on its website. Welsh Newspapers Online will allow the researcher not only to browse and read digital copies of the original page but also, by adopting Optical Character Recognition technology, to search for words, names and dates across all 1 million pages simultaneously.

The first newspaper to be published in Wales was the *Cambrian*, published in Swansea in 1804; the collection of local and national historical newspapers, from this date until 1910, are a rich resource for family and community historians, helping to give an insight into the daily lives of our ancestors and the communities they lived in.

Remember, that the Library can provide access to original or microfilm copies of later newspapers and many titles can also be accessed in the reading rooms through online subscription sites such Times Digital Archive, 19th Century British Library newspapers, and Newsbank available free of charge to Library users. If you are able to read Welsh, or know someone who can help you, the many *papurau bro* (community newspapers) established in the 1970s and 1980s should not be ignored. Copies of these papers from all over Wales are housed at the Library, and feature historical articles and photographs each month.

Further Reading

Cofrestri Plwyf Cymru/Parish Registers of Wales ed. C J Williams and J Watts-Williams (2000)

Cofrestri Anghydffurfiol Cymru/Nonconformist Registers of Wales ed. Dafydd Ifans (1994)

Robert Davies, *The Tithe Maps of Wales* (1999)

W. Ll. Davies, *The National Library of Wales: a survey of its history, contents, and its activities* (1937)

Rhidian Griffiths, *Y ddinas ar y bryn: Llyfrgell Genedlaethol Cymru trwy luniau: The city on the hill : The National Library of Wales in pictures* (2007)

David Jenkins, *A Refuge in Peace and War: The National Library of Wales to 1952* (2002)

Glyn Parry, *A Guide to the Records of the Courts of Great Sessions* (1995)

Helen Watt, *Welsh Manors and their Records* (2000)

The National Library of Wales also produces a number of information leaflets on various subjects including:

Family History
Church in Wales Records
Probate Records
Maps
Photographs
Newspapers
Sources for the History of Houses

For copies please contact the Enquiries Service as previously stated.

4. Welsh Pedigrees and Heraldry

Michael Siddons

Although pedigrees had always played an important role in society in Wales, heraldry was an import from outside, arriving much later in Wales than in England.

Pedigrees

Giraldus Cambrensis referred in the twelfth century to the importance of their pedigrees to the Welsh, saying that they were more desirous of marrying into noble families than into wealthy ones. 'Even the common people retain their genealogy, and can not only readily recount the names of their grandfathers and great-grandfathers, but even refer back to the sixth or seventh generation, or beyond them.'[1]

In Welsh law it was necessary for each person to know his pedigree, because the rights and duties of each member of society depended on his place in a kinship. Land, for example, was not held by individuals but by a kinship.[2] The legal texts contain terms for relationship as far as the seventh degree.[3] Even when this need disappeared with the Acts of Union with England of 1536 and 1542 the Welsh continued to give great importance to their pedigrees. The Welshman's love of pedigree and pride in noble descent was a subject of scorn to the English. William of Worcester wrote to John Paston in 1457: 'I sende a bille of the namys endyted to my maister and yow, to see and laugh at theyr Wellsh names descended of old pedigréis'.[4]

In the beginning pedigrees were transmitted by heart, and it was some centuries before they were written down. The earliest surviving genealogical texts were first written down in the ninth century, and a few of them in the twelfth and thirteenth centuries. They contain the pedigrees of the princely lines, including lesser ones such as those of Arwystli and Gwent, together with the pedigrees of ancient heroes and saints, and some other leading families. Some of these pedigrees go back into the Dark Ages. It is believed that the earliest surviving texts of the pedigrees date from *c.*1100, and two others from the thirteenth century, but most of the original pedigrees did not survive, and we now have only later copies. The earliest texts have been edited by Dr Peter Bartrum.[5]

A knowledge of the pedigrees of the princes and the other important families formed an important part of the learning of the bards, who in addressing their patrons sang of their ancient noble lineage, often at great length. From the fifteenth century onwards we have collections of pedigrees of the princes and noblemen by each generation of bards.[6] Very little evidence was recorded for the earliest part of the pedigrees, and the bards, with few exceptions, did not give dates or sources, but where it is possible to check the traditional pedigrees against record evidence, they are found to be surprisingly accurate.[7]

In the latter part of the fifteenth century the bards began to talk of 'the fifteen tribes of Gwynedd', and to list them. Gutun Owain referred to 'One of the XV tribes', and he probably had a list of them, although the lists which we have today are from a little later. These lists all agree, with one or two variations. Other groupings included 'the five royal tribes of Wales'.[8]

The majority of the well-known Welsh families claimed to be descended from a relatively small number of 'patriarchs' who lived centuries earlier, of whom a few had no historical existence.[9] Because the number of families claiming descent from some of these patriarchs was so great, they were divided into sections, each section descending from an ancestor who can be described as an intermediate ancestor, himself descended from the original patriarch. Examples of this division are the descendants of Tudur Trefor and Bleddyn ap Cynfyn:

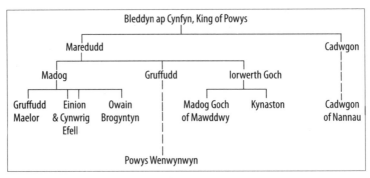

Figure 1:
Subdivisions of the descendants of Bleddyn ap Cynfyn.

From the late sixteenth century the bardic system began to decline, the chief factors including the decline in the quality of the poetry and the anglicisation of the gentry. It was fortunate that this period also saw the appearance of a number of gentlemen antiquarians, the foremost of whom were George Owen (d. 1611) of Henllys, Nevern, in the south,[10] and Robert Vaughan (d. 1667) of Hengwrt near Dolgellau, in the north.[11] These enjoyed friendly relations with the bards, and as a result of this many of the manuscripts of the bards were saved together with much of the traditional learning of the Welsh.

Most of the manuscripts of Gruffudd Hiraethog, the leading bard of the mid-sixteenth century, came to his disciple Wiliam Llŷn (d. 1580), who in his will left all his manuscripts to Rhys Cain (d. 1618), whose son Siôn Cain (d. 1650) transferred the whole collection to Robert Vaughan of Hengwrt. Robert Vaughan left them, together with a great many other manuscripts which he had acquired, including the bards' manuscripts of verse, and his own great collection of pedigrees,[12] to his descendants. In 1859 the whole collection came to W. W. E. Wynne (1801–80), of Peniarth, and now forms the Peniarth collection in the National Library of Wales. Some of George Owen of Henllys' manuscripts are held in the National Library of Wales, and others in the British Library and the College of Arms.

The bards wrote in Welsh, but most of the gentleman antiquarians, although they were also Welsh-speaking, were educated in England and wrote mostly in English. Their work was in a more modern style, giving dates and sources for the pedigrees. The later deputy heralds were chosen from among them.[13]

In the seventeenth century several comprehensive collections of pedigrees were compiled, with a great effort to record every descendant, whatever his position in society. Such collections were made by Peter Ellis (d. 1637), Jacob Chaloner (d. 1631), Robert Vaughan of Hengwrt (d. 1667), Griffith Hughes (*fl.* 1634–65), Owen Salesbury of Rug and John Salesbury of Erbistock (collection of *c.*1630–70), David Edwardes of Rhyd-y-gors (d.1690), William Lewes of Llwynderw (d. 1722) and Hugh Thomas (1673–1720).[14] The last of these great collections, based on the earlier ones and completed *c.*1770, is the Golden Grove Book, compiled by Evan Evans of Carmarthen.[15]

After editing the early Welsh genealogical texts Dr Bartrum went on to make a detailed study of the traditional pedigrees over a period extending from the earliest pedigrees until the generation born in the early sixteenth century. He examined all the earliest available texts in order to select the most trustworthy ones. The fruit of this work is two very important series of pedigrees, which give the most reliable texts available.[16] It is important to understand that the purpose of these collections was to put the traditional pedigrees into order, and to correct the errors made in copying and re-copying earlier manuscripts. Dr Bartrum did not seek to base each pedigree on record evidence, but was ready to use such evidence when he came across it. These collections are fully indexed for personal names and places. A very important element of the indexes of personal names is that they indicate for each individual the earliest manuscripts in which he or she is mentioned. The reader can therefore know to what extent these sources are contemporary with the individual concerned. With these volumes there is no need for the non-specialist to consult the original manuscripts, and of course published texts are much easier to read than the manuscripts.[17] Because of the lack of surnames in Wales in earlier days and the consequent importance of place-names, these collections of pedigrees are an essential tool for the study of any aspect of mediaeval Wales, whether historical, literary or geographical, and Aberystwyth University is making them progressively available online, with the additions and corrections incorporated.[18]

Two valuable volumes are *Welsh Family History: A Guide to Research* and *Second Stages in Researching Welsh Ancestry*, edited by John and Sheila Rowlands, which treat all aspects of genealogy and family history.[19] The first of these contains a discussion of the genealogies in books and manuscripts.[20]

Heraldry

Heraldry has been defined as the systematic use of hereditary devices centred on the shield. The practice of decorating the shields of knights with symbols began in the twelfth century in England, northern France, Flanders and Luxembourg, and spread to other countries of western Europe. The practice was widespread among the knightly class by the end of the thirteenth century.[21] One of the chief causes of this development was the wearing of closed helmets, which made it impossible to recognise a knight in battle or in the tournaments which were so popular in feudal society at that period. Each knight chose emblems to adorn his shield, and before long the same emblems adorned the linen coat which he wore over his armour for protection against the heat of the sun, and also the covering of his horse. Similar emblems were placed on banners or standards. This pattern of emblems was called a coat of arms. Knights later began to decorate their helmets with emblems called crests. The widespread present-day use of the word 'crest' to mean a coat of arms is incorrect, and should be avoided.

Wales did not form part of this international society, and except for the Marches, where Anglo-Normans had replaced the native rulers, the feudal system had not developed. As a result, heraldry reached Wales much later than England. Only a handful of native Welshmen had coats of arms before 1350, and they were not widely adopted before the middle of the fifteenth century. The earliest arms recorded were those of Gruffudd ap Llywelyn of Gwynedd (d. 1244), and his sons Llywelyn, prince of Wales (d. 1282) and Dafydd (d. 1283), and Gruffudd ap Gwenwynwyn of Powys (d. 1286) and his sons.[22] Apart from these members of princely families most of the Welshmen whose arms were recorded early took part in English knightly society, most often through military service.

Immigration into Wales began soon after the Norman conquest of England in 1066, especially in the south and the east. A number of foreigners settled in Wales from then on, either as military followers of the lords who had replaced the native lords, or in more peaceful ways.[23] Because these lords were members of the knightly class in England, many of them also having lands in England, it is not surprising that they and those who came with them followed English heraldic practice. As a result there is more heraldic evidence for them than for the native Welsh in the period before 1350.[24]

Every type of emblem or device can be used in a coat of arms, including animals and birds, or geometric figures such as crosses, chevrons, or anything else. In the beginning the pattern of the charges was simple, but after a generation or two most of the simple designs had been chosen, and the need was felt for a system and rules. It was accepted that colour should not be placed on colour, nor metal on metal. The metals were yellow, representing gold, and white, representing silver, and the colours were black, red, blue and green. The reason for this convention was that there was a greater contrast between metal and colour, which made for easier recognition. Animal furs were also used for patterns, such as ermine and squirrel. With the adoption of rules and the increasing complexity of design, experts became necessary. These were called heralds, and the study of coats of arms was called heraldry. Coats of arms became hereditary in the male line, and if more than one member of a family was active at the same time, it was necessary to distinguish between them. The original coat of arms was borne by the head of the family, while the other members made alterations, called differences, by a change either of the colours or of the charges. For example, Dafydd ap Gruffudd of Gwynedd kept the design of his elder brother Llywelyn's coat, but changed the colours.[25]

Another later development was the placing of more than one coat on the same shield. This practice is called quartering. According to the rules of arms the descendants of a daughter who is heiress or co-heiress to her father, or whose brother or brothers are without descendants, may quarter on the same shield the coat of their father with that of their mother. They are considered to represent both families. If this happens several times in the same family an additional coat may be placed on the shield each time.

Although the early bards, when singing the praises of their patrons, often described them as 'dragon', 'lion', or 'eagle', these were heroic epithets and not heraldic, and for the earliest real description of a coat of arms in Welsh we have to wait until c.1351–9, for a poem addressed by Gruffudd Gryg to Einion ap Gruffudd ap Hywel of Chwilog, which contains the lines:

Aeth, dyro gwpl i'th darian
A thri fflŵr-de-lis i'th ran,
Yn gydwynion ei gadu
Y sydd iawn mewn maes o ddu.[26]

[Put a chevron on your shield,
Three fleur-de-lis for your part,
Leaving them all white,
That is right in a field of black.]

But in general the bards largely ignored heraldry until the mid-fifteenth century, when some of them, such as Lewis Glyn Cothi (*fl.* 1447–89), referred to it widely in their work, and it became part of the lore of the bards. Lewis described and painted coats of arms in manuscripts which have survived in his own hand.[27] Another well-known bard who introduced heraldry into his work was Gutun Owain (*fl.*1450–98). But some of the most prominent bards, such as Guto'r Glyn (*c.*1435–*c.*1493), continued to ignore heraldry in their poetry.

Some bards, who came to be called herald bards, took a particular interest in genealogy and heraldry. They made collections of pedigrees and coats of arms, and recorded the arms which they saw in churches and houses. Coats of arms were attributed to each of the fifteen tribes of Gwynedd and the five royal tribes, and to the intermediate ancestors such as those in Figure 1. Rhys Cain of Oswestry (d. 1618) and his son Siôn Cain (d. 1650) are considered to have been the last herald bards.

From the end of the fifteenth century pedigrees of the gentry were compiled in the form of long rolls, many of them decorated with coats of arms, showing the subject's descent from the princes and notable ancestors, and also the relation with important contemporaries, such as Queen Elizabeth I, the Herberts or the Cecils.[28]

Although Wales lost its independence in 1282, it did not form part of the kingdom until the Acts of Union in 1536 and 1542, and the traditional Welsh society and culture remained to a large extent unchanged. Although the English heralds visited parts of the southern and eastern March in *c.*1480 and 1531, Wales was left largely to itself from an heraldic point of view until 1550, when Edward VI ordered Fulk ap Hywel, a Welshman who was the Lancaster Herald of Arms, to make an official heraldic visitation of Wales. Unfortunately he was convicted of forging a seal in 1551, and his visitation did not take place.[29]

The difference of language and social structure in Wales, and the need for better recording of Welsh arms and pedigrees led to the appointment by the English heralds of deputy heralds, and two traditionally-trained herald bards, namely Gruffudd Hiraethog (d. 1564) and Lewys Dwnn (appointed 1586, d. c.1616), were appointed deputy heralds for the whole of Wales, and visited the gentry throughout Wales, recording their pedigrees and heraldry.[30] These were succeeded by deputies appointed for parts of Wales only, most of them chosen from among the gentleman antiquarians. Welsh gentlemen began to study in England, either at university or the inns of court, and also to visit the heralds in London where they became familiar with English practice, often obtaining confirmation of their arms, and in some cases also the grant of a crest. With the increasing influence of the heralds, Welsh heraldry moved gradually nearer to English heraldry, although the old habits died hard.[31]

Welsh heraldry therefore developed largely independently until the mid-sixteenth century,

Heraldic genealogical roll of John Hughes, incumbent of Llanwrin by Rhys Cain (NLW, WPR 22)
With the permission of Dr Michael Powell Siddons and the National Library of Wales

and there were significant differences in heraldic practice between England and Wales:

1. In the early days the Welsh paid little respect to the conventions concerning metal on metal and colour on colour.

2. The Welsh did not often differentiate their arms to indicate the place of each individual in the family.

3. The Welsh did not follow consistently the rules for quartering coats of arms, and often quartered the arms of their most distinguished ancestors. The wooden panel of Charles Lloyd (b. 1613) of Dolobran, Meifod, and his wife Elizabeth Stanley, of an English family, is a good example. This panel bears the arms of husband and wife side by side on the same shield. On her side the presence of each quartering can be explained by descent from an heiress, according to the rule. But this rule is not followed on Charles Lloyd's side.[32]

4. The greatest difference, however, was the practice of retrospective attribution of coats of arms. With a certain logic the Welsh reasoned that since coats of arms were hereditary, the arms borne by present-day men must have been those borne by their ancestors, and took this reasoning back to attribute the arms to the original 'patriarch' who founded the lineage, who lived before the days of heraldry, and was even in some cases a legendary figure. A step further was to argue that since these were the arms of the patriarch, they must also be those of all his descendants, who thus had the right to bear them.[33] The effect of this was that many families bore the same coat of arms.

    Retrospective attribution occurred in other countries, arms being attributed to the saints, Christ and the Trinity, to Arthur and his knights, the 'Nine Worthies', and other ancient heroes, but the difference in Wales was that the arms so attributed were borne by later families 'by inheritance'.

    As mentioned earlier, since the families claiming descent from some of the patriarchs were so numerous, they were later divided into sections, each family in the section descending from an intermediate ancestor. Each of these intermediate ancestors was attributed a coat of arms, which was considered to have descended to the families descended from him and borne instead of the coat of the original patriarch.[34]

5. One of the results of this retrospective attribution was the possibility of quartering a large number of coats of arms, many of them representing historical pre-heraldic ancestors, and sometimes even legendary supposed ancestors. This led to some grotesque examples of multi-quartering: the Lloyd family of Stockton, for example, quartered no less than 323 coats on the same shield, including multiple repetition of series of coats.[35]

6. Since the origins of so many traditional Welsh pedigrees are traced back so far in time compared to many English families, and the descent traced to a limited number of 'patriarchs', the coat of arms more often tells us more from which long-distant patriarch the bearer claims descent, and little or nothing about his immediate family. For example, many families in south-west Wales claimed to be descendants of Urien, a sixth-century ruler, and all bear the coat attributed to him. Some of these families bore these coats by the mid-fifteenth century, so that they now have more than 500 years of historical use behind them.

Until relatively recently most Welsh families did not have fixed family surnames, and expressed their names as X, son or daughter of Y: thus Dafydd ap Gwilym was Dafydd the son of Gwilym. When fixed names were taken, in some cases one brother took their father's name as a fixed surname, another their grandfather's name. As a result many families with different surnames claim descent from the same distant ancestor. In the same way, families now bearing the same surname are not necessarily related at all. A great number of Welsh names are simply derived from Christian names, Williams, Thomas, etc. Names beginning with vowels gave, for example Bowen from ab Owen, or Powell from ap Hywel. Other surnames were derived from epithets, such as Gwyn or Wynn (white), Llwyd (grey), Gough (red), Vaughan (from *fychan*, often used for younger).

Another type of heraldic emblem or device is the badge. A well-known badge is that of three ostrich feathers, borne by the Prince of Wales as heir to the throne. Noblemen began to use badges in the fourteenth century on a type of flag called a standard, a long flag with tapering ends, and they were also borne by their followers.[36] Examples are the raven of Sir Rhys ap Thomas (d. 1525) and the dragon with a bloody hand in its mouth of the Herberts. Sir Rhys ap Thomas was referred to by the poets as 'the raven', or 'the great raven', from his badge.

Arms and badges were also used to adorn seals, windows, tapestries, curtains, furniture, sepulchral monuments, houses and so on.

The right to a coat of arms

A coat of arms does not belong to a name, but to a family. One sometimes sees commercial offers of 'the coat of arms of your name', but these are quite worthless. The fact that a particular Vaughan family has a coat of arms, for example, does not mean that all Vaughan families have a right to the same coat. The right to an officially recognised coat of arms is limited either to those belonging to a family whose right has been recognised in the past, or today by the heralds in the College of Arms in London, or else to someone who has himself or herself received a grant of arms from the heralds. Most of the old traditional Welsh coats have been recognised by the heralds.

NOTES

1   Giraldus Cambrensis, *The Description of Wales*, Book 1, chapter 17, paragraph 1.
2   For the structure of society and the importance of kinship in Wales see R.R. Davies, *History of Wales, II, 1063-1415, Conquest, Coexistence and Change* (1987), 115-29; and A. D. Carr, *Medieval Anglesey* (1982), new edition published in 2011; chapters V, VI.
3   These terms are listed in the Welsh Law books, e.g. *Llyfr Colan*, ed. Dafydd Jenkins (1993), 16, 265. See also Francis Jones, 'Approach to Welsh Genealogy', *Trans. Cymm.*, 1948, 317.
4   Norman Davis (ed.), *Paston Letters and Papers of the Fifteenth Century* (2 vols, 1971-6), I. 525 (no. 321).
5   P. C. Bartrum, *Early Welsh Genealogical Tracts* (1966).
6   Dr Bartrum published three valuable articles on the genealogical manuscripts: Peter C. Bartrum, 'Notes on the Welsh genealogical manuscripts', *Trans. Cymmr.*,

1968, pt. 1, 63-98; 'Further notes on the Welsh genealogical manuscripts', *ibid.*, 1976, 102-118; 'Notes on the Welsh genealogical manuscripts (Part III), *ibid.*, 1988, 37-46.

7   One of the first to refer to his sources was Gruffudd Hiraethog. See P.C.Bartrum, 'Genealogical sources quoted by Gruffudd Hiraethog', *NLWJ*, XXVI (1989-90), 1-9.

8   For the five royal tribes of Wales see P.C.Bartrum, 'Pedigrees of the Welsh Tribal Patriarchs', *NLWJ*, XIII (1963-4), 125, which also gives the members of another group, of less importance; and for the fifteen tribes of Gwynedd see idem, 'Hen lwythau Gwynedd a'r Mars', *NLWJ*, XII (1961-2), appendix, 230-2.

9   'Pedigrees of the Welsh Tribal Patriarchs', *NLWJ*, vol.XIII (1963), pp.93-146, and the same, continued in *ibid.*, vol.XV (1967), pp.157-66).

10   B. G. Charles, *George Owen of Henllys : A Welsh Elizabethan* (1973).

11   *Oxford Dictionary of National Biography* [ODNB], s.n. Robert Powell Vaughan.

12   NLW, Peniarth MS 287.

13   Michael Powell Siddons, *The Development of Welsh Heraldry* [*DWH*], 4 vols (1991-2006), I, 313-21.

14   These collections are described in the articles referred to in note 6.

15   Carmarthen Record Office, 'Golden Grove Book', 4 vols. For Evan Evans see Daniel Huws, 'Evan Evans of Carmarthen: Compiler of the Golden Grove Book', *The Carmarthenshire Antiquary*, xlv (2009), 61-3.

16   P. C. Bartrum, *Welsh Genealogies AD 300-1400* (8 vols, 1974) [WG 1], and *Welsh Genealogies AD 1400-1500* (18 vols, 1983) [WG 2]. The National Library has since published a series of additions and corrections to these volumes.

17   The use of the collections is explained in Michael Powell Siddons, 'Using Peter Bartrum's *Welsh Genealogies*', in *Second Stages in Researching Welsh Ancestry*, ed. John and Sheila Rowlands (1999), 134-46.

18   Aberystwyth University, Bartrum Project. Internet: cadair.aber.ac.uk. In progress ; the present state of the project can be consulted by typing in the box [search Cadair] the name of the tribe, family, district or index required.

19   Published in 1998 and 1999.

20   Michael Powell Siddons, 'Printed and manuscript pedigrees', pp. 211-19; T. Ceiri Griffith's study *Achau rhai o deuluoedd hen siroedd Caernarfon, Meirionnydd a Threfaldwyn* (2003)

21   Useful books on heraldry are Thomas Woodcock and J. M. Robinson, *The Oxford Guide to Heraldry* (1988); *Boutell's Heraldry*, ed. J. P. Brooke-Little (1983). Welsh heraldry is treated in *DWH*.

22   *DWH*, I, frontispiece and plates XXI, XXII, and figs 94, 96-7.

23   The descendants of these incomers were called *Advenae* in the pedigree books.

24   The dates of appearance of coats of arms in Wales are given in *DWH*, vol. I, 402-15.

25   *DWH*, I, plate XXII.

26   Quoted in *DWH*, I, 73.

27   Heraldry in Welsh poetry is discussed in *DWH*, I, ch. 4, and in Lewis Glyn Cothi's poetry in DWH, I, 77-119.

28   See Michael Powell Siddons, *Welsh Pedigree Rolls* (1996); idem, 'Welsh pedigree rolls – additions and corrections', *NLWJ*, XXXII (2001-2), 433-42.

29   See *DWH*, I, 304, 309, 386.

30   For the Welsh deputy heralds see *DWH*, I, 313-21. Gruffudd Hiraethog and Lewys Dwnn are noticed in *ODNB*. Gruffudd Hiraethog's genealogical manuscripts are described by P. C. Bartrum in 'Further notes', 106-10, and Lewys Dwnn's visitation manuscripts were edited by S. R. Meyrick with a number of inaccuracies in *The Heraldic Visitations of Wales, by Lewys Dwnn* (2 vols, 1846). For Lewys' visitation in Meirionnydd see *History of Merioneth*, II, J. Beverley Smith and Llinos Beverley

Smith (eds.) (2001), 632-3.

31   The Welsh deputy heralds are discussed in *DWH*, I, 313-21.

32   See *DWH*, I, 231, and IV, frontispiece.

33   See the examples of the arms of Urien and Iestyn ap Gwrgan in *DWH*, I, 195-7.

34   See Fig. 1 for an example of this subdivision among intermediate ancestors.

35   See *The Oxford Guide to Heraldry*, pl. 25.

36   Standards are illustrated in *DWH*, I, pl. XX, and *DWH*, IV, pl. XI. Badges are discussed in Michael Powell Siddons, *Heraldic Badges in England and Wales* (4 vols, 2009).

5. The State Church and Nonconformity in Wales

J. Gwynfor Jones

Doubtless the history of religion in Wales has produced a large number of volumes and articles, extensive in their content and scholarship, by authors who either publish transcriptions of sources of all kinds so as to reveal the growth and development of the Christian faith in its relation with local history or who use sources in monographs or articles to discuss aspects of the faith in Wales, principally from the period of the Protestant Reformation from the sixteenth century onwards. These works are published in Welsh or English, and essential information is made available which is very helpful to the historian who wishes to extend the span of his or her research in the history of religious establishments in Wales. A large number of official and unofficial booklets are published on churches and chapels for the tourist market, many of them suitable for tracing the origins of cathedrals, parochial and Nonconformist churches in rural and urban centres. For more detailed information on churches and chapels of historical importance in many areas in Wales see *Public Access to Cadw-Aided Buildings/ Mynediad Cyhoeddus i'r Adeiladau a Gynorthwyir gan Cadw* (1999); for references to religious sites and others preserved by the National Assembly, see the series 'The Buildings of Wales', published by the University of Wales Press together with the Penguin Publishing

Company and the volumes on *Powys* (1979), *Clwyd* (1986), *Pembrokshire* (2004), *Carmarthenshire and Ceredigion* (2006), *Gwynedd* (2009) and *Powys* (2013).

A significant amount of archival material has survived on the Middle Ages to study local history and family history, and other sources such as formal diocesan records which are recorded chiefly in Latin. Yet R. I. Jack, in his chapter entitled 'Ecclesiastical Records' in *Medieval Wales* (1977), 127–60 offers a useful guide together with John le Neve, *Fasti Ecclesiae Anglicanae, 1310–60*: XI *Welsh Dioceses* (1965); J. Conway Davies (ed.), *Episcopal Acts and Cognate Documents relating to Welsh Dioceses, 1066–1272* (Historical Society of the Church in Wales, 1 (1946); 2 (1948), 3 (1949); R. F. Isaacson (ed.), *The Episcopal Registers of St David's, 1277–1283* (2005). Many secondary volumes also reflect much of the religious life of the Middle Ages and supply relevant information about areas and persons in Wales whose names appear in public library archives. Among the most prominent are Glanmor Williams, *The Welsh Church from Conquest to Reformation* (1962), *Glamorgan County History*, 3, chapter 3, 87–166, *History of Merioneth*, eds J. Beverley Smith and Llinos Beverley Smith, 2, *The Middle Ages* (2001), 254–96, F. G. Cowley, *The Monastic Orders in South Wales, 1066–1349* (1977) and D. H. Williams, *The Welsh Cistercians* (2 vols, 1984).

There is a vast amount of literary material, sources and secondary studies on the early Protestant Reformation period in Wales. Key volumes which have examined that movement across the century and its impact on momentous religious changes from the sixteenth century down to the Victorian age, have been published chiefly to record diocesan and parochial administration in Wales. The volumes by Browne Willis are among the best of their day and deal with the four diocesan cathedrals, namely St David's (1717), Llandaff (1719), Bangor (1721) and St Asaph (1801) under the general title *A Survey of the Cathedral Church*.

There is much detail in D. R. Thomas' three volumes *History of the Diocese of St Asaph* (1908–13) and A. J. Pryce's two volumes, *The Diocese of Bangor in the Sixteenth Century* (1923) and *The Diocese of Bangor during Three Centuries* (1929), deal with episcopal registers in the diocese, and are key sources to understand the structure of religious life in that diocese. In *JWEH*, 2 (1985), 7–26, Madeleine Gray

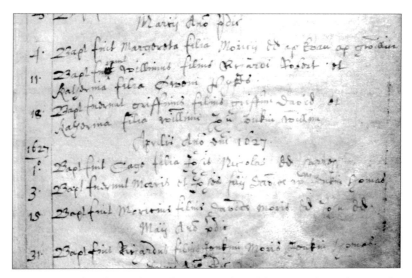

Parish Register, St Ishmael, Carmarthenshire: Baptisms (1626–7)
With the permission of the Carmarthenshire Record Office.
Note: The entries 4 March (the Welsh format of the name Margaret, daughter of 'Morris David ap Evan ap Gwillim'), and 1 April, that is, the first day of the year 1627; before 1752 the year commenced on 25 March

provides a detailed essay on the ecclesiastical church records in Gwent in 1603, and in the same journal offers a similar contribution on Bangor diocese in the last years of the sixteenth century (*JWEH*, 5 (1988), 7–26. Her studies continue in *JWRH* on the diocese of St Asaph in 1563, 1 (1993), 1–40, Llandaff, 2 (1994), 31–95 and St David's, 5 (1997), 29–56.

Substantial contributions were made by J. A. Bradney to the history of the diocese of Llandaff in *Llandaff Records* (5 vols 1905–14) containing the details of parish records, copies of episcopal letters to 1812 together with the Catalogues of the Dean's Law Books and Chapter House since 1575 and those of the Bishop's since 1660. Glanmor Williams has contributed more than anyone to the history of the Protestant Reformation in sixteenth-century Wales, and in his volumes and essays numerous references are made to sources that highlight religious order and organisation, as well as theological disputes and the leaders who promoted or resisted that movement, his most important volume being *Wales and the Reformation* (1999). He has also published numerous articles on the growth of early Protestantism in the diocese of St David's, for example 'The Second volume of St David's Registers, 1554–64' in *BBCS*, 14 (1952), 45–54, 125–38. See also Barrie Williams' publication of his doctoral thesis 'The Welsh Clergy, 1558–1642' (Ph.D. dissertation The Open University 1998). In NLW Cwrtmawr MS. 203 John Jones, Gellilyfdy, provides a collection of religious carols, and Llewelyn Siôn, the Glamorgan bard from Llangewydd, has copied a large number of free-metre poems known as *cwndidau* in NLW MS. 13070. The fullest collection of poems of this *genre* is found in L. S. Hopkin James and T. C. Evans (eds.), *Hen Gwndidau, Carolau a Chywyddau* (1910).

To measure the amount of Roman Catholic activity in Wales from the last decades of the sixteenth to the eighteenth centuries several recusant rolls survive which are stored, together with gaol files of the Great Sessions, in the National Library of Wales. E. G. Jones' small but valuable volume *Cymru a'r Hen Ffydd* (1951) is a useful guide in this field as well as his article 'Catholic recusancy in the counties of Denbigh, Flint and Montgomery, 1581–1625', *Trans. Cymmr.*, 1945, 114–33. Similar studies of value on recusants in south-east Wales are published by F. H. Pugh, 'Glamorgan recusants 1577–1611' and 'Monmouthshire recusants in the reigns of Elizabeth I and James I' in *South Wales and Monmouth Record Society Publications*, nos 3 and 4 (1954, 1957), 49–68, 57–110, 471–506.

In the National Library of Wales episcopal records are kept for each of the Welsh dioceses, consisting of formal episcopal probate records before 1858 in the consistory courts of the four dioceses together with the archdeaconry of Brecknock, Hawarden and Chester consistory courts. Original wills and administrative bonds are housed there as well dating back to about 1600 (excepting Bangor circa 1635).

For records post-1858, the year when probate was transferred to the civil probate registries in Wales and England, wills are proven and administered either in the Family Department of the main central registries in Somerset House or a local registry. Copies of all wills prepared in those registries are deposited in Somerset House. Until 1942 second copies of wills were kept in local registries and bound in volumes of registered wills, and copies are kept in the National Library of Wales. See J. Conway Davies, 'The Records of the Church in Wales', *NLWJ*, 4 (1945), 1–34, and *A Guide to the Department of Manuscripts and Records in the National Library of Wales*, ed. Daniel Huws (1994), 22–35. For further information on parish records of Wales, owned by

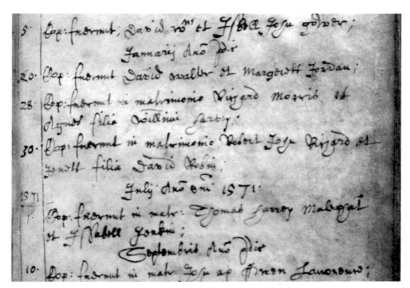

Parish Register, St Ishmael, Carmarthenshire: Marriages (1571)
With the permission of the Carmarthenshire Record Office
*Note: The entries for January which refer to the year 1570, and the
entry for 10 September 1571 for the Welsh format of the name John ap
Owen Lawrence (who married Katherin Owen David)*

the state in 1837, see C. J. Williams and J. Watts-Williams (eds),
Cofrestri Plwyf Cymru/Parish Registers of Wales (2000), Nia Henson
(ed.), *Bangor Probate Records, 1 Pre-1700* (NLW Probate Indexes, no.
1, 1980) and Nansi C. Jones (ed.), *NLW Probate Indexes, no. 2:
Archdeaconry of Brecon Archdeaconry Probate Records, 1 Pre-1660*
(1989). In these parish records, births, marriages and deaths were
listed, and E. G. Wright's contribution 'A Survey of parish records in
the diocese of Bangor', *TAAS*, 1959, 44–52, and the summary of parish
records in Llandaff diocese pre-1836 in *A Digest of the Parish Records
within the diocese of Llandaff previous to 1836* (1905) are very useful.

Of advantage also would be to browse in the *National Index of
Parish Records*, V, *South Midlands and the Welsh Border*, eds D. J. H.
Steel, H. E. F. Steel and C. W. Field (1966), 79–92, and R. W.
McDonald's article 'Cofrestri Plwyf Cymru', in *NLWJ*, 19 (1975–6), 112–
31. Among the published collections of parish records see Alice Audley
(ed.), *Conway Parish Registers, 1541–1793* (1900).

Most of the register entries are short and factual, but some

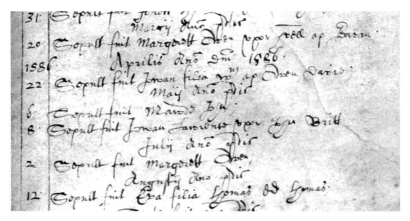

Parish Register, St Ishmael, Carmarthenshire: Deaths (1586)
With the permission of the Carmarthenshire Record Office
Note: The location of the entries for 20 March and 22 April,
indicating that the year had commenced on 25 March.

interesting additional information is added in many parish records which reflect social conditions and circumstances. For example, while registering the death of a young girl in 1840, the vicar of Llanbadarn Fynydd added that she was a magician. 'The young woman was bewitched a little before her death', he stated, 'and in grief from that belief she died'. In St Donat's, in the Vale of Glamorgan, registers for 1783 the death of a young girl is recorded of smallpox after her parents came there to exhibit a puppet show. The record of Elizabeth Cadwaladr, a vagrant from Llangernyw, Denbighshire, who died in 1698 by the roadside, is a sad comment on personal and social deprivation. About the same period the body of a poor man called Thomas in the Llanidloes area was exhumed because it was thought that he had money in his coat pocket (see R. W. McDonald's article, cited above, 122–30). Similar notes are found in several other records and they all reveal poverty and hardship in rural Wales in periods of economic depression.

The growth and development of Nonconformity in Wales from the middle years of the seventeenth century and earlier provided a marked increase in the number and variety of sources and secondary literature published as volumes, articles and explanatory notes. Geraint H. Jenkins' *Protestant Dissenters in Wales 1639–1689* (1992) contains a useful selection of source material with commentary on a crucial period in the history of early dissent, and J. G. Jones, *Crefydd a Chymdeithas:*

Astudiaethau ar Hanes y Ffydd Brotestannaidd yng Nghymru c.1559–1750 (2007) provides a variety of studies which examine aspects of Anglican, dissenting and Methodist trends.

Of immense importance also in this field of study are the substantial volumes by Thomas Richards on early Welsh Puritanism. Of the five published by him on that movement from 1639 to 1719, one is in Welsh, namely *Piwritaniaeth a Pholitics, 1689–716* (1927), a study of the political dimensions to early religious dissent in Wales. Richards also published several leading articles such as 'Eglwys Llanfaches', a study of the first Congregationalist church established in Wales (1639), in *Trans. Cymmr.*, 1941, 150–84 and '*Declarasiwn 1687: tipyn o'i hanes a barn Cymru amdano*', *TWBHS* (1924), 1–46. For the condition of Glamorgan clergy during the Commonwealth and Protectorate see Phillip Jenkins' extended study 'The suffering of the clergy: the Church in Glamorgan during the Interregnum', *JWEH*, 3 (1986), 1–17, 4 (1987), 9–41, 5 (1988), 73–80. As background to the archives the short contribution by E. D. Jones 'Nonconformist records in Wales' should be consulted in W. R. Powell, 'Protestant Nonconformity Records: Protestant Nonconformist Records and the Local Historian', *Archives*, 5, 25 (1961), 9–10 and Brynley F. Roberts 'Welsh Nonconformist Archives' in *JWEH*, 3 (1986), 61–72. The pioneering work for that century doubtless is the history of Congregationalism in Wales by T. Rees and J. Thomas, *Hanes Eglwysi Annibynnol Cymru* (4 vols, 1871–5) and J. Thomas, vol. 5 (1891). Among contributions from the later generations of historians, include those of R. Tudur Jones, especially *Hanes Annibynwyr Cymru*, translated as *Congregationalism in Wales* (2004), edited by Robert Pope from the original volume published in Welsh in 1966, and B. G. Owens, 'Anghydffurfwyr Cymru 1660–62' in *Y Cofiadur*, 32 (1962), 3–91; 'Cofrestri'r Ymneilltuwyr', *TWBHS*, 1968, 31–49, 'Ffynonellau newydd', *ibid.*, 1972, 33–50 and 'Llawysgrifau Coleg y Bedyddwyr, Bangor', *ibid.*, 1973, 32–54.

In the sphere of advancing Nonconformity from the seventeenth century onwards substantial contributions have been available in articles and notes in Anglican and Nonconformist journals which enriched denominational literature: *Yr Ymofynydd* (1847), *TWBHS* (1901), *JHSPCW* (1914), *Y Cofiadur* (1923) and *Bathafarn* (1946). Valuable articles are published in the *JHSChW* (1949–90) and its successors, *JWEH* (1984–92), *WJRH* (1993–2005), the *WJRH* (2006) and the chapter entitled 'Nonconformity' by Muriel Bowen Evans in *Welsh Family History*, edited by John Rowlands and others, together with Dafydd Ifans' volume on Welsh Nonconformist registers entitled *Cofrestri Anghydffurfwyr Cymru* (1994). In Nonconformist journals contributions appear which trace the history of meeting houses (conventicles) and the lives of prominent individuals in the religious life of their period from the Protestant Reformation down to the years when the Puritan movement emerged to about 1700. Alongside articles by R. Tudur Jones and B. G. Owens (cited above) a list of Welsh Baptist leaders is available during the critical period 1660–62 in *TWBHS* (1962), 3–93. See also the indices available from 1923 to 1992 in *Y Cofiadur*, 57 (1992), 16–26 by Trevor Watts and Gareth O. Watts. Of value is D. Rhys Phillips' 'Rhestr Aelodau Ilston (16 October 1656)' in the same journal (1928), 1–107, and 'Cofrestri'r Ymneilltuwyr' by B. G. Owens in *TWBHS* (1968), 31–49. Thomas Richards reveals details of the religious census of 1676 in *Trans. Cymmr.*, app. (1925–6), 1–118.

An immense amount of sources are available for eighteenth-century religious and educational activity. Detailed monographs of these themes have appeared for that century, the most comprehensive and valuable volumes being Geraint H. Jenkins' *Literature, Religion and Society in Wales, 1660–1730* (1978) and *The Foundations of Modern Wales c.1642–1780* (1987), which contains chapters, with source references, on the condition of the Anglican church, charity school movements and the Methodist Revival. M. G. Jones' *The Charity School Movement* (1914) is also of particular value, 266–325, pp. 388–410 and Mary Clement (ed.), *Correspondence and Minutes of the SPCK relating to Wales 1699–1740* (1952) and her *The SPCK and Wales 1699–1740* (1954) and *Correspondence and Records of the SPG relating to Wales 1701–1750* (1973). .

For detailed studies and published sources of Griffith Jones, Llanddowror, and his Circulating Schools see *The Welch Piety* (1737–76) as well as two volumes by W. Moses Williams (ed.), *Selections from the Welch Piety* (1737–76) and 'The Friends of Griffith Jones' in *Y Cymmrodor* (1939). E. Morgan (ed.) *Letters of Griffith Jones ... to Mrs Bevan* (1832) is of immense value as source material to understand Griffith Jones' mind and aspirations as recorded in his correspondence with his patron.

For the development of the Methodist Revival see John Hughes,

Rhulen Church (Radnorshire)

Methodistiaeth Cymru (1851–6) and Gomer M. Roberts (ed.), *Hanes Methodistiaeth Galfinaidd Cymru*, 1. *Y Deffroad Mawr* (1973), and 2. *Cynnydd y Corff* (1978) together with the recently published third volume, *Y Twf a'r Cadarnhau c.1814–1914*, edited by J. G. Jones (2011), and *The History of Welsh Calvinistic Methodism, III: Growth and Consolidation* (*c.1814–1914*), also edited by J. G. Jones (2013). All three volumes contain a mass of information, primary and secondary, which reveal the major developments in the history of the denomination. For detailed information on the religious life in Glamorgan between the restoration of monarchy (1660) and the latter half of the eighteenth century consult Gomer M. Roberts 'Religion and Education in Glamorgan 1660–c.1775) in Glanmor Williams (ed.), *Glamorgan County History*, 3 *Early Modern Glamorgan* (1974), 431–535.

Useful archival material is found on the growth of Calvinistic Methodism in its historical journal (*JHSPCW*) by several historians such as Tom Beynon, M. H. Jones, Richard Tibbott, Gomer M. Roberts and J. E. Wynne Davies, all of whom have contributed extensively in this field of study. Detailed knowledge is also available in *The Trevecka MSS Supplement* (1940), *Selected Trevecka Letters*, 1 (1742–1747) (1956) and 2 (1747–1794) (1962), both volumes edited by Gomer M. Roberts. 'The Archives of the Calvinistic Methodist or Presbyterian Church of Wales', NLWJ, 5 (1947), 13–49 by Gildas Tibbott and K.

Monica Davies is particularly useful, and *Calendar of Trevecka Letters*, edited by B. S. Schlenther and E. M. White (2003), is indispensable for historians of the Revival for it contains abstracts of letters by Harris and others from 1697 to 1768, the whole collection being essential sources for a detailed study of Methodism. See also E. M. White *Praidd Bach y Bugail Mawr: Seiadau Methodistaidd De-orllewin Cymru 1737–1750* (1995), a study of Methodist societies in south-west Wales in mid-century, and similar volumes which form studies basic to regional studies of Methodism. Also by the same author the condition of the Anglican Church is examined in a contribution entitled '"A poor benighted church"? Church and Society in Mid-Eighteenth-Century Wales', published in R. R. Davies and Geraint H. Jenkins (eds), *From Medieval to Modern Wales: Historical Essays in Honour of Kenneth O. Morgan and Ralph Griffiths* (2004), 123–41.

Among regional studies of Nonconformist churches are W. Hobley, *Hanes Methodistiaeth Arfon* (6 vols 1910–24); Gomer M. Roberts *Methodistiaeth fy Mro ... yn Dwyrain Myrddin* (1938); W. Griffith, *Methodistiaeth Fore Môn, 1740–1751* (1955) and G. P. Owen, *Methodistiaeth Llŷn ac Eifionydd* (1978). For full details of selective Calvinistic Methodist publications down to 1981 see D. Ben Rees, *Haneswyr yr Hen Gorff* (1981), 85–110, a survey of Calvinistic Methodist historians, a work which contains very useful source references. The wider geographical repercussions of Methodism are discussed in a substantial monograph by David Ceri Jones, *'A Glorious Work in the World': Welsh Methodism and the International Evangelical Revival, 1735–1750* (2004), and the newly-published collaborative study of Wesleyan and Calvinistic Methodism in England and Wales entitled *The Elect Methodists* by D. Ceri Jones, B. S. Schlenther and Eryn M. White (2012), which adds a new approach to Methodist studies.

Detailed studies of prominent leaders among the Congregationalists, Baptists and Unitarians need to be consulted, especially the works of R. Tudur Jones, *Hanes Annibynwyr Cymru* (cited above), T. M. Bassett, *The Welsh Baptists* (1977), the author's translation of the original Welsh version published in the same year, and D. Elwyn Davies, *Y Smotiau Duon: Braslun o Hanes y Traddodiad Rhyddfrydiaeth ac Undodiaeth* (1981), a history of Unitarian causes in west Wales. For Wesleyan Methodism three standard volumes by Hugh

Jones, *Hanes Wesleyaeth yng Nghymru* (4 vols 1911–13) are available, as well as A. H. Williams, *Welsh Wesleyan Methodism* (1935) and *John Wesley in Wales* (1971), a source-based volume on Wesley's travels and correspondence in Wales, and Lionel Madden (ed.), *Methodism in Wales* (2003). A statistical study has been published of Wesleyan chapels in the Welsh provinces by Eric Edwards in *Yr Eglwys Fethodistaidd* (1980) and the appendix in 1987. Several archival articles published in *Bathafarn* are also extremely valuable. The papers of W. H. Evans ('Gwyllt y Mynydd') are deposited among Bangor University manuscripts, and their details are published by Thomas Richards in *Bathafarn*, 1, (1946), 54–6.

Membership statistics relating to many churches are often published in denominational journals, such as Isaac Thomas 'Y Gronfa Gynulleidfaol ac Annibynwyr' in *Y Cofiadur*, 28 (1958), 3–32, B. G. Owens, 'Llawysgrifau Coleg y Bedyddwyr, Bangor', *TWBHS* (1973), 32–54, and David Jones provides a pioneering and exhaustive study of denominational statistics of chapels in Wales and England 1814–1914, in *Hanes Methodistiaeth Galfinaidd Cymru*, 3 (2011). The official Archive of the Presbyterian Church of Wales (*Y Greirfa*) is housed in the National Library of Wales, a prime denominational repository cared for over many years by K. Monica Davies.

Archives for the nineteenth century reveal how prolific sources for historical studies of Nonconformist history are to assist those interested in the history of religion. Volumes and articles are available to study the Anglican Church and Nonconformists alike. Two key articles by Walter T. Morgan, 'The Diocese of St David's in the nineteenth century', *JHSChW*, 21 (1971), 5–49; 22 (1972), 12–48; 23 (1973), 18–55, and his discussion of consistory courts in the same diocese, again in *JHSChW*, 7 (1957), 5–24, 8 (1958), 58–81 are of particular value when examining legal affairs in the Anglican Church. Likewise, in Nonconformist libraries there are vast numbers of biographies, autobiographies and denominational histories, besides the weighty theological material which appeared consistently in newspapers and denominational journals. Full information is available on sources of this nature in Calvinistic Methodist repositories, as recorded by D. Ben Rees in *Haneswyr yr Hen Gorff*.

Among the most popular biographies in their day and age were those written by Owen Thomas, *John Jones, Talsarn* (2 vols, 1874) and

Register Book, Capel Als, Llanelli (1844–51)
With the permission of the Carmarthenshire Record Office
Note: The various occupations of the members of Capel Als Independent
church, and the signature of the Rev. David Rees, the minister of Capel
Als (1829–69) and the editor of the journal Y Diwygiwr (1835–65)

Cofiant y Parchedig Henry Rees (2 vols, 1890) as well as J. T Jones, *Cofiant Christmas Evans* (1938), D. S. Jones, *Cofiant William Williams o'r Wern* (1894), J. P. Roberts and T. Hughes, *Cofiant John Evans, Eglwysbach* (1903), William Pritchard, *John Elias a'i Oes* (1911) and Goronwy P. Owen's edited version of John Elias' autobiography, *Hunangofiant John Elias* (1974).

Among the denominational leaders in mid nineteenth-century Wales, David Rees, minister of Capel Als, Llanelli, and Lewis Edwards of Bala, have both been commemorated in handsome biographies by Iorwerth Jones, *David Rees y Cynhyrfwr* (1971), and by Trebor Lloyd Evans. *Lewis Edwards: Ei Fywyd a'i Waith* (1967) and Densil Morgan, *Lewis Edwards* (2009). An English-language version of the two volumes by John Morgan Jones and William Morgan, *Y Tadau Methodistaidd* (1897), entitled *The Calvinistic Methodist Fathers of Wales*, translated by John Aaron (2008), contains immense information on leading ministers in the period when Calvinistic Methodism became a powerful force in Welsh Nonconformity. Volumes in this genre not only contain a mass of useful material relating to the

Register Book, Capel Als, Llanelli (1854–8)
With the permission of the Carmarthenshire Record Office.
*Note: The reference to John Evans, 'Shop boy', received into
membership on 19 April, 1857, and 'Expelled for a rascally dishonest
conduct in business'. Also, Mary Edwards, formerly a member of
Capel y Graig, Tre-lech, who had been 'Excluded for uncleanness'*

rise of Nonconformity using archival material but often add valuable social and theological comment and interpretation.

From 1898 onwards, obituaries of ministers are included in the *Calvinistic Methodist Year Book* together with annual reports and minutes of Unions and General Assemblies, Associations, Quarterly Meetings and related bodies, recording in detail the seasonal and annual administrative and other functions of denominations. Centenary and bi-centenary booklets are in large supply recording the details of origins, chapel-building and ministerial and lay leadership. Only two Presbyterial histories have been published, namely R. H. Evans, (ed.), *Hanes Henaduriaeth Dyffryn Clwyd* (1986) and J. G. Jones, *Her y Ffydd: Ddoe, Heddiw ac Yfory: Hanes Henaduriaeth Dwyrain Morgannwg 1876–2005* (2006).

Large numbers of histories of individual denominational causes and chapels have appeared, such as Trebor Lloyd Evans, *Y Cathedral Anghydffurfiol Cymraeg* (1972) [Y Tabernacl Congregational chapel, Morriston], Gomer M. Roberts, *Y Ddinas Gadarn: Hanes Eglwys Jewin, Llundain* (1974) [Jewin Calvinistic Methodist chapel London], R. T. Jenkins, *Hanes Cynulleidfaol Hen Gapel Llanuwchllyn* (1937) [the historic Congregational chapel at Llanuwchllyn, Merioneth], and W. Ambrose Bebb, *Canrif o Hanes y 'Twr Gwyn', 1854–1954* (1954) ['Twr Gwyn' Calvinistic Methodist chapel in Bangor].

Meurig Owen has recorded the history of several Presbyterian chapels in London in articles and in a volume *Ymofyn am yr Hen Lwybrau: Hanes rhai o Hen Eglwysi Presbyteraidd Cymru yn Llundain* (2001).

Several county and other libraries house archives of all kinds, original and secondary relating to religious bodies such as, for example, Cardiff City Library and Lampeter and Bangor University libraries. The 1851 Religious Census in Wales, the only one to be held, is a prime source for knowledge of chapels of all denominations, their numbers and statistics in the mid-Victorian era and published in two volumes, the first for South Wales edited by Ieuan Gwynedd Jones and David Williams in 1976 and the second by Jones for North Wales in 1981. In both volumes evidence is supplied to measure the success of Nonconformity in Wales. The census was held on Sunday morning 30 March 1851 and it was estimated that 80 per cent of congregations throughout the Principality were predominantly Nonconformist. Several studies are available to assess the significance of the census in different regions of Wales, for example Ieuan Gwynedd Jones 'Denominalisation in Swansea and District: A Study of the Ecclesiastical Census of 1851', *Morgannwg*, 12 (1968), 67–96; idem, 'Denominalisation in Caernarfonshire in the mid-nineteenth century as shown in the Religious Census of 1851', *TCaerns.HS*, 31 (1970), 78–114.

The Anglican church was losing ground by the mid-nineteenth century and diocesan standards were declining in rural and industrial parishes. That was clear in Llandaff diocese over the previous century as shown by J. R. Guy, *The Diocese of Llandaff in 1763: The primary visitation of Bishop Ewer* (1991). A century later the situation had deteriorated owing to economic and social circumstances in an age of industrial expansion. Roger Brown has contributed substantially to the history of the Anglican Church in Wales and its episcopacy in an age of community disruption and hardship. Among his chief works are *In Pursuit of the Welsh Episcopate: Appointments to Welsh Sees 1840–1905* (2005), and *Ten Clerical Lives: Essays relating to the Victorian Church in Wales* (2005). The contribution of E. T. Davies in this field, tracing the background of the Anglican Church, is also of importance, such as *Religion in the Industrial Revolution in South Wales* (1969).

A. V. Jones' detailed study of Nonconformist chapels in Aberdare and the surrounding area, entitled *Chapels of the Cynon Valley/Capeli*

Maesyronnen Chapel (Radnorshire)

Cwm Cynon (2004), containing valuable source material, is a useful guide to the religious culture of a valley community. In 2009 Huw Edwards published *Capeli Llanelli: Our Rich Heritage*, an immensely valuable study of Llanelli chapels amply illustrated with commentary.

The official volumes in the early twentieth century which supply the most information on the condition of religion in Wales are those known as the *Report of the Royal Commission on the Church of England and other Religious Bodies in Wales and Monmouthshire* (seven volumes, 1910). Their publication marks a further step towards the disestablishment of the Church in Wales, revealing that there was a revival in that Church and examining the major differences between Anglicans and Nonconformists and the degree of co-operation between them. In these sumptuous volumes a wealth of evidence is uncovered, not only on religion in Wales on the eve of the Great War (1914–18), but also on aspects of society in rural and urban Wales and on the views of religious leaders of all denominations on the spiritual condition, as reflected in their pastoral work in urban, rural and industrial Wales.

This commission was formed on 21 June 1906 following the religious revival in 1904–5, when Wales was ignited with an evangelical spirit led principally by Evan Roberts, Loughor, and his co-revivalists. Many volumes and articles have been published on this revival, including D. M. Phillips' extensive study of Roberts entitled *Evan*

Roberts: The Great Welsh Revivalist and his Work (1906), translated by the author into Welsh as *Evan Roberts a'i Waith* (1912). It is a dated and unbalanced study which is still valuable in that it contains useful data; Eifion Evans, *Revival Comes to Wales: The Story of the 1859 Revival in Wales* (1991 reprint); *idem, Fire in the Thatch* (1996 repr; *idem, The Welsh Revival of 1904* (1997 reprint); N. Gibbard (ed.), *Nefol Dân: Agweddau ar Ddiwygiad 1904* (1997); *idem, Fire on the Altar: A History and Evaluation of the 1904–05 Welsh Revival* (2005); *On the Wings of the Dove: The International Effects of the 1904–05 Revival* (2002). All these works, though they are designed to follow the course of the revival and interpret its significance, do contain useful source material for further study of the twentieth century.

The newspaper press of the period also contained detailed references to individual revival meetings in all parts of Wales and beyond, especially *Y Drysorfa, Y Dysgedydd, Seren Gomer, Y Traethodydd, Yr Ymofynnydd, Bathafarn, Baner ac Amserau Cymru, Western Mail* and *South Wales Daily News*.

Recent historians in the post Second World War period have researched into numerous aspects of Welsh religious history, for example R. Tudur Jones, the doyen among them, whose substantial volumes have enlightened the historian's knowledge and understanding of Nonconformity. Among the most significant are his history of the Congregational Union – *Yr Undeb: Hanes Undeb yr Annibynwyr Cymraeg 1872–1972* (1972) – and two volumes *Ffydd ac Argyfwng Cenedl 1890–1914* (1981–2), translated into English in one volume edited by Robert Pope and translated by Sylvia Prys Jones, entitled *Faith and the Crisis of a Nation: Wales 1890–1914* (2004). In 1998 a selection of some of his most substantial articles were edited in a volume edited by D. Densil Morgan entitled *Grym y Gair a Fflam y Ffydd: Ysgrifau ar Hanes Crefydd yng Nghymru* (1998). Morgan himself is another prolific author who combines religion, theology and history most ably in his many volumes, providing sources which enable historians to deepen their knowledge and understanding of Nonconformity in Wales. Among his works appear *The Span of the Cross: Christian Religion and Society in Wales, 1914–2000* (1999, 2nd ed. 2011), *Wales and the Word: Historical Perspectives on Religion and Welsh Identity* (2008) and *Cedyrn Canrif: Crefydd a Chymdeithas yng Nghymru'r Ugeinfed Ganrif* (2007), which contains studies of some giants among Christian scholars in Wales such as J. E. Daniel, Ivor Oswy Davies, Pennar Davies and R. Tudur Jones.

Robert Pope has also written extensively on the social impact of the Labour movement on religion in the early twentieth century and has published *Building Jerusalem: Nonconformity, Labour and the Social Question in Wales 1906–1939* (1998), followed by *Seeking God's Kingdom: The Nonconformist Social Gospel in Wales 1906–1939* (1999) and *Codi Muriau Duw: Anghydffurfiaeth ac Anghydffurfwyr Cymru'r Ugeinfed Ganrif* (2005).

The story of the Disestablishment relies mainly on the work of K. O. Morgan, *Wales in British Politics, 1868–1922* (1963) and his booklet *Freedom or Sacrilege? A History of the Campaign for Welsh Disestablishment* (1965), and the *Royal Commission* (1910), cited above, is also very useful. M. H. Bell's *Disestablishment in Ireland and Wales* (1969), especially chapters 7 and 9, draws interesting comparisons between disestablishment activities in the two countries.

Nonconformity reached its peak in the first two decades of the twentieth century, and R. Tudur Jones contributed a statistical study of religion in Glamorgan in 1905–06 in *Glamorgan County History*, 6, chapter 12, 245–64.

After the Great War a gradual but certain decline is evident, but leaders continued to hold their services and meetings despite the economic and social difficulties in the critical years between two World Wars. A vast number of statistics are available relating to the condition of chapel buildings and financial matters in this and earlier periods when chapel-building revealed interesting architectural features. Studies have appeared which give the reader a valuable insight into the material culture of Nonconformity, such as Penri Jones, *Capeli Cymru* (1980), Anthony Jones, *Welsh Chapels* (1996) and D. Huw Owen's *The Chapels of Wales* (2012), the fullest and most useful of these studies. It would also be advisable for readers to consult past numbers of the newsletter *CAPEL*, launched in May 1986, for information about a large selection of chapels in all parts of Wales. Also the *Royal Commission on the Ancient and Historical Monuments in Wales*, in conjunction with *CAPEL*, has listed online the names of all Nonconformist chapels in Wales (*www.cbhc.gov.uk/coflein*).

References have already been made to the variety of religious archives deposited in county or regional libraries. In the Glamorgan

County Archives, for example, archives are available relating to the Society of Friends in Wales, together with early dissenting sources of Y Groes-wen chapel near Caerphilly for the years 1793 and 1916, the archives of the English Baptist Association in south-east Wales (1910–69), records of Croes-y-parc Baptist chapel near St Fagans, and those for the Cardiff Wesleyan circuit. Similar archival material is deposited in other libraries and much of it has been transcribed and published in denominational and local county history journals. All such archives prove to be of immense value to local and other historians who study social and religious trends in regions and localities.

In view of the wealth of material that is available on the Church in Wales and Nonconformist causes in Wales it would be opportune for those interested in researching into such archives to inquire with chapel secretaries and other officials as to their whereabouts since they are vital sources for social and cultural history. The danger is that many may have been neglected, lost or even destroyed, for denominations, excepting the Presbyterian Church of Wales, do not have a central repository to house them. Church leaders and officials should be made aware of the importance of protecting this heritage because archives are priceless treasures. Only by accident quite often are such sources preserved, and in such threatening circumstances church officials and those involved in local religious studies need to make efforts to ensure their protection to the future in Wales.

6. Probate Documents and Local History

Gerald Morgan

If your will is anything like mine, you're sure to think that wills are remarkably dull, with little of value for the historian. If so, then think again. Take, for example, the will of Elizabeth Lloyd of Cwmnewidion in the parish of Llanfihangel-y-Creuddyn, north Cardiganshire, made in 1744. Elizabeth was a widow, and her only child, Charles, was dead. She was the owner of the small mansion of Cwmnewidion in the Ystwyth valley, along with Cwmnewidion mill, eight farms and two cottages in Llanfihangel-y-Creuddyn. She made her will because she had taken in and raised her granddaughter Ann, Charles Lloyd's illegitimate daughter. Despite her illegitimate status, Ann was acknowledged by the will as heiress to the Cwmnewidion estate.[1]

Elizabeth Lloyd lived on for more than two decades; she watched Ann grow up and marry one Cornelius Griffiths. Three children were born before the old lady herself died in 1768, having made a codicil to her will to acknowledge her three great-grandchildren. But alas for her plans; Ann's marriage was a disaster. Cornelius was a wastrel, who first mortgaged Cwmnewidion to Lord Lisburne of Crosswood in 1777 and sometime after 1781 lost the whole estate to his aristocratic neighbour.

Most wills do not reveal such dramas, or throw such light onto the history of a small estate, but that story should be enough to prove that wills and probate documents are not necessarily dull. Probate documents are often essential in all kinds of research: the history of a

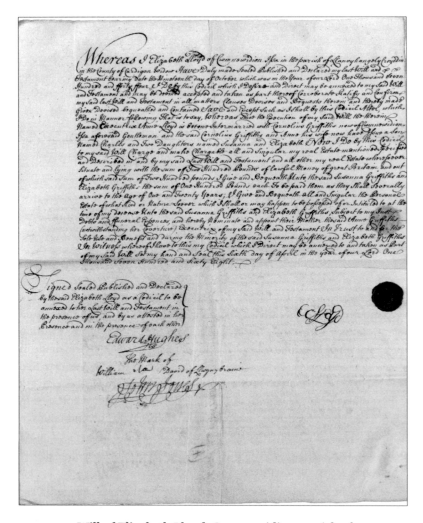

Will of Elizabeth Lloyd, Cwmnewidion, parish of
Llanfihangel y Creuddun, Ceredigion (1744)
[NLW, Crosswood Deeds, 1, 847]
With the permission of the National Library of Wales

community, an estate, a family, agriculture, trade, furniture – on so many aspects of social history. We may look briefly at the parish history aspect. There are probate documents for every historic Welsh parish, and they can all be read online. One can enter either a known name, with the person's parish and calling if known. Alternatively one can look at all the wills from a particular parish, either for the whole period up to 1858 or for a period of your choice. One can contrast urban and rural wills. Or one can look for professions or callings; for example, documents survive from Bangor diocese up to 1858 for 190 shopkeepers, called 'mercers' in the earlier period. Their inventories can be particularly interesting.[2] Blacksmiths, glovemakers and other craftsmen leave evidence of their trades, as well as master mariners. The variation of occuptions noted for testators becomes ever more varied: by the nineteenth century one can find wills in Wales for one or more of the following: baker, chaise driver, clockmaker, draper, glazier, innkeeper, lace manufacturer, magistrate's clerk, surgeon and tailor.

Handwriting in wills from 1700 onwards is usually readable with little difficulty, although there can be difficulties with place-names, personal names and abbreviations. This is far more the case in earlier wills: a good deal of practice is needed, especially with documents from before 1650. Elizabethan handwriting is not easy for the beginner. Fortunately, the opening paragraphs of most wills are similar; Thus, the following is typical, with some variations, of thousands of wills:

> In the name of god Amen the xiith daye of december in the yeare of our Lorde god 1607 I Richard Thomas ap David of the parish of Cardigan in the county of Cardigan and diocese of St Davids weake in body but stronge in mynde and of sounde and perfecte memorie lawde and praise be to Almyghtie god doe make this my Testamente contayninge herein my Last will in maner and forme folowinge ...

These are not the words of the testator but the priest, using a pro forma, and are most helpful in learning to read these documents. Personal and place-names are often more difficult, often occurring only once in a will.[3] It's good learning practice to copy a few whole wills and inventories at first, but with time comes familiarity, and most wills can be summarised rather than copied whole. One should always note the copy or summary by its reference number, and examine the note of

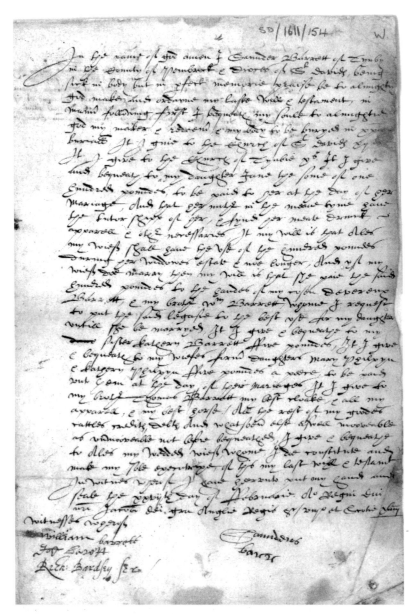

Will of Saunders Barrett, Tenby (1611) [NLW, SD/1611/154]
With the permission of the National Library of Wales.
*Note: The accompanying inventory reveals that Saunders Barrett sold,
in his shop at Tenby, a range of fabrics*

probate which is usually to be found on the back of the document. This may be difficult to read, but they may include the name of the church lawyer before whom the will was proved, and of course the date of proving. Most wills were proved at the diocesan offices of Carmarthen (for St David's), Llandaff, Bangor and St Asaph. The archdeaconry of Brecon managed its area wills, and the peculiar of Hawarden was also a separate case. But with time a number of more local priests could be empowered to grant probate, thus easing the difficulties of travel for the executors, who were often women – men frequently trusted their widows more than their sons.

Wills often come with a variety of documents. There may be an inventory of goods, valued by two men of the deceased's neighbourhood. These may give us a good idea of the man's occupation if it is not noted elsewhere. They may also suggest a degree of his wealth, but there is a caveat. Part of the executor's duty was to keep an account of how the legacies were paid and what costs were involved. These accounts were usually destroyed, but the rare survivals show that a man who owned plenty of goods was actually in quite serious debt.[4] Deeds of bond or administration, in Latin until 1732, often accompany wills; they simply bound the executors and two helpers, all named with status, to execute the will or pay a penalty. Sometimes there are letters, written by local gentlemen on behalf of poorer neighbours, urging the church probate officials to be quick and not to charge too much. There could, of course, be cases of disputed wills, which are interesting because they generated a good deal of paperwork. The original witnesses, the executor, and the disputing party had to appear at the diocesan court. A questionnaire was drawn up and each person interrogated. Unfortunately from the historian's point of view these cases are rare – only one in several hundred wills is likely to have been disputed.

Contrary to popular belief, it was not only rich people who made wills; farmers, miners, sailors, craftsmen and even paupers made wills. But even today fewer than half the adult population make wills, and the proportion was certainly much smaller during the sixteenth to nineteenth centuries. Property might be divided by family agreement; wills may also have been destroyed where there was no danger of disputes. Women certainly made wills, as in the case of Elizabeth Lloyd. As today, women tended to outlive men, and the widowed state was common. Married women did not normally make wills because at law their husbands owned all their property, unless they were heiresses when they married, had children, had been widowed and married again. In that case they might make a will to ensure that the children of the first marriage received their due. Spinsters could also make wills, though they are rare – almost every woman seems to have been married, though this impression is the result of the documentation, which is only a sample of the population. Many a man made it a condition of his widow receiving generous treatment (that is, more than her legal thirds) that it should last only so long as she remained unmarried, otherwise it would revert to his children. This was not a wish born of misogyny or the desire to control her from beyond the grave. It was simply to ensure fairness for his own children, since the second husband should maintain his wife and their children from his own wealth.

Women rarely figure in the routine documents of government and local administration. Widows paid rents and some other dues, and they also appear most interestingly in court proceedings, especially crime. But when a man made a will he named all his close female relatives – mother, wife, sisters, daughters, granddaughters, and sometimes aunts, cousins and nieces. No one should be left out. Three needs would be satisfied by the legacies: in the case of the widow-to-be, the will usually stipulates that she should have 'her thirds', in other words a third of the testator's goods and money. He might well leave her a separate gift, a horse perhaps, or a piece of furniture. A widow could also expect her children to provide her with bed and board. The widow's third was a share laid down by the Church in medieval times and maintained later by rural custom; another third would go to the children, and the last third to good causes, which naturally included the Church. After the Reformation in England and Wales the shares for good causes dwindled in most cases to a small sum for the cathedral church of the diocese, while the children benefited. There might also be small gifts to the parish church, or gifts to the local poor.

An estimate of the financial worth of women can be made simply by averaging the value of their inventories with those of an equivalent number of men. In rural parishes it tends to the ratio of 1:3. Of course, we are not comparing like with like; a man carried the responsibility for his family, the widow for herself only – and only widows and the very occasional spinster left inventories. The lists often tell us of women's economic lives. Elliw ferch Rees, of Llangoedmor, died in 1609. She had no farm stock at all, but her inventory indicates how she survived economically. She left a baking trough and small quantities of corn, two flitches of bacon, a winnowing sheet, and 18 shillings in cash. So she was baking bread, salting bacon, helping with the harvest, and lending small sums to her neighbours: many women did this task of small banking for those about them. Richer women lent out large sums, to men as well as women; debts are often listed and the networks can be traced into neighbouring parishes. Women's wills are characterised by considerable attention to detail – there must be something for everyone, so to speak.

Wealthy widows' wills tell us much about their lives. Thus Margaret Stedman of Strata Florida, parish of Caron, died at a great age in 1617. She had been a Breconshire heiress before her marriage to John Stedman. His property had passed to his son James, who was clearly dying at the same time as his mother. She divided her inherited lands between James and her two younger sons so that they should not be landless. She divided her cash resources and her wardrobe between her five daughters; the clothes are lovingly detailed. Margaret was especially concerned for her granddaughter Margaret, who was apparently an orphan. The girl is left a large stock of farm animals, and the old lady, seeing that the girl needed a guardian, overlooked her three sons in favour of her son-in-law Marmaduke Lloyd of Maesyfelin, Lampeter, the wealthiest man in the county. Particularly touching is her bequest of her jewellery, again lovingly detailed, to her daughter-in-law Katherine, so that 'she shall leave [them] to John Stedman her son as a relic of memory of my love to my grandchild'.

Returning to the main body of men's wills, the testator had to think of his daughters. It was a father's obligation, if he had the wherewithal, to provide a dowry for every unmarried girl. Farmers usually left a share of the farm stock to them, to be taken to their husbands on marriage either as stock or money. Married daughters would have been dowried already, and could expect only a token gift. Sons, too, would expect their share. Younger sons would have a specified number of items, while the rest would go to the eldest son. Either the widow or the eldest son would usually be named executor.

Naturally there are limitations to the extent the local historian may be able to use probate documents, though in previous paragraphs their importance for the lives of women, otherwise so poorly documented, is obvious. In rural parishes the great majority of wills were made by farmers. They and their parishes are named, but rarely are their farms named, which is a severe drawback, since most farm names survive to the present day. It must also be remembered that wills were not normally used to bequeath land belonging to the testator, though secondary properties might be mentioned, especially if they were tenancies, not freehold. At this point some terms used in connection with property must be listed, as well as a few others:

catells, chattels	not cattle in the bovine sense, but inanimate moveable goods
heriot	a fee payable to the landlord by a tenant on his inheriting a tenancy at his father's death
mansion	the principal home of the testator; not necessarily a grand house
messuage	a farm with a farmhouse
capital messuage	the home farm of the owner of several farms
parcel	a piece of land without a farmhouse
pilcorn	oats, or a mixture of barley and oats
teal	a measure of corn
tenement	a farm rented by a tenant from its owner

Examination of a number of farmers' wills for a particular area (one or more parishes) can give a reasonable idea of the state of farming.

A farmer whose inventory includes good quantities of cereals may be assumed to have been working good arable land, but corn was grown at virtually all levels except open sheep and cattle pasture. it has often been assumed that the Welsh uplands were economically marginal, but Nia M. W. Powell has argued forcefully that this was far from being the case.[5] For example, Phylip ap Howel, immediate ancestor of the Powells of Llechwedd Dyrys and Nanteos in Ceredigion, died in 1589. He was of Ysbyty Cynfyn, east of Aberystwyth, high in the Cambrian mountains, and he left a valuable inventory including numerous sheep and cattle, and clearly he had been purchasing farms in the lowlands nearer the sea. He is described as 'yeoman', his sons as 'gentlemen', and later descendants were titled 'esquire'. They owed their original wealth to the upland country.

Inventory of John Jackson, Carmarthen (1693)
[NLW, SD/1693/217]
With the permission of the National Library of Wales
Note: The goods listed in this inventory, including pocket pistols,
brass compasses, razors and gold rings, indicate that John Jackson
dealt mainly in hardware

Farmers' inventories give us a good idea of the kind of agriculture they were practising, though allowance has to be made for the season at which an individual list was made. All goods are priced, and one might expect a slow but steady increase in the values of farm animals between, say, 1600 and 1700, but there is little evidence for such inflation, at least in the west Wales inventories. Cattle and horses were far more valuable than sheep, which in their turn were more valuable than pigs and poultry. Goats appear in inventories in the sixteenth and seventeenth centuries, and are priced at half the value of a sheep, but then they disappear. 'Poultry' can refer either to fowls or to trivial items.

Wills can show evidence of family plotting. Morgan ap Philip ap Howell, of Llanbadarn Fawr, died in 1622, with only an illegitimate daughter surviving him. The family heir to his considerable wealth was his younger brother David. Morgan, however, wanted to ensure a dowry and a good marriage for his daughter, so had a will drawn up – not on paper, but on huge vellum sheets – listing all his lands by name. Morgan left a life interest in all the estate to his wife, and then laid down that 'the right heir at law' should pay his daugher £700 if he wanted the estate. Whether David actually paid up is unknown; he certainly took the lands.

As well as the farmers who dominated rural society, other trades and callings are represented, as well as the craftsmen and sailors already mentioned. There is enough evidence in probate records to develop a social history of the priests of the Established Church. It is quite clear that vicars and rectors in rural livings would spend much time farming. Many of them seem to have been possessed of few, if any, books (though this may reflect the ignorance of the valuers). But William Evans of Llanddewibrefi, who died in 1602, left a valuable inventory. He had owned a total of five horses, thrity-three cattle and sixty-four sheep. More interestingly, he was clearly an early Puritan, who had owned a Tremelius Bible, Calvin's *Institutions*, and thirty other books. (Tremelius was a Protestant who translated the Hebrew and Greek biblical texts into Latin.)

Many priests owned or rented farmland as well as using church glebe-land. But there were poor priests too. The poorest of all was John Hughes, curate of Trefilan, who died in 1614. He owned one horse, two blankets, a pillow and a sheet, all kept in a chest, and valued at £1 15s 8d. He left his clothes – 'my best doublet, 2 of my best bands, shirt, shoes, hat, jerkin and breeches' – to his illegitimate son. What a contrast with William Evans.

The wills of several hundred Welsh clergymen survive for the seventeenth and eighteenth centuries, a primising topic for research.

Perceptive readers may be intrigued by the fact that Welsh testators, who must before 1858 have been largely Welsh-speaking, and often monoglot, managed to leave documents that are apparently all in English. The only commonly-used Welsh word is *wyr*, meaning a grandchild of either sex, and occasionally a great-niece or great-nephew, now written *ŵyr*. In fact, of the 180,101 sets of Church in Wales probate documents in the National Library, more than a thousand sets contain at least one document in Welsh, 700 of them from the Bangor diocese. One must understand the usual testamentary procedure to grasp what was going on.

Wills were typically made on the testator's deathbed, usually with family, friends and neighbours offering moral support. Before 1700 it was usual to call in the parish priest, who would be paid for his services, often with a sheep from the inventory. Virtually all parish priests were Welsh-speaking, but almost always more literate in English than in Welsh. The dying person would dictate his wishes in Welsh to the priest, who would make notes, and then draw up a formal document in English, using the kind of pro forma mentioned above. A single instance demonstrates the procedure. The formal will of Harry Prichard of Penllech, Caernarfon, who died in 1763, is in English, but there is a simple list, under his name, of the legacies to members of his family, and a longer bequest to his wife written in Welsh. The Welsh document is the note made of the testator's wishes.

Very slowly it became understood that, contrary to popular belief, there was no absolute ban on the use of Welsh in formal procedures. And so from 1660 a trickle of documents appeared in Welsh, and were invariably granted probate as legal documents. The number slowly increased after 1700 as more laymen and fewer parish priests were involved, and it was still increasing when suddenly, from 1858, all wills were sent to London, and it is no longer possible to research the subject. Welsh-language wills sometimes bear evidence of dialect use in a way that barely appears in their English counterparts, and Welsh-language inventories are rich in agricultural terminology.

Space doesn't allow a more expansive treatment of this fascinating subject, which can bring individuals and their joys and sorrows back to life, telling us of people of whom we would otherwise know nothing. Some published material on the subject is available either on sale or in libraries, but there is much to do, especially in Wales. For guides see, for example, J. S. Gibson, *Wills and Where to Find Them* (1974); A. J. Camp, *Wills and their Whereabouts* (1978); Jane Cox, *Wills, Inventories and Death Duties: a Provisional Guide* (1988). For English terms, see Stuart A. Raymond, *Words from Wills and other Probate Records* (2004).

NOTES

1 NLW Crosswood Deeds, I, 847. (In the case of all other wills cited in this chapter, they can be found on the NLW website by going via the Wills/Ewyllysiau button, and then giving the date, diocese, and testator's name.)

2 Gerald Morgan, 'Retail Therapy in Seventeenth-century West Wales', *Ceredigion*, 15 (2005), 1–20. Ibid, 'West Wales Mariners' Wills 1650–1859', *National Library of Wales Journal*, xxx 2 (1997), 197–206

3 For the problem of understanding Welsh personal names, see Gerald Morgan, 'Welsh Names in Welsh Wills', *The Local Historian* (August 1995) 178–85. See also J and S. Rowlands (eds.), *Second Stages in Researching Welsh Ancestry* (FFHS, 1999) esp. Chapters 10 and 11.

4 See, however, Peter Spufford, *Index to the Probate Accounts of England and Wales* (2 vols: British Record Society, 1999). For Welsh examples, Gerald Morgan, 'Brecon Probate Accounts', *Brycheiniog*, 31 (1998–99), 43–48

5 Nia M. W. Powell, '"Near the margin of existence"? Upland Prosperity in Wales during the Early Modern Period'. *Studia Celtica* 41 (2007), 137–62

7. Family Knowledge and Records

Evan James

The first source for tracing ancestry is the information given by the family, and particularly by the oldest relatives. A tape recorder can be very valuable when collecting their reminiscences. If they can put their recollections on paper, all the better. Preparing a list of questions to ask them could help jog their memories.

It is probable that some of the relatives have a family Bible, birth certificates, newspaper cuttings, etc. which prove how members of the family are related to each other. Photographs of the family would be very valuable in maintaining interest. One should remember to note the names of persons and places, and give an estimate of the date on a piece of paper attached to the photograph, or write faintly on the reverse, before all recognition is lost.

They should also be asked where their ancestors and other relatives were buried. Besides recording every relevant monumental inscription, a photograph should be taken of each grave. It is important to look at other gravestones nearby because relatives were often buried close to each other. It should be remembered that the date of death and age are not always correct on a gravestone. It should also be realised that many years could elapse before placing a commemorative stone on the grave, and that those who arranged to erect the gravestone became uncertain of the facts, particularly the year of death and age of the deceased.

Occasionally some are commemorated on a gravestone though they were buried elsewhere. The place of burial may be revealed, particularly for soldiers who were buried abroad, or mariners lost at sea. Cremation was made lawful in 1902. The ashes of the deceased are often returned to the local graveyard and placed in the grave of a relative or with a small plaque in a special plot in the graveyard reserved for urns.

Besides gravestones there are many monuments inside churches and chapels, as well as windows, furniture and books dedicated to the memory of particular members. Monuments in memory of those who lost their lives in war may also be found there, as well as in village halls, schools, colleges and outside in public places.

In the southern half of Ceredigion no gravestone earlier than the eighteenth century has been found (although Iolo Morganwg saw in Strata Florida graveyard about the year 1799 one with the date 1684 on it). A few gravestones dating from the eighteenth century are to be found in parish churchyards in Ceredigion (and as many as 27 of them are still to be seen in Strata Florida churchyard). On family altar tombs the head of the family is often given, the date of his death, name of his home and his age, as well as similar information about his wife and some of his children.

On very small stones there is space only for the initials of the deceased and perhaps the year of death and age, e.g. M.T. / AG / 54 / 1768 in Tregaron churchyard. In the parish register is recorded:

Margaret Thomas buried 21 May 1768 aged 54

In Lampeter churchyard a large area has been set aside for graves marked by small stones with two letters and a number on each one, e.g.:

H.P. / No. 1420. This corresponds to record 1420 in the local workhouse register namely 'Henry Parker, died 27 Feb 1931 aged 66

Before 1800 most of the monumental inscriptions are in English, although three languages – Latin, English and Welsh – are on the grave of Peter Davies 'of Glyn' in Llanbadarn Odwyn churchyard, who died on 30 August 1766 aged forty-one years:

Tempore Disce Mori Brevis est haec vita perennis
Longa haec senti: tunc mors tibi dona Dabit.

Accom-plish'd now is all my strife
my happy soul is gone.
I lost the Pains of mortal life
The glorious Prise I won.
Mi es yn rhydd o'r carchar Prydd
lle rwyf ddarllenydd hygar
Mi ges yn wych Gyfnewid gwiw
Cael ne[foed]d Duw'n lle Daiar.

At Ystrad Meurig there is an inscription in Latin only, on the grave of one of the headmasters of the famous school held in the building near the church. At Aberporth there are several Welsh inscriptions from the end of the eighteenth century, one of which is translated here as follows:

Here lie the bodies of 5 of the children of Dafydd Evan, Llwyncoed:
Evan who died 24 June 1791 (6 days), etc.

However, the corresponding records in the parish register are for the children of *David Evans*. Welsh was used more and more regularly as the century progressed, except that the wealthiest families and some priests, merchants and town residents continued to use English. In Lampeter churchyard there are sixty-seven gravestones for Polish people, most of them in Polish.

With time the surface of a gravestone may be so weathered as to make the inscription difficult to read. On a sunny day a mirror can be of assistance by reflecting the sunlight from one side onto the surface of the stone to create shadows in the dents in the letters. On a cloudy day a wide tube with one end cut at an angle may be used, placing that end close to the

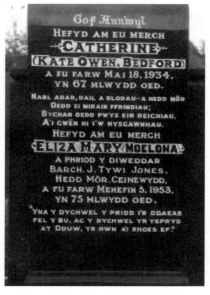

The gravestone of the author Eliza Mary Jones, 'Moelona', Capel Hawen Graveyard, Rhydlewis, Ceredigion

surface of the stone so that the letters are lit from the side. Wiping across the surface of the stone lightly with a damp sponge can also make the letters easier to read. If there is ivy, lichen or moss hiding the inscription, one has to be very careful when trying to remove them so as not to damage the surface of the stone and alter the appearance of some of the letters.

One of the advantages of a gravestone as a source of records is that information about more than one person can be recorded on a stone as well as the relationship between them, even if one is buried half a century later than the other – information that is usually difficult to correlate using a register of burials. It should be remembered also that it is not the date of burial that is usually given on a gravestone, but the date of death. The name of a mariner lost at sea or a soldier buried in a foreign country may be on the family gravestone, but there would be no reference to them in a burials register. However, the name of the soldier would probably be on a monument to all the soldiers of the district who lost their lives.

The gravestone of Joseph Joseph, 1863, and his second wife, Llwynrhydowen [old chapel] graveyard, Rhydowen, Ceredigion

It is only comparatively recently that ordinary people have taken to the custom of erecting a monument on a grave, and the earliest one to survive in Bangor Teifi churchyard is one in memory of Samuel Jones who died in 1809. But it is likely that the stone was not erected until 1845, when Hannah, Samuel's sister, died. In the same parish there are only two inscriptions dating from the decade 1821–1830 whilst there are twenty-five persons recorded in the burials register. By the decade 1871–1880 there were thirty records of burial and twenty-four inscriptions on graves.

On some of the earlier graves the name of the father was used as the second name and the wife was given her maiden name, since the use of surnames did not become common in

114

some districts till the beginning of the nineteenth century. In the churchyard of Llandysiliogogo, Ceredigion, can be seen in Welsh:

> Evan Jenkin, Cefncoedbach, who died 5 April 1834 aged seventy-three
> Catherine his wife, who died 27 February 1813 aged forty-two
> Margaret their daughter who died 19 March 1825 aged seventeen
> Daniel their son who died 13 October 1833 aged twenty-eight
> Ebenezer their son who died 8 October 1835 aged twenty-six

But in the parish register the names that were recorded were Evan Jenkins, Catherine John, Daniel Evans and Ebenezer Evans. There is no record of Margaret's burial.

Very many monumental inscriptions have been transcribed and indexed by individuals, often members of Family History Societies. Many of these indexed transcriptions may be found in record offices, local libraries, the National Library of Wales and more and more on the Web. There has been much tidying and re-arranging of graveyards during the second half of the twentieth century as has happened in Llandysiliogogo churchyard. The inscriptions were recorded in 1971, and also in 1997, when it was found that several of the stones had been relocated in two rows with no family connection between one stone and the next. In addition it was found that as many as thirty of the stones were missing. A copy of both layouts is at the National Library of Wales.

Further reading

E. L. James and M. A. James, *Monumental Inscriptions with Indexes*, Volume 1 (1995), Volume 19 (2011). Transcriptions and indexes of monumental inscriptions of some of the parishes of south Ceredigion. Copies are available at the National Library of Wales, Ceredigion Record Office and Ceredigion Library, Aberystwyth.

The gravestone of the Rev. Peter Joseph, 1857, minister of Llwynrhydowen Unitarian church, Llwynrhydowen [old chapel] graveyard, Rhydowen, Ceredigion

8. Criminal Records

Glyn Parry

Wales law courts – be they Crown courts, ecclesiastical courts or private courts such as manorial courts – touched the lives of a substantial proportion of the Welsh people in one way or another. Statistics are scarce before 1805 though we now know that almost 20,000 individuals were indicted before the Court of Great Sessions between 1730 and 1830. In the absence of a professional police force until the 1850s, almost all criminal prosecutions were private prosecutions which adds another 15–18,000 individuals who had to appear in Court to prosecute those 20,000 indicted (a number of accused were prosecuted by the same prosecutor, which explains why the figure for prosecutors is lower than the number prosecuted). If we add to these two figures the number of witnesses who appeared before the Court to give evidence as well as the jurors, then the number could well approach 100,000. In 1899 the petty sessions courts in Wales heard 55,027 cases, or one case for every thirty-six people living in Wales, assuming that no one was accused twice. A rapid survey of the caseload of the ecclesiastical courts of the archdeaconries of Brecon and Carmarthen suggests that approximately 2,000 people were summoned before the two courts between 1700 and 1755 – a period when the ecclesiastical courts were in serious decline. Court records, then, are a vital source for both local and family history.

This chapter will survey in very general terms the criminal records of the following courts: diocesan or consistory courts whether covering the whole bishopric or just the archdeaconry; manorial courts; courts of petty sessions; Court of Great Sessions in Wales, assize courts and Quarter Sessions. It will not look at records of civil actions apart from those that were heard before the Great Sessions, nor will it look at the records of the Council of Wales and the Marches because so few case records have survived. The records of the central law courts in London (Kings Bench, Common Pleas, Exchequer and Chancery) are vast and will not be directly addressed here, but the most important records of the Great Sessions almost all duplicated the records of these central courts, in form if not in content.

Cover of Launched to Eternity, Crime and Punishment 1700–1900 (Glyn Parry, 2001)

Diocesan or consistory courts

It might surprise many people to realise just how much authority the diocesan courts (also called Bishop's courts) had over the everyday lives of the people of Wales. As we shall see, the diocesan courts had authority, for example, to hear cases against people for drinking and/or playing on the Sabbath; for refusing – without good reason – to frequent church on Sunday; refusing to attend communion; for sexual/moral offences such as adultery and fornication; and marital breakdown.[1] The courts also heard cases relating to the Church itself, such as non-payment of tithes and clerical misbehaviour. Today, almost all the diocesan court's authority has been swept away. In Wales the ancient bishoprics of St Asaph, Bangor and Llandaf had a single court, whereas the other ancient diocese, St David's, because of its huge geographical size, had four archdeaconial courts instead of a single diocesan court, namely Brecon, Cardigan, St Davids and Carmarthen. The ecclesiastical court's main business, when it was fully functional, was the granting of probate and the granting of faculties to enable churches to alter or repair church buildings or graveyards. There is no need here to stress how important probate records (both wills and inventories) are to family and local history, but faculties are also key to the history of church buildings, both internal and external. Faculties had to be obtained (and still have to be obtained today) from the church courts in order to carry out any work both within and without the building from major alterations such as installing new pews to minor changes such as erecting a plaque on a church wall.

What kind of cases were brought before the consistory courts against individuals?

To judge from the records of the archdeaconry of Brecon from 1662 to 1700 and from 1750 to 1760 the commonest prosecution was for non-payment of tithes (also called subtraction of tithes). We can be fairly certain, however, that such cases did not result from a refusal to pay on principle (as happened during the Tithe War in Wales in the 1880s, for example) but was the result of either poverty or an abhorrence of paying taxes in general. The second most prevalent prosecution was for slander. Such cases are particularly interesting since the prosecutor's complaint would include the slanderous words in question, in the language in which they were spoken. These are one of those rare written

A contemporary illustration of the murder of William Powell,
Glynareth, Esq. (1769) [NLW Mss. 232061D, p. 2]
With the permission of the National Library of Wales

records where we can actually hear ordinary people conversing (or at least insulting) other ordinary people in Welsh and in English. Such records have been widely used by English historians to study inter-personal relations in post-Reformation England, and by Richard Suggett in Wales.[2] Other cases heard by the consistory courts included drunkenness; illegitimate children; assaults on clergymen; clandestine marriages; frequenting conventicles (unauthorised assemblies for worship) (pre-1689); pew disputes and sexual misbehaviour. It should also be noted that licencing Nonconformist chapels after 1689 was the responsibility of both the diocesan courts and the Quarter Sessions.

What kind of records did the Welsh consistory courts create?
Firstly, Act Books. These volumes usually note the appearance of individuals summoned, the next step(s) in the legal process, a list of all documents filed in each cause, and the court's judgement. They serve as indexes to the court's business and are invaluable for those interested in the minutiae of the court's legal process. Unfortunately, they are often extremely difficult to use, especially before 1732 when they are in Latin. The handwriting often leaves a lot to be desired and the court clerks habitually used abbreviations now often difficult to decipher. Moreover, they rarely give details about the causes themselves, that is, what the disputes were all about. This can be done by consulting the second type of record – pleadings in individual causes. Legal process in the diocesan courts was quite complicated, with clients being able to submit a variety of legal documents or pleadings before judgement, the most important and informative of which was the libel (from the Latin *libellus,* meaning a booklet) and the defendant's response. It is these two legal instruments that add flesh to the bare bones of the Act Books.

With the close of the legal process and arguments in court, the chair of the court (usually the chancellor of the diocese sitting without a jury) would pronounce judgement. Diocesan courts could not inflict physical punishments such as whipping offenders, nor could they sentence anyone to prison. Indeed, the role of these courts was not punishment as such but reconciliation and reformation of the offender. The court's usual punishment was penance, that is, it could order the offender to stand dressed in a white sheet before the church congregation and admit his or her guilt: it was in effect a kind of communal punishment. The final sanction in the court's disciplinary armoury was excommunication. This meant that excommunicated persons could not prosecute anyone in a court of law; could not give evidence in court; could not be an executor of a will; could not be a child's guardian. More significant, perhaps, no person was to have any business dealings with an excommunicate, nor could anyone support him or her in any way, nor could anyone offer shelter to an excommunicate, on pain of being excommunicated themselves. Indeed, Margaret, the wife of William Powell of Llanhamlach, Breconshire, was prosecuted in 1682 for attending an excommunicate's funeral.

All the records of the Welsh diocesan courts are held by the National Library of Wales, but it is readily apparent that a substantial proportion of the records have long been lost. The courts were established sometime during the Middle Ages but there are no pleadings relating to individual prosecutions until the second half of the seventeenth century, and of the diocese of St Asaph not until 1826. The Act Books have fared better. The earliest are those for St Asaph (1580) and the archdeaconries of Carmarthen (1590) and Brecon (1661). They are available for the diocese of Llandaf from 1688, but Bangor not until 1730. All the extant Act Books are currently being digitised by Family Search and will eventually be available free of charge on its website.

From the seventeenth century the power and authority of the diocesan courts was in steady decline. They lost the right to prove wills and to hear cases relating to broken marriages in 1857 but long before then the secular courts had managed to establish jurisdiction over, for example, libel and slander (there are examples of this in the records of the Court of Great Sessions from the 1730s onwards) and tithes. Apart from granting probate and faculties, the court of the archdeaconry of Brecon heard only three other causes between 1827 and 1829. Today, the court's jurisdiction is confined to clerical misbehaviour, apart from bishops. One fundamental weakness of the consistory courts, which no doubt contributed to their decline, was their inability to enforce attendance on those summoned to appear. Time and time again we find innumerable examples in the records of individuals simply ignoring their summons to attend and to threats of excommunication. The only means for the courts to secure attendance was to enlist the help of the secular courts.

Manorial courts

A manor was a geographical unit owned by a landowner. As an owner or lord of a manor the landowner had certain rights not only over the land but also over his tenants as well and, to a lesser extent, over freeholders within the manor. The rights of the lord and of his tenants were defined by the custom of the manor and not by common law, which meant that both landlord and tenants rights varied from manor to manor. Manorial lords (though by no means all of them) had also been granted limited rights by the Crown to try criminals, as we shall see. As a result two types of manorial courts developed: the court baron, which dealt with routine manorial business, and the court leet, which dealt with crimes or misdemeanours committed within the manor. In practice, however, the records often do not distinguish between the two courts. Whilst using manorial court records it is well to remember that manors varied enormously in size. For example, the manor of Mefenydd in Ceredigion extended between 15 and 20 miles from the sea, whilst the manors or lordships of Brecon, Denbigh and Glamorgan were larger than some of the historic counties of Wales. Manorial and parochial boundaries rarely matched: some manors were entirely within a single parish; other manors included a number of parishes, whilst some parishes could include a number of manors (Llancarfan in Glamorgan, for example, included five manors within its boundaries).

The main business of a manorial court was to record land transactions by the tenants of the manor and such transactions could be conveyances, mortgages, leases, devises in wills or trusts for example. All these transactions needed the permission of the manorial lord (for a fee). In order to execute such transactions the land in question had to be conveyed (strictly speaking it had to be surrendered) in open court to the lord, or more likely to his steward as the lord's chief manorial officer. The steward would then admit the new owner to the land. These transactions were then enrolled on the manorial court roll and the incoming tenant would receive a copy of the relevant part of the roll. Hence, this type of landholding was called copyhold.

Courts baron also entertained cases against individual tenants or freeholders of the manor for breaches of manorial rules, bye-laws or custom. We find cases for overpasturing the manor's common land; neglecting to maintain roads in a decent state of repair; neglecting to clean or scour ditches; leading animals through another's cornfield or moving someone else's animals from one field to another. All such cases involved the communal wellbeing of the manor; but manorial tenants could also bring private prosecutions for debt against fellow tenants provided the debt in question was less than £2.

As was mentioned earlier, the court leet had a right – but a very limited right – to hear criminal prosecutions. It could hear cases for petty theft, assault and affray, for example, but the most serious cases were reserved for the Crown courts. Courts leet could, however, punish transgressors, usually by fining them.

Apart from the manorial court roll already mentioned, manorial courts created a series of other valuable records for the study of family and local or community history. These included, firstly, manorial surveys which give a wealth of details about rents, duties and services owned by the tenants to the lord, such as free labour during harvest; grinding corn at the lord's mill; donation of poultry at Christmas and carrying coal or timber to the lord's mansion. Secondly, custumals, which list all the manorial tenants; rents owed; lands held; and duties or obligations owed. Thirdly, extents which are unbelievably detailed since they contain a valuation of everything within the manor – every building, every scrap of land, every obligation and all the produce paid as rent instead of money. Extents measure the value of a manor if it were to be leased for a year and not its sale price. However these three manorial records were not drawn up very frequently, unlike the abundant manorial rentals, which note the names of tenants, their holding and the amounts of rent paid.

Manorial courts were genuinely important to the manorial community and this is reflected in the heavy use made by historians of their records. They have been exploited to portray the relationships between individual tenants and their neighbours, their family and other community members as well as for analysing the way communities policed themselves. The manorial rolls, especially the enrolled details of landed transactions, have been used extensively (but not in Wales) to study the patterns of landownership – were some families acquiring more land at the expense of their neighbours; were outsiders acquiring land and if so why – and the long term stability of manorial communities – were the same families resident in the manor for several generations, and so on. However, what makes manorial records key to local and family history in Wales is the fact that they are almost the only significant records available from approximately the fourteenth century until Tudor times.

The starting point for researching all the catalogued Welsh manorial records held by Welsh repositories is the computerised Manorial Documents Register maintained by The National Archives (*www.nationalarchives.gov.uk/mdr*) which can be searched online. However, studying manorial records is not plain sailing. All the records are in Latin until 1732 (apart from the 1650s) and are heavily abbreviated, and whilst these usually follow a standard pattern some of the abbreviations were quite often unique to a single manor or indeed to a single clerk who wrote them! Worse, the manors entered into a period of steady decline from roughly the mid-sixteenth century onwards. They lost their limited criminal jurisdiction to the Crown courts (mainly Quarter Sessions) and the parish became much more important as an administrative unit and gradually took over responsibility for the upkeep of roads and the poor, for example. In the long run what eventually killed off the manors, however, was not their loss of criminal jurisdiction or local responsibilities but the fact that more and more landed transactions were executed in the steward's or local solicitor's office rather than in open court. This was the death knell for the manorial court: no business meant no court, no court meant no records. This decline is readily apparent in the deteriorating quality of the records themselves from the seventeenth century onwards, especially the court rolls – the backbone of manorial records. Instead of parchment rolls we have untidy, hurriedly written scraps of paper filed loosely and haphazardly together.

Courts of Petty Sessions

Unlike the Great Sessions and Quarter Sessions in Wales, petty sessions were not established by an Act of Parliament and it is therefore impossible to give a firm date when they began. Their roots, however, can be traced to Quarter Sessions adjournments in the seventeenth century, which transferred responsibility for some court cases to a local justice of the peace who would listen to the case in his front parlour. As central government's administrative demands on Quarter Sessions became heavier and heavier from about 1600 onwards, more and more business was delegated to single or pairs of justices of the peace. Unfortunately, a robust administrative regime was not imposed on these ad hoc courts until the middle of the nineteenth century, with the inevitable result that few Welsh petty sessions records have survived before 1850 (Anglesey has the earliest records going back to 1792). Despite this, the petty sessions records are by far the most important of the Welsh court records discussed in this chapter for family and community history. The reason for this is extremely simple: the overwhelming majority of criminal prosecutions by the end of the eighteenth century – and certainly by the middle of the nineteenth – were heard before petty sessions. It was estimated in 1857 that petty sessions heard twenty times as many cases as all the other courts combined. By the end of the nineteenth century, petty sessions heard 80 per cent of all criminal prosecutions in Great Britain.

Mid nineteenth-century parliamentary statutes imposed stricter administrative practices and procedures on petty sessions (which means better records) as well as enlarging its responsibilities. In 1848 all petty sessions were compelled to transfer details of fines, papers relating to individual prosecutions, and witnesses' statements to Quarter Sessions. In 1847 the Juvenile Delinquency Act gave the courts the right to hear cases against children under the age of fourteen. A few years later they were empowered to hear all cases of theft of goods less than 25 pence, which was raised in 1879 to £2.

The courts were already listening to cases of drunkenness, misbehaviour, refusal to pay rates, non-payment of maintenance by fathers of illegitimate children and vagrancy. They also held non-criminal but locally important administrative functions including licencing of pubs and clubs, storage of explosives, and, from 1927, registration of adopted children.

The most useful petty sessions records are the court registers (including the juvenile offenders' registers) and the magistrates' minute books. The registers contain summaries of all cases that came before the courts whilst the minute books contain the prosecution's evidence (usually the arresting police officer's); age of the defendant if under sixteen years old; and sentence or punishment where appropriate. Before diving into the registers, however, it is worth remembering that these volumes have been indexed, usually at the front. Glancing through the indexes can dramatically cut down on the amount of research work needed to trace relevant offences or specific offences. Any research on Welsh petty sessions records (and indeed any serious historical research on Wales) must begin with the Archives Network Wales (ANW) website (*http://www.archivesnetworkwales.info/*). ANW contains summary descriptions of over 4,700 of the main catalogued archives held in Welsh repositories, including all the catalogued petty sessions records held by Welsh county archives services.

What kind of criminal cases came before the petty session courts?

To judge from the records of the Aberaeron and Lower Ilar petty session court the main types of cases heard – in declining numerical order – were orders to fathers of illegitimate children to pay maintenance; petty thefts; begging or vagrancy; refusal or inability to pay taxes, drunkenness and fishing offences. It does not follow of course that this pattern was replicated elsewhere. In Aberystwyth in 1902, for example, the most frequent offences dealt with by the magistrates were 'drunkenness' and 'drunk and disorderly' cases. But in the same year Aberystwyth magistrates also hear cases for allowing chimneys to catch fire, driving a horse and cart too fast, selling adulterated milk, holding a lottery, whilst a serving maid was prosecuted for shaking a mat in the street! Poaching cases were also heard at petty sessions.

Without doubt, petty sessions records give a very vivid (if blinkered) view of Welsh communities from roughly the mid nineteenth century onwards. (They can also be very humorous on occasions.) More than anything else, they totally undermine the age-old image of late nineteenth-century Wales as a staid, sober, moral and deeply religious people. They show quite clearly that in that period drunkenness, bastardy and petty theft were very common phenomenon.

Court of Great Sessions

The Courts of Great Sessions was established by the so-called Second Act of Union of 1543 and it remained on the statute book until the courts were abolished in 1830 and replaced by the assize courts. The Act empowered the Courts of Great Sessions to hear all pleas of the Crown 'in as large and ample a manner' as the Court of King's Bench and to hold pleas and real actions in 'as large and ample a manner' as the Court of Common Pleas. This in effect meant that the Great Sessions had extensive jurisdiction over both civil and criminal cases; it also managed to acquire jurisdiction over equity causes. The courts sat twice a year in each of the Welsh counties apart from Monmouthshire which, for administrative convenience, was allocated to the Oxford assize circuit.

The twelve remaining counties were arranged into four circuits: North Wales (Anglesey, Caernarfonshire and Merioneth); Chester (Flintshire, Denbighshire and Montgomeryshire); Brecon (Breconshire, Glamorgan and Radnorshire) and the Carmarthen circuit (Carmarthenshire, Cardiganshire and Pembrokeshire). All the records of the court are held by the National Library of Wales.

The overwhelming majority of the court's time was taken up by civil actions, the main record of which are the plea rolls until about 1700. After 1700, however, only those actions that reached issue (i.e. the parties to the action had agreed on what they disagreed, that is, what the issues in dispute actually were) were enrolled on the plea rolls. By 1700 at the latest, only a tiny minority of civil actions ever reached issue; the overwhelming majority had either been abandoned or settled out of court. Plea rolls, then, include details of the plaintiff's case (called declaration or bill), the defendant's answer (called the plea), and, where the case had been argued in court before a jury, the judgement. Most civil actions are mundane cases of simple debt punctuated now and again by actions concerning title to land, breaches of contract, cases of assault wherein the plaintiff is seeking financial compensation and cases of slander.

Finding records of actions in the plea rolls relating to specific localities or families can be a daunting and time-consuming task. There are no modern indexes, but a series of very useful contemporary indexes do survive called docket rolls. They index every civil action before the courts, including actions which did not reach issue. They note the names of the parties, the names of their solicitors, what stage the action has reached, the nature of the dispute and the defendant's plea. However, there is no indication where the litigants lived nor – in landed actions – the location of those lands. The docket rolls are currently being digitised by Family Search of the Genealogical Society of Utah and will eventually be accessible free of charge online.

The main records of the criminal side of the Court of Great Sessions are the gaol files. The files include indictments, calendars of prisoners to be tried by the courts and (from around 1800) calendars of prisoners sentenced to terms of imprisonment by other courts – mainly Quarter Sessions; examinations and depositions of prosecutors and witnesses; bonds or recognisances of prosecutors and witnesses to appear in court to prosecute or to give evidence and coroner's inquests. Examinations of witnesses are by far the most interesting documents since they provide vivid cameos of the everyday life of ordinary people, but great care should be taken when using some of the documents in the gaol files, especially indictments, since many of the 'facts' rehearsed in them are simply incorrect. Often the date of the offence, the occupation of the accused and even the location of the alleged offence are incorrect. Sometimes the date of the offence is the date when the accused was arrested and similarly the place of arrest is supposedly the place where the offence took place. The latter in particular makes writing local history particularly difficult. Nevertheless, some of these errors may be corrected by comparing the indictments with bonds or recognisances which are factually correct. The same problems are also present in Quarter Sessions indictments.

There are no modern indexes for the gaol files but a number of contemporary indexes are available. The most comprehensive are the Crown Books but, unfortunately, they only survive for Flintshire. Another series of indexes are the Black Books, but these are only available for the Brecon circuit and even then only from 1726. Earlier index-type records which should be utilised are the Calendar Rolls of Indictments: these survive for Radnorshire, 1555–1569; Glamorgan, 1555–1601; Cardiganshire,1542–1602 and Pembrokeshire, 1542–1674.

However, the most useful finding aid by far is the Crime and Punishment database hosted by the National Library of Wales. This is an online searchable database of the gaol files from 1730 until 1830. The database can be searched by names of the accused or prosecutor; abode and occupation of the accused; date and type of offences; location of offences; pleas; verdicts and sentences. The pre-1730 gaol files are currently being digitised by Family Search and will in due course be freely available on its website. For the last twenty-five years of the Court's existence the Criminal Registers are also very comprehensive (see below under Assize Records). The Great Sessions Order Books can also be used as indexes to the gaol files since these contain a formal record of the court's judgements and decisions and include, therefore, orders to punish convicted offenders. These are available for the North Wales, Chester and Brecon circuits: the equivalent for the Carmarthen circuit are called Precipe Books.

As has already been indicated, gaol files also include coroner's inquests, which are extremely useful for both local and family history.

They can be used for evidence of murders; suicides; shipwrecks; industrial mining and traffic accidents, and innumerable domestic accidents involving both adults and children. However, a substantial proportion of the inquests were never filed with the records of the courts, because they were considered to be the private property of the coroner until the 1920s and as such there was no legal obligation on him (always a him) to transfer his records to the court. There are no indexes, contemporary or otherwise, for the coroner's indexes apart from Murray Chapman's calendars of the Montgomeryshire gaol files (see Further Reading for details).

Even though the Court of Great Sessions held a jurisdiction in equity from its very foundation, records of its equity or chancery proceedings are extremely rare before 1690 (1730 for the Chester circuit): most evidence for pre-1690 proceedings is in fact to be found amongst estate records. The overwhelming majority of pre-1690 Welsh equity causes were heard either in the Court of Chancery in London or before the Council of the Marches in Wales until it was abolished in 1689 and, even after 1689, most were heard in London. The main difference between equity and common law was that equity looked at the spirit rather than the letter of the law; at the purpose of deeds and documents and human actions. As a result, a substantial proportion of equity causes involve disputes over marriage settlements, wills, trusts and other family disputes.

The fundamental equity records are the litigant's pleadings and the most important (and most prevalent) of these are the complainant or orator's bill of complaint (the complainant being the common law equivalent of plaintiff) and the defendant's answer to the complaint. After conclusion of pleadings the court would issue written interrogatories or questions to be asked of witnesses locally. If the cause came to be argued before the court – and only a small minority were – the judges would pronounce judgement or decree, but quite often before judgement the court would order its chief administrative officer – the Registrar – to write up a detailed report, especially if financial accounts were involved and these are extremely valuable.

The basic place to search equity records for family history is not the pleadings files (bearing in mind that they also include interrogatories). Nor is it the decree books or the registrar's papers, but contemporary indexes to the pleadings, called Bill Books. Even though they name the

Cheque cashed at a bank by Thomas Davies, a clerk at the Dafen
tinworks, a few minutes before he was murdered by David Rees
[Mus. 411a]
With the permission of the Carmarthenshire Record Office

complainants and the defendants as well as the date of the filing of the
pleadings, they do not give any information whatsoever about the
nature of the dispute nor where the litigants lived. For local or
community history, there is currently no option but to trawl through
all the records.

Assize records
The Court of Great Sessions was abolished in 1830 and replaced by the
English assize courts, which in turn were abolished in 1972 and replaced
by the Crown Courts. The four Great Sessions circuits were
amalgamated to form two new circuits: North Wales and Chester
(Cheshire's separate jurisdiction – the Palatinate – was also abolished
in 1830) and the South Wales circuit. All the records are held at The
National Archives. The assize records created the same kind of records
as the Great Sessions, though indictments and depositions are filed
separately. It is advisable, as with the Great Sessions, to search
contemporary indexes first rather than the actual records themselves.
These indexes are variously called Minute Books, Gaol Books or Agenda
Books. However, the fundamental index for criminal proceedings
before the assize courts, and indeed for the Quarter Sessions, from 1805
until 1892 are the Criminal Registers held at The National Archives
which were created by the Home Office from returns sent in by the
assize courts, the Quarter Sessions and the Great Sessions until 1830.
The Registers give the name of all accused who were tried before the

A CALENDAR

OF THE

Criminal Prisoners,

Confined in His Majesty's Gaol, at Cardiff:

Who are to be Tried or Disposed of, at the Great Sessions to be held at Cardiff. for the said County;

On SATURDAY, the 23rd of AUGUST, 1828.

BEFORE THE

Honorable N. G. CLARKE, Esquire,

AND THE

Honorable ROBERT MATHEW CASBERD, Esquire.

R. F. JENNER, Esquire, Sheriff.

No.	Name.	Age.	Trade, &c.	OFFENCE.	Sentence.
1.	*Benjamin Harris,*	28,	*Labourer,*	Committed 19th June, 1828, by J. B. Bruce, Esq. charged on the oaths of Evan Williams and others, with breaking into his house, situate at Newbridge, and stealing a Coat and other wearing apparel therefrom.	*Guilty Sentence of Death Recorded*
2.	*Thomas Morgan,*	20,	*Boatman,*	Committed 26th July, 1828, by The Rev. G. Thomas, Clerk, charged upon the oaths of William Rees and others, with having stolen three Iron Chains, of the value of ten shillings, the goods and chattels of The Marquis of Bute.	*Guilty One year Imprisonment*
3.	*Evan Smith,*	32,	*Miller,*	Committed 2nd August, 1828, by F. Fredricks, Esq. and The Rev. T. Gronow, Clerk, charged on the oath of John Thomas, with having received several sums of Money to the amount of fourteen shillings, for and on his account, and did fraudulently and feloniously embezzle and secrete the same.	*acquitted*
4.	*John Davies,*	23,	*Smith,*	Committed 9th August, 1828, by W. Forman, Esq. charged on the oaths of Giles Williams and others, with having feloniously stolen one silver Watch, from the dwelling house of the said Giles Williams, situate at Hyrwain, in the parish of Aberdare, his property.	*Verdict Guilty*

A calendar of prisoners in Glamorgan who were to be tried in 1828, with their ages, occupations and offences, and also their sentences and penalties added by one of the court clerks
With the permission of the National Library of Wales

three courts in Wales; details of offences; verdicts; sentences where appropriate and which court hears the case. The Criminal Registers are the basic starting point for a general search of the most serious offences committed in Wales after 1805. The Registers are held by The National Archives, but microfilm copies of cases tried in Wales are held by the National Library of Wales and they are also available online for a fee (*ancestry.com*).

Quarter Sessions

As the title suggests, Quarter Sessions met four times a year in each county, though not necessarily in the same place. They held important administrative functions, which are discussed in Chapter 9; here we will concentrate on the courts' criminal work. Generally, only minor criminal offences were heard by the court, such as assaults, misdemeanours and thefts of goods valued at less than 5 pence, but this situation was altered considerably by Sir Robert Peel's legal reforms during his period as Home Secretary in the 1820s. The number of capital offences had increased substantially from 1688 until 1815, from around fifty to about 290. The results of this Bloody Code, as it was known, was not only to make such offences as sheep-stealing, theft of goods worth over 25 pence or tearing down a sapling capital offences, but also to remove some crimes from the jurisdiction of the Quarter Sessions to the Great Sessions, since the former could not pass down the death sentence, though it could sentence some convicted offenders to transportation. Peel's reforms, however, reversed this process by eventually abolishing almost all capital offences. In 1820 the Great Sessions heard twice as many indictable offences as all the Welsh quarter sessions courts combined: by 1850 the Quarter Sessions heard three times as many of the same offences as the assize courts in Wales. One result of this transfer –together with the increasing administrative workload of the Quarter Sessions and new legislation -was the transfer of more and minor offences to the petty sessions.

The most important records as far as crime is concerned are the Quarter Sessions rolls. Their contents are very similar to the Great Sessions gaol files already described, that is, indictments, recognisances and depositions of witnesses. Other records created by the courts should be used as indexes, the most important of which are the Order Books and Minute Books, which give details about the accused,

Ruthin Gaol/Record Office

the offences, plea, verdict and sentence. The basic starting point for researching Quarter Sessions records is the previously mentioned Archive Network Wales.

Between them court records of the various courts in Wales offer a very vivid portrait of communities along the length and breadth of the country across the centuries, and illuminate matters totally unrelated to crime and criminals; nevertheless, these sources are not unbiased versions of events. They need to be handled with care and woven very carefully with other sources to achieve as balanced a history as possible of our communities. Finally, it may be worth remembering that only a very small percentage (as is the case today) of crimes were ever reported to the authorities, perhaps only one in ten.

NOTES

[1] It is important to remember that ecclesiastical courts could not grant a divorce in today's meaning of the word. The courts could, however, annul marriages because they were judged to be invalid on grounds of, for example, bigamy, consanginuity or sexual impotence which granted the right to the couple to marry again (though strictly speaking they were never married in the first place), or they could grant a legal separation ('bed and board') on grounds of cruelty or adultery, but the couple were not allowed to remarry.

[2] Richard Suggett, 'Slander in Early-modern Wales', BBCS, 39 (1992), 119-153.

Further Reading

Ecclesiastical courts

The standard works on the Welsh ecclesiastical courts are Walter. T. Morgan, 'The Consistory Courts of the Diocese of St David's 1660-1858' (unpublished University of Wales, MA thesis) and his article 'The Consistory Courts of the Diocese of St David's' in *JHSChW*, 6 (1957), 5–24. A specialist work on Church court records is Dorothy M. Owen, *The Records of the Established Church in England, Excluding Parochial Records* (1970).

Manorial courts

The best work on Welsh manorial records is Helen Watt, *Welsh Manors and their records; with an introduction on the Origins and Development of the Manorial System in England and Wales to the Sixteenth Century by Michael Rogers* (2000). Another useful work is Mary Ellis, *Using Manorial Records* (c.1994). Anyone wanting to master the complex medieval manorial records should start with P. D. A. Harvey, *Manorial Records* (1984). Examples of works (amongst hundreds of publications) which utilises manorial records to portray English manorial communities are Marjorie Keniston McIntosh, *Autonomy and Community: The Royal Manor of Havering, 1200-1500* (1986) and *A Community Transformed: the Manor and Liberty of Havering, 1500–1620* (1991). A good example of the types of cases that came before a manorial court work is George Eyre Evans, *Aberystwyth and its Court Leet* (1903).

Petty sessions

I am not aware of any substantial work on the petty sessions in Wales; recourse must be had then to books on the sessions in England, though these are horribly dated by now. Amongst them are Sidney and Beatrice Webb, *English Local Government from the Revolution to the Municipal Corporations Act: the Parish and the County* (1906); Bertram Osborne, *Justices of the Peace, 1361-1848: A History of the Justices of the Peace for the Counties of England* (1960). For a particularly fine example of how to use and interpret the records see David J.V. Jones, *Crime in Nineteenth Century Wales* (1992).

Court of Great Sessions

See Glyn Parry, *A Guide to the Records of Great Sessions in Wales* (1995) and W. Llewelyn Williams, *An Account of the King's Court of Great Sessions in Wales* (1916). The best way to familiarise with the handwriting and abbreviations is to compare the original records with Murray Chapman's superb transcripts in *Criminal proceedings in the Montgomeryshire Court of Great Sessions: transcript of commonwealth gaol files 1650-1660* (1996);

Montgomeryshire Court of Great Sessions: calendar of criminal proceedings 1541–1570 (2004), Montgomeryshire Court of Great Sessions: Gaol Files 1571–1580 (2008); *Montgomeryshire Court of Great Sessions Gaol Files: 1581–1590* (2010) and *Montgomeryshire Court of Great Sessions: Calendar of Gaol Files 1591–1595* (2010)

Assize courts

The best works on the assize courts are two books by J. S. Cockburn: *Calendar of Assize Records. Home Circuit Indictments; Elizabeth I and James I, Introduction* (1985) and *A History of English Assizes, 1558–1714* (1972). Even though both discuss the assizes courts before they were introduced to Wales they are still highly relevant, especially the former. For a brief introduction and a summary list of the Welsh assize records held at The National Archives (*http://www.nationalarchives.gov.uk/records/research-guides/assizes-key-welsh-1831-1971.htm*)

Courts of Quarter Sessions

Once again, nothing of substance has been published on the Quarter Sessions courts and their records covering all of Wales. The best currently available are the introductory sections of the catalogues of Quarter Sessions records published by some of the Welsh County Archives Services. More generally, see Sir Thomas Skyrme, *History of the Justices of the Peace* (1991), and for sessions rolls of a single county in the 1860s see Susan C. Ellis, 'Observations of Anglesey life through the Quarter Sessions Rolls, 1860–1869', *TAAS* (1986), pp. 117–146).

9. Local Government

Helen Palmer

What is Local Government ?

Local government usually consists of a range of services provided for the smooth running of the community it serves. Local government often carries out the commands of central government as they are expressed through Acts of Parliament. The central government often makes a strategic decision about how things should be done, passes an Act of Parliament and then it is up to local government to make sure that the new statute is enacted.

In the past local government services have been supplied by a wide range of organisations. The people who administered these organisations were sometimes appointed by the central government, sometimes selected from within the community and sometimes elected by the votes of the community.

This chapter will look at some of the different kinds of Local Government, the records it produced and the research uses for those documents.

Wales Before 1536

The traditional local government unit in Wales was the *cwmwd* (commote) whose origins extend back to the Dark Ages. The local administrative system in Wales was transformed as a result of the Edwardian Conquest (1277-84) and the shires of Anglesey, Caernarfon, Merioneth, Flint, Cardigan and Carmarthen were established at this time. Another post-conquest development was the substitution of Welsh law: *cyfraith Hywel* (the law of Hywel) by English law. The leading officer in the medieval shire was the sheriff, implementing the government's policy, collecting taxes and dispensing justice in the sheriff's court. By the early modern period the office had become largely honorific as much of his work was taken over by Justices of the Peace (see The Quarter Sessions). A combination of English and Welsh law, known as 'the custom of the March' was practised in the Marcher lordships which comprised the other areas of Wales. These were converted into the shires of Denbigh, Montgomery, Radnor, Brecknock, Glamorgan, Monmouth and Pembroke as a result of the Acts of Union (1536-43), which also largely ensured the introduction in Wales of English legal procedures.

The Manor

In the Middle Ages in rural areas the manor was the principal unit of local government administration with which the ordinary person came into contact. All land actually belonged to the monarch, but in exchange for the promise of military service the king awarded land to favoured individuals, who in their turn would grant smaller estates to their own followers. These estates – manors – existed principally to support the household of its owner. Manors could vary in size, scope and structure – some were coterminous with villages, whilst elsewhere a village was divided up between two or more manors. Elsewhere again, a manor could incorporate several villages, or consist of a manorial centre with outlying properties. The people who lived in the manor might be freemen or bondmen. The latter were only allowed to leave the manor with the lord's permission and had to serve the lord of the manor in many different ways.

The manor usually consisted of a whole series of components which together provided the potential for a successful rural micro-economy. This included not only the different types of lands and farming practiced, but also the people who undertook all the work (the tenants). At the centre of the manor was the residence (the 'manor house') and its home farm, sometimes known as the demesne farm, with (perhaps) dovecots, barns and granaries, stables and fishpond.

With this might be the manor court in which the lord of the manor exercised his private jurisdiction over his tenants and freeholders who had to attend the court sessions and be bound by the court's decisions. Although the manor court (like other law courts) could and did fine people who did not abide by its regulations it was essentially more of an administrative body, overseeing the life of the community. The court was presided over by the steward, who was the representative of the lord of the manor. Matters were presented to the court by a jury of local people giving reports or accusations in response to specific questions asked by the steward. Much of the work was carried out at the court baron, where farming practices were regulated, land conveyed and disputes between tenants settled. In manors where lords had been given special judicial rights from the Crown, courts leet were also held, with authority to determine misdemeanours. Often the separate jurisdictions were combined in one court and the rolls presenting its decisions contain the work of each. The courts had powers of punishments beyond fines (see Chapter 8).

The remainder of the manor might include the homes of the tenants, a warren (both a place where rabbits were bred for food and a status symbol – the 'right of free warren' was a franchise awarded by the monarch to kill small game in a defined area), fisheries and marsh (again, a potential source of foodstuffs), parkland for grazing and for deer, woods for fuel, mills for grinding corn, pasture and arable land for the growing of crops and raising of domestic animals. There would probably be regular markets and fairs. It was usual to have a church situated within the manor; the relationship between the manor and the church's ecclesiastical parish can be a little complicated.

The tenants of a manor paid rents and laboured for the lord of the manor in exchange for having a safe and stable environment in which to live. They were subject to various obligations like having to get their corn ground at the manor's own mill – which could be more expensive than a rival miller whose services they were *not* allowed to use.

Manorial records

Manorial documents are considered to be so important that they are protected by law, and local government record offices keep them with the special permission of The National Archives at Kew. There is a very useful Manorial Documents Register available online as part of The National Archives website, including a section devoted to Welsh manorial documents, many of which are at the National Library of

Wales in Aberystwyth, and in local government record offices. Some of the documents most likely to survive are:

- Surveys – written descriptions of the property, these describe the assets of the manor, including boundaries, acreages and tenants' rights and obligations.
- Custumals – similar to surveys, these described the customs of the manor, details of the land, services and rents owed to the lord of the manor, the classes of tenants and the lord's obligations.
- Financial accounts of the manor.
- Court records which consist of the manorial court rolls (the 'minute books' of the courts). These can be in heavily-abbreviated Latin, and therefore rather difficult to use. They record the proceedings of the court.

The Quarter Sessions

The Quarter Sessions were law courts which had the most important administrative role in local government at county level for over 500 years; before 1888 there was no clear distinction between local

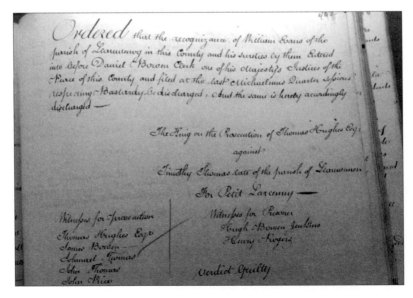

Quarter Sessions volume, Llanwenog
With the permission of Ceredigion Archives

138

government and the local administration of justice, as both matters were dealt with by Justices of the Peace. It was their duty to meet (or 'sit') four times a year at Quarter Sessions, listen to criminal cases, enquire into the upkeep of the highways, roads and bridges (see 'The parish') and ensure that the county rate was used properly.

The Quarter Sessions were created as a result of the need for Justices of the Peace to meet regularly to deal with administrative matters and criminality in the county. An Act of Parliament of 1361 created the role of Justice of the Peace (also known as JPs and magistrates). JPs were to be men of the county who were well informed about the area in which they lived and 'of good social standing'; in practice this meant the position was open only to men with a minimum property qualification, so most magistrates were landowners and gentry. Although the position of magistrate enjoyed considerable status there was also a lot of work involved. In the eighteenth century an increase in the number of clergy acting as magistrates indicated a reduction in the number of gentry willing to undertake the duties of a JP – and consequently a more administratively active and committed magistracy evolved, as the status-conscious gentry departed. In the 1830s, the Commission of the Peace (as it was also known) was opened to men with 'commercial wealth' earned from business and since then magistrates have been drawn from more diverse parts of society. The position of JP has always been unsalaried, with salaried officials (such as the Clerk) who could advise, and execute the JP's wishes. Female magistrates began to appear in Wales between 1915 and 1920. The appointment of all Justices of the Peace had (and has) to be approved by central government.

What was the county rate ?
Rates are a form of local taxation. Anyone with sufficient wealth or income became a ratepayer, and several different rates were raised to support local government. The county rate was used to pay for things like the upkeep of bridges, the county gaol, and the running of the court of Quarter Sessions. It was set by the Justices of the Peace.

Records of the Quarter Sessions
The survival of Quarter Sessions records is by no means uniform. Different counties may have very different collections of records. Many

of the records dealt with the administration of justice (see Chapter 8 for these records), but others show the administrative function of the courts. These include the Order Books which record orders made by the court, often to the County Treasurer for payments.

As it was the duty of the JPs to ensure that Acts of Parliament were executed at a local level, they dealt with hugely diverse matters such as putting children into apprenticeships; ensuring the dead were buried only in wool; licensing drovers, pedlars and chimney sweeps; approving plans for new gaols and other public buildings; overseeing factory conditions; the registration of dissenting ministers, and even (during the Commonwealth period) performing marriage ceremonies.

The Borough (sometimes the 'Corporation') and its Council

What is a borough ?
Some towns grow naturally, from settlements at significant geographical locations such as a fording place on a river, a defensible place, or the meeting point of valleys, whilst other were founded where a need for their presence – often a military need – was felt, either by the king, by barons or by monastic lords. Where towns were established they were furnished with markets, market places and tenements (or burgages) suitable for traders. In medieval England and parts of Wales the most basic liberty enjoyed by towns with borough status was that of burgage tenure. This meant in effect that the tenants or burgesses owed no manorial obligations to their lord other than their rent. Burgage tenure was a 'mobile' tenure which the burgess could sell, alienate, mortgage or bequest without the need for a licence from his overlord. Burgesses were granted the right to freedom from toll and the right to hold fairs and markets. Other borough privileges could vary from place to place.

During the twelfth century the usual practice was for burgesses to lease a borough from their lord, the towns' revenues (rents, tolls, court fines etc.) being composed into a fixed annual sum called a 'farm'. In royal boroughs the revenues were collected by the reeve, an official of the king who also presided over the courts. Towns became really 'free' when the townspeople secured the right to appoint their own officials including the reeve, and paying their annual dues to the lord corporately rather than individually.

Enlistment of the Royal Cardigan Militia, 1827–8
With the permission of Ceredigion Archives

Borough courts

By the twelfth century, serious crime was not usually the province of the borough court, but some boroughs maintained coroners who kept records of crimes pending the arrival of the (royal) justices.

Many boroughs did have extensive jurisdiction over their inhabitants in civil cases. Actions might be brought against visiting merchants; deeds concerning town property might be enrolled as was the probate on wills.

Documents of the borough

The Charter

Although borough status did not depend on having a charter, many towns obtained them. The rights and liberties of the borough would be granted by the monarch in a royal charter, or by the lord (either secular or ecclesiastical) if the borough was non-royal. From time to time borough charters would be reissued or updated. In the fourteenth century new charters known as Charters of Incorporation appeared. Incorporation made the town a 'person' in the eyes of the law by bestowing on it the 'five points':

- The right to perpetual succession.
- A common seal. The seal was the method of validating documents before literacy was widespread. Individuals and institutions had seals of varying complexity. Seals of important institutions (like bishops, or, especially, the monarch) would have very large and beautiful seals, which would be attached by ribbon or cord to the documents they issued. Less wealthy individuals had smaller seals. Today's 'signet ring' had its origin in the personal seal, which would be pushed into warm wax at the bottom of a document to prove it represented the owner's wishes.
- To sue and be sued.
- To hold lands.
- To issue bye-laws.

Minute books

For the day-to-day administration of the borough a minute book was used, which recorded the decisions by which all the varied business of the town was conducted.

Judicial

Boroughs often had their own courts, separate to the County Quarter Sessions. Proceedings of the Borough Court may survive, including court pleas, jury verdicts, enrolled deeds, wills, debts and the records of inquests. There may also be Civil Court records such as debt cases.

Financial
The borough kept accounts of the corporation and individuals, including the Mayor's accounts, Chamberlain's accounts, audit books, receipts rolls, rentals and records of locally-raised taxation.

Freeman and apprenticeship records
Records of Freemen admitted to the borough (on borough court rolls at an earlier period), applications for freedom etc. and apprenticeship registers.

Architectural plans and maps
Early maps of towns, and architectural drawings for buildings and structures either built by, or the responsibility of the corporation.

Estates
Title deeds, leases etc, registers of leases and counterparts of leases granted by the town.

Coroners' rolls
Records of the coroner into unexpected or violent deaths. The office dates from 1194 in England, and 1284 in Wales. In practice, surviving records are much more recent; many do not survive.

Poll books and papers concerned with elections
The right to vote has, for most of its history, been limited by gender and wealth. Poll books show who voted in an election and for whom (before the secret ballot was introduced) and there may be other records such as electoral registers (from the 1832 Reform Act onwards), posters, and documents showing how the election was conducted.

Bye-laws

Records of the Guilds, Chantries and other fraternities which the borough supported

Records of trusts
Established to administer benefactions received by the burgesses such as grammar schools or hospitals.

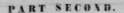

List of voters, Register of electors, Borough of Aberystwyth 1865–6
With the permission of Ceredigion Archives

The Parish

The parish was originally an ecclesiastical unit which was adopted as a civil administrative unit. For much of its history the ecclesiastical and administrative aspects of the parish were loosely interconnected – for instance, parish records of the vestry meetings might be kept in the parish chest in the church; the meetings themselves were held in the church vestry.

Pre-Reformation responsibility for local administration fell upon the parish and the manorial courts, and the monasteries dealt with much of the relief of the poor. After the dissolution of the monasteries, and as the manorial system declined, the parish inherited and adopted many of the responsibilities of these two bodies.

The parish was the central unit of local administration by the early seventeenth century, although much of its work was overseen by the JPs at Quarter Sessions. The importance of the parish to local government lasted over 200 years, though its actions were changed by numerous Acts of Parliament along the way.

Parochial local government depended on a regular meeting called the Vestry, at which decisions were made. There were two types of vestry, the General Vestry and the Select Vestry. The General or Open Vestry was ostensibly open to everyone in the parish, but as this was generally an impractical method of conducting local government it was usually a much smaller group known as the Closed or Select Vestry which made the decisions and administered the finances of the parish.

Meetings could take place in the church vestry but often occurred in more congenial surroundings such as a local house or inn. Both members of the Established Church and Nonconformists might be involved in the Vestry, particularly in the nineteenth century. Its decisions, recorded in the Vestry Books or Vestry Minutes, affected the whole community; it had the power to levy rates and to appoint the parish officers.

Parish Officers

A series of annually appointed unpaid parish officers administered the responsibilities of the parish. These offices were compulsory (although there were sometimes ways of wriggling out of them), and they were in general not paid (although they might receive certain allowances) .

The officials were:

- The churchwardens – often two, sometimes one appointed with 'church' approval, and the other the 'people's choice' through the vestry.
- The parish constable
- The overseers of the poor
- The surveyor of highways

The records produced by these officials showed the civil administration of the parish. They were traditionally kept with the registers of baptism, marriage and burial (which, although recording religious events in the lives of parishioners, also served a civil purpose themselves until the introduction of civil registration and certification in 1837), often in the church itself.

The principal documents of the parish are as follows:

Vestry Books (or Minutes)

In 1818 an Act made the keeping of Vestry Minutes compulsory. Many parishes had already maintained them for years, however. They record the decisions of the Vestry meetings. As with all minutes they are not likely to be detailed. They should be signed to signify the general agreement of the meeting. Sometimes they demonstrate the relationship between the Select Vestry and the General Vestry.

Rate Books

Parishes were allowed to levy rates, but that also meant they had the responsibility to assess which members of the parish community had to pay those rates and how much they had to pay. The resultant lists and rates books give the names of individuals, often accompanied by the name of their dwelling. The amount for which individuals are assessed can give an indication of their social status within the parish.

Until the early part of the eighteenth century rates were often collected as a single, general levy, but thereafter they tended to be split up and separate demands were made for the Poor Rate and for the General or Church rate for the upkeep of the parish church.

Churchwardens' and Overseers' Accounts

The use of rates for the upkeep of the fabric of the church and other parish facilities was recorded in the Churchwardens' Accounts. These may include payments to tradesmen for repairs to the church and associated parish buildings. It should also include payment for the bread and wine for the Communion in the parish church at Christmas, Easter, Whitsun and All Saints Day.

Records of the Overseers of the Poor

The manner in which the rates used for the upkeep of the poor were spent are contained in the Accounts of the Overseers of the Poor. Payments were made to paupers, either in actual money or 'relief in kind', which could be food, fuel or clothing, or anything else deemed necessary for the welfare of the pauper (such as alcohol!). When a pauper died the parish might have to pay for the coffin and funeral expenses.

Settlement and Removal

Because parishes were concerned to ensure that they maintained only those poor people who were truly their responsibility the system of 'settlement' grew up. One gained the right of settlement by either renting property to an annual value of £10, or by paying the poor rate or by serving an apprenticeship within the parish or by serving as a parish officer. A wife automatically took the place of settlement of her husband and children usually took the place of settlement of their father, except in the case of an illegitimate child, where settlement was determined by place of birth. When someone needed relief but was suspected of being the responsibility of another parish, the Vestry Books may record that they were to be examined before the Justices of the Peace. Settlement enquiry papers ('Examinations as to Settlement') may sometimes be found which give details of the examinee's life.

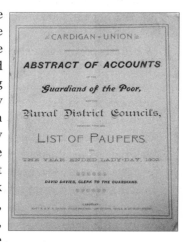

Abstract of accounts, list of paupers, Cardigan Union
With the permission of Ceredigion Archives

Apprenticeships

Parishes would try to off-load their pauper children on to other (sometimes distant) parishes into apprenticeships. It was hoped that a child with a trade would rise above the status of pauper, but as apprenticeship within a parish gave right of settlement, it also meant that the receiving parish had to assume responsibility for poor relief for that person if it became necessary. Apprenticeship papers were therefore important in demonstrating those for whom the parish no longer had responsibility!

Bonds of Indemnity (Bastardy Bonds)

Illegitimate children (and their mothers) could be a financial burden to a parish, so from the mid-eighteenth century it was common for the father of an illegitimate child to enter into a bond of indemnity (more colloquially known as Bastardy Bonds) with a parish whereby he would bear the cost of supporting the child should it become chargeable to the parish.

Records of the Overseers of the Highways

From the Highways Act of 1555 to 1835 the responsibility for the maintenance of most roads within a parish lay with the parish administration. In the eighteenth and nineteenth centuries there was also (still) a common-law liability on the parish to maintain the highways in its area, but in practical terms the responsibility for these arterial routes was often devolved to Turnpike Trusts.

The overseer was empowered to raise a local rate and his accounts had to be approved at the end of his office. He was answerable to the JPs at Quarter Sessions, who might demand work to be undertaken on neglected stretches of road.

The overseer was responsible for supervising statute labour, whereby local people had to work for several days each year in repairing the roads.

In 1835 a new system was introduced whereby JPs appointed paid surveyors for groups of parishes, and the whole system became more 'professional'.

Records of the Parish Constable

This was originally a manorial office, but in the seventeenth and eighteenth centuries it became a parish responsibility.

The constable was empowered to raise taxes and had to keep accounts which were examined at the end of his time in office. He could be responsible for the stocks, the pillory and the lock-up, for raising the hue and cry, for whipping vagrants, securing prisoners, and escorting them to the local Quarter Sessions.

The constable might also collect all the rates levied within the parish, national taxes (such as the poll tax, hearth tax and land tax – when and where applicable) and the raising of the local militia (see below). He might also be responsible for weights and measures and making sure ale-houses were licensed at Quarter Sessions. Where parish records fail, the Quarter Sessions records may sometimes reveal the work of the parish constable.

The County Militia

The Lords Lieutenants of the county were obliged to raise a quota of men for service locally in support of the regular army, under a series of Militia Acts. In times of war these men might have to go much further afield. Each parish had to provide its quota of men, and if sufficient volunteers were not forthcoming, then the able-bodied men of the parish could be balloted to make up the quota. The parish had to support dependants of a man chosen by ballot, which could be expensive if he had a big family. To avoid this parishes would sometimes arrange to pay for a substitute (usually a single man from another parish) to go instead. Parish papers may exist to show the workings of this process.

Control of Vermin

Vestry books often record the destruction of wildlife whose existence was seen as prejudicial to the well-being of the parish. Polecats, owls, birds of prey, hedgehogs, foxes, badgers and weasels were all killed in large numbers and records of their killing, by whom, and the payment allotted by the Vestry for this, may be recorded.

Tithes

The idea of tithes came from the injunction to Moses and Jacob in the Bible to give one tenth of all the produce of their land for the work of God. The 'great tithes' of corn and hay and the 'small tithes' of livestock, wool and non-cereal crops went to support the rector of a parish who in returned maintained the chancel of the church and saw to the provision of church worship.

At the Reformation tithe rights belonging to the monasteries were confiscated by the Crown and sold off (or granted) to various owners known as lay proprietors. This led to about one third of all tithes being owned by lay people rather than the Church – in addition, some clergy and ecclesiastical institutions leased the collection of tithes to laymen.

Originally tithes were payable in kind and sometimes the precise customs to be followed in collecting tithes are detailed in glebe terriers (documents recording ecclesiastical property). In some parishes, by the Early Modern period farmers paid a fixed *modus* instead (goods commuted to a sum of money).

Collecting tithes in kind was difficult and unpopular. Parliamentary Enclosure, and the Acts by which it was allowed to happen, provided an opportunity to settle matters by allotting land to the tithe owners in lieu of tithes.

The question of commutation of tithes was discussed seriously from the early nineteenth century, and by the 1830s the need for reform was acknowledged by the Church of England, which acquiesced in the passing of the Tithe Commutation Act in 1836 whereby tithes were converted into rent charge payments based on the price of grain at the time.

Tithe Maps

The Tithe Commissioners hoped to produce 'A General Register and Survey of Real Property', comparable in its detail to the eleventh-century Domesday Book, as a result of the Tithe Commutation Act 1836.

The two most important tithe documents held by the parish were the tithe map and schedule or apportionment. The map was hand-drawn, usually at a large scale of about 25" : 1 mile. It showed every parcel of land, road, path and dwelling and each of these was numbered. The schedule or apportionment contained a list of the same numbers showing who owned and who occupied each parcel of land. There may be a preamble noting the extent and use of the arable land which was liable to tithe, the names of all tithe owners and all customary payments which were made in lieu of tithe. The acreage and the tithe payment appear against each property. There may be details of field names and land use.

Diminishing significance of the parish

Throughout the nineteenth century the importance and significance of the parish as a unit of local government diminished as its duties were taken over by other bodies, in a century which saw central government seeking to control local government much more closely.

Boards, Trusts, Commissions, Authorities and Companies

During the eighteenth and nineteenth century as towns and cities grew, and industry developed, local government began to divide more noticeably into urban and rural administrations. In the rural areas the JPs still did the majority of the administration, but in towns elected Boards were often responsible for specific areas of local government. Boards were constituted for particular purposes, usually to deal with a single issue.

A series of local and private Acts of Parliament created Turnpike Trusts, drainage boards, improvement or pavement commissioners, municipal water and gas companies. The Act would provide for the creation of a Board of Commissioners composed of *ex officio* and elected members, and gave the Board the authority to raise a rate to undertake limited tasks.

When several towns had applied for similar local or private Acts, eventually a general Act might be passed which other authorities could adopt if they wished. Other Acts of Parliament insisted that local Boards be constituted for particular purposes.

Turnpike Trusts

These were set up to provide a well-maintained road network on popular routes. The road-building was privately financed, and returns on investment came from charging tolls on particular stretches of road. The 'turnpikes' were the barrier placed across the road to stop the traffic when collecting the toll. In parts of Wales, opposition to the Turnpike Trusts and their charges resulted in the Rebecca Riots and significant local unrest. As a result County Roads Boards were introduced in some areas.

Minute books of the Turnpike Trusts and County Roads Boards may be held in local authority record offices, along with financial records of the company, including those relating to individual toll houses in some cases. There is a preserved toll house at the St Fagans: National History Museum.

Highway Boards

Highway Boards were set up in rural areas under the Highways Act of 1835 and the Highways Act 1862 to maintain roads in the area. The Act in 1835 abolished statute labour (see Records of the Overseers of the

Highways, above) and allowed a highway rate to be levied. Parishes could join together as highway district authorities and employ a paid district surveyor. This was permissive legislation, and did not have to be undertaken. However, the Highways Act 1862 empowered JPs to *compulsorily* unite parishes into Highway Districts run by a Highways Board where they thought it necessary. In 1878 the rural sanitary authorities often took over responsibility for the Highways Boards. Following the Local Government Act of 1894 the responsibilities of Highways Boards passed to the Rural District Councils, whose new Highways Committee often carried on using the same minute books as the old Board.

Burial Boards

In the 1850s the increased number of people living – and dying – in towns and cities meant that there was no longer sufficient room to bury in urban churchyards.

A series of Acts were passed to allow local government to create cemeteries on the edges of towns. Acts allowed the Vestry to set up a Burial Board to administer civil cemeteries; minute books and accounts may survive to show how the Board performed, and there should be burial registers and other records relating to burial, which may be useful to genealogists.

School Boards

Following the Education Act of 1870 any place without adequate educational provision for children could set up a School Board and build a school, with state assistance. The locally-elected School Board was responsible for the administration of the school. This system continued until County Councils took on the responsibility after 1902. School Boards kept minute books and financial records which may be in local government record offices.

Poor Law Unions, Boards of Guardians and the Workhouse

The direct care of the poor passed from the parish with The Poor Law Amendment Act of 1834 which saw the creation of Unions, and Union Workhouses. Parishes were grouped together into 'Unions' managed by elected Boards of Guardians, and a Union Workhouse was built in a convenient town. Instead of looking after the poor locally, parishes paid the Union to either keep its paupers in the workhouse (known as 'indoor relief') or have money paid to them at home ('out relief'). There were economies of scale and standardization of procedures in this method of poor relief. The Boards of Guardians were responsible to the Poor Law Commission, and records reflecting this relationship may be found in The National Archives at Kew. Because of the attempted standardization of procedures, workhouses were issued with numerous registers, journals, ledgers and other documents in which details of local poor law administration had to be recorded. Local government record offices often house very large collections of these records (where they have survived) which may provide valuable insights into both the local management of the poor and the lives of pauper ancestors.

Urban and Rural Sanitary Authorities

Although a series of Acts had been passed in the nineteenth century relating to public health, they tended to be focused on particular areas, or permissive rather than compulsory. However, the Public Health Acts of 1872 mapped out the whole of England and Wales into Urban and Rural Sanitary Districts, the former having more powers than the latter as urban areas were perceived as posing more threats to human health at the time. The Rural Sanitary Authorities covered the same areas as the Poor Law Unions, *minus* any urban areas, The Authorities were tasked with improving public health by regulating threats to public health such as the pollution of watercourses, and the investigation of 'nuisances' such as insanitary waste heaps .

The 1888 Local Government Act – County Councils

This Act sought to bring together many of the responsibilities that the Quarter Sessions, the boards and authorities had been developing, and entrust them all to a single new body – the County Councils. The Act said that the Councils should 'be entrusted with the management of the administrative and financial business of that county and shall consist of the chairman, aldermen and councillors'. What was really significant was that the men who ran the Council were elected and not appointed, introducing democracy to the highest level of local government.

From the Quarter Sessions the County Councils got these rights and responsibilities, amongst others:

- To make, assess and levy rates, and then to spend the money they had raised.
- To borrow money.
- To own and administer county buildings (including shire halls, county halls etc., asylums for pauper lunatics, reformatory and industrial schools, but not prisons which had been nationalised under an act of 1877).
- To administer and maintain some, but not all, roads and bridges.
- The licensing of places for music, dancing and racecourses.
- To oversee the work of the County Treasurer, Surveyor, Public Analyst and officer employed under the Explosives Act of 1875 (who kept a register of those in the county licensed to keep explosives!).
- To maintain the Coroner (these were formerly elected by freeholders in the county ; under an Act of 1887 they were appointed by the County Council).
- To execute Acts relating to contagious diseases of animals, destructive insects, fish conservancy, wild birds, and weights and measures.
- The power to appoint a Medical Officer of Health.

The County Councils inherited some of the records of the Quarter Sessions and they also sometimes inherited its personnel. Many of the Clerks of the Peace became the first Clerks of the County Council, whilst many JPs became the first councillors elected to it.

The County Councils set up a number of committees to reflect the work it undertook. In the early days of the Council typical examples might be the 'Roads and Bridges Committee' and the 'Weights and Measures Committee'. All the committees produced minutes about their discussions and decisions which were published and should be available at local government record offices.

Council minutes can be much more interesting than one might suppose!

In 1902 under the Education Act of that year, County Councils acquired the responsibility for elementary education from the School Boards and British and National Schools. Thereafter detailed minutes of the Education Committee should be available.

i. The 1894 Local Government Act

This Act of Parliament created a second tier of local government, replacing the Urban and Rural Sanitary Boards or Authorities with Urban and Rural District Councils. The Act also created Parish Councils, which effectively replaced the old parish administration of the Vestry. This formally acknowledged the separation of ecclesiastical and civil local government. In Wales, the Parish Council was replaced in 1974 by the Community Council.

ii. Records of Parish and Community Councils

As Parish Councils were set up in 1894 the Minute Books of the Council should date back to this time. Parish Council records are linguistically significant in that they are the first local government records in modern Wales to be routinely recorded in Welsh.

In addition to the minute books there should be financial records showing how the parish council spent its money, and there may also be correspondence with the district and county council, with parishioners, and with businesses with which the parish council dealt. Some parishes acquired particular additional responsibilities such as cemeteries, in which case these records too may be available.

Parish records are often deposited at local government record offices, but they may also be held by the successor body, the Community Council. Community Councils were created under the 1972 Local Government Act. There is a right of access to the records under the Freedom of Information Act 2000.

Local Government Act 1929

As a result of this further Local Government Act in 1930 County Councils acquired the remaining duties of the Poor Law Unions – although they had been responsible for the provision of asylums and other public health services from their foundation. From this date it is worth consulting County Council minute books for records of the Public Assistance Committees. Their work concentrated on vagrancy and providing 'outdoor relief' (see Poor Law Unions, above). The after-effects of the First World War, and the subsequent depression meant that in addition to the tramps and vagrants who had formerly used the 'casual wards' of the workhouse as they made their way round the country, there were now many unemployed seeking work who were similarly itinerant, and it was felt by the County Councils that these men deserved better accommodation than the 'tramping class'. The need for 'out-relief' was another consequence of unemployment, coupled with a rise in the standard of living and inflation, which left the elderly and sick with less buying-power. The Unemployment Assistance Board was set up to provide relief for the unemployed, transferring the responsibility from the County Council to a national government body.

Local Government re-organisations

Local Government Act 1972

This Act, which came into force in 1974, marked the end of the old system of counties, county boroughs, urban and district councils. Its effect in Wales was to create larger counties by amalgamating several smaller ones. The distinction between town and country local government was largely erased by abolishing the county boroughs and making them the centres of mixed urban and rural authorities. It provided a two-tier system of local government where the County Council provided the higher tier and District Councils provided the second tier. The size and shape of the District Councils often reflected the geographical region of the old, smaller, abolished County Councils. Below the District Council was the Community Council, which replaced the Parish Council (see above) and took on similar responsibilities and powers.

Responsibility for the functions of local government was divided between the County and the District. Education, consumer protection, libraries, social services and traffic and highways were managed by the County, whilst cemeteries, environmental health, housing and the collection of the rates were managed by the Districts. Other function such as tourism, arts and recreation, planning and footpaths might be managed by either authority, or both.

Local Government Act 1994

The Local Government (Wales) Act 1994, which came into force on 1 April 1996 has been the most recent reorganisation of local government in Wales . This created twenty-two unitary authorities which provide all local government services other than those provided by the community councils. There are fourteen local authority record offices in Wales, some of which include the records of more than one current unitary authority, and the records of more than one of the old pre-1974 counties.

Further Reading

In an amazingly wide field, the reader can refer particularly to: Helen Watt, *Welsh Manors and their Records* (2000) for the early period; W. E. Tate, The Parish Chest (1983), and relevant sections of David Hey (ed.), *The Oxford Companion to Family and Local History* (2008). For example, see the chapter by R. W. Hoyle on 'Local Government', and David Hey's chapter on 'The Poor'.

10. The Census

Beryl Evans

This chapter aims to provide basic information about the census for both family and community historians. The census returns, as they are most commonly referred to, contain vital information for all social and economic historians interested in the Victorian era and later. The census can be used to study a family or to undertake a detailed study of a township, parish or even county. A study over several censuses can show changes in how our families lived and worked, depopulation in rural areas, increase of population in urban areas, changes in language patterns and occupations. Use of the census returns by local historians can help create a demographic analysis of an area; analyse household, family and community structures; study trades and occupations, and help map migration patterns. With the detailed descriptions of enumeration district boundaries the information could be used in conjunction with tithe maps and later ordnance survey maps.

As the census was only taken every decade other sources should be used to create a broader picture of families and communities; sources include civil registration records, parish records, trade directories and probate records.

A census of the population of England and Wales has taken place every decade since 1801, except for 1941 when war intervened. The early returns from 1801 to 1831 were merely statistical tables and hold no genealogical content. The government at the time merely wanted to know the number of people living in each area, their age groups, sex and occupations. Subsequently, after the central offices had collated the information from census enumerators, most of the original schedules (or forms) were destroyed, but some have survived, showing the names of head of households and number of occupants. The early censuses, 1801–1831, were taken by overseers and clergy. Some questions were asked of the overseer and others of the clergy. In order to gather the statistical information necessary they may have compiled lists of names to assist them. Occasionally these lists have survived; there are very few for Wales:

1801
Amlwch, Llannerch-y-medd, Llanwenllwyfo (Bangor University Archives, Bangor Mss 1488)

1811
Clocaenog (Denbighshire Record Office, PD/20/1/46)

1821
Beaumaris (Bangor University Archives, Beaumaris and Anglesey Mss 2/19-20)
Llandygwydd (Pembrokeshire Archives, HDX/158/87)
Llanarthney (Carmarthenshire Archive Service, CPR/35/43)
Gresford (Allington, Marfod and Hoseley townships only)
(Denbighshire Record Office, PD 34/1/32/)
Henllan (Denbighshire Record Office, PD/38/1/315)
Northop (including Flint Town) (Flintshire Record Office, P/45/1/201)

1831
Northop (Flintshire Record Office, P/45/1/202)
Mold (Llwynegin township only) (Flintshire Record Office, P/40/1/58)
Penstrowed (Powys County Archives Office, M/EP/47/2/MT/1)

The census was taken on a Sunday night as this was probably the most likely night of the week when the majority of people would be at home. The dates of census night are as follows:

1801	10 March	1841	6 June	1881	3 April
1811	27 May	1851	30 March	1891	5 April
1821	28 May	1861	7 April	1901	31 March
1831	29 May	1871	2 April	1911	2 April

From 1841 onwards things changed and more information was gathered for the census and the enumerator's books were officially preserved, therefore this is the first census providing any information of value for the historian. There are a few areas of Wales missing from census returns, in particular the 1861 census, a full list of officially missing records can be found at *http://www.findmypast.co.uk/help-and-advice/knowledge-base/census/known-issues*.

The basis of the census registration districts was that of the civil registration districts established in 1836. The Superintendent Registrar's districts were used as administrative units and were numbered. The published tables for each census would be in numerical order, Wales (including Monmouthshire) being number 11. There were later changes to the districts therefore some areas changed from one district to another over time, so this is worth bearing in mind if for some reason you cannot find an area in a particular district. Information maps showing Registration and Census districts for 1837 to 1851 and 1852 to 1946 can be purchased from *www.ihgs.ac.uk* and are available at local archive offices and the National Library of Wales for consultation.

Each of the Superintendent Registrar's districts is divided into sub-districts and these in turn into enumeration districts. The enumeration districts varied in size as they depended on the size of population, but it usually covered about 200 households, enumeration districts consisted of parishes and townships as appropriate.

The process of taking a census has been documented in detail in other publications noted in 'Further Reading'. Basically an enumerator would distribute a schedule to each household in his designated area during the week prior to census night (which was always on a Sunday with varying dates as previously noted). Each head of household was to complete the form giving details of all who were present in the household on census night, whether it was their usual place of residence or not. They were not to include anyone who was not present. The enumerator then returned on the Monday to collect completed schedules; if they were uncompleted he had to fill them in by asking the householder for the information.

The information was then copied into the enumerator's books and handed to the local registrar. They were then checked before being sent to London, where the information was gathered and analysed and published as a Parliamentary Paper in the form of a series of tables relating to various topics. The original schedules were subsequently destroyed. This was the pattern for all census returns from 1841 to 1901.

The original enumerator's books for the census from 1841 to 1911 and original schedules for 1911 are in the custody of The National Archives, Kew. No manuscript returns are held for 1801 to 1831, but a few lists may occasionally be found in local county archive offices, see *Local Census Listings 1522–1930* for further details. Those for Wales have already been listed. The returns are closed for 100 years due to the personal information they contain; the latest available is 1911. The 1921 census will be released in January 2022. No returns are available for 1931: they were destroyed by fire during 1942 and no census was taken in 1941 due to the Second World War.

The 1841 census was the first in which personal information was recorded and later made available. The form asked for name of place (address); whether a house was inhabited or not, or being built; names of each person in the abode; age and sex; profession, trade or of independent means; whether born in the same county; whether born in Scotland, Ireland or Foreign Parts. Unfortunately the information given was not always accurate; the address was often given as the township or parish and did not differ throughout, making identification of a particular property difficult. The names of all persons at a property on census night were to be recorded, starting with the head of household. No relationships are shown in this early census; therefore, errors could be made between siblings and a husband and wife without evidence from other sources. Only one forename was recorded. The age column in 1841 does not show the correct age except for children under fifteen; all other ages are rounded down to the nearest figure divisible by five and this should be remembered when age discrepancies appear during later census searches. Ages given to the enumerator could also be incorrect, and so comparison of details from other census returns and other sources would be advisable.

The 'occupation' column often did not record anything for a woman as they often worked seasonally, casually or part-time. The 1841 census does not record the place of birth, only if this was the same as the place of residency; therefore this is of little use to family historians. One original census enumerator's book for Wales exists outside the holdings of The National Archives: that of Wrexham town, was found in a second

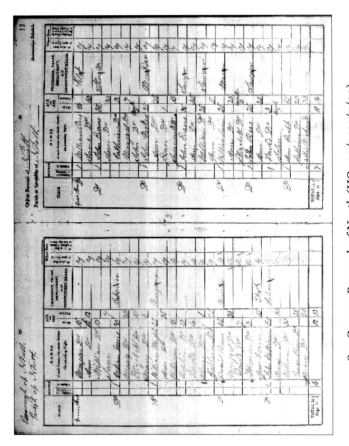

1841 Census, Borough of Neath (HO 107/1421/7/23)

Reproduced with the permission of The National Archives, London, and findmypast.co.uk

Note: This is an example of the limited amount of information provided in the 1841 Census and also the way that the age was noted to the nearest five years beneath the actual age

hand bookshop and is now held at the Denbighshire Records Office (DD/DM/228/62).

From 1851 onwards the returns became more detailed. More geographical information could be given under street, place or road and name or number of house; name and surname in the household on census night; for the first time the relationship to the head of the household; condition – whether married, single or widowed; age (male or female); rank, profession or occupation; where born – this time to include parish and county of birth; for the first time also a column asking 'Blind' or 'Deaf and Dumb'. Each household was given a number by the enumerator; this can be used to ensure information for an enumeration district is complete.

One census that is hardly mentioned is the 'Census of Accommodation at Worship' or better known as the 1851 Religious Census. This census has only been taken once, when the Government wanted to find out exactly what religious provision was made across England and Wales. The census was taken on Sunday 30 March 1851. A schedule was distributed to each church, chapel and religious establishment throughout England and Wales and was later collected by a census officer. Unlike other censuses this one did not record any names, but was to gather statistical evidence of those attending a service and was completely voluntary.

The information requested was: name and description of church or chapel; location; when first consecrated; circumstances established; if built after 1800 who built it and at what cost; whether endowed financially; number of spaces 'free' or 'other'; number attending on census day in morning, afternoon and evening services; and average attendance over a twelve-month period.

All details relating to Wales have been transcribed in two volumes: *The Religious Census of 1851: A Calendar of the Returns relating to Wales*, Volume 1 – South Wales and Volume 2 – North Wales. The following is an example of information that can be found and can be useful for the local and family historian alike relating to religious establishments in the area where their ancestors lived:

Llansantffraid Parish, Aberayron (District), Cardiganshire

Nebo. Independent.
Erected: 1809; rebuilt 1833
Space: free; other 150; standing 100
Present: morn. 170; aft. 125 scholars; even. 120 (see below)
Average: church members, 96.
Remarks: Chiefly a place of worship, but it has been occasionally employed as a Day School. The Sunday School is always held therein. The Chapel will hold about 400 persons. Evening: Either a sermon or a prayer meeting at which on an average, 120 persons attend.

In this part, grown up persons and regular members of the churches as well as very young children regularly attend Sunday Schools.
Thomas Jones. Independent Minister.

The 1891 census was important for Wales as this was the first time the language question was included: 'Language spoken – English, Welsh or Both'. Prior to this census there was no information relating to those who spoke Welsh. Even in 1891, the statistics were not accurate, as some parishes administered under English Registration Districts, such as the Ceiriog Valley in Denbighshire and parts of Radnorshire and Montgomeryshire, did not receive the schedules that included the language question. Officially, over the whole country 60 per cent could speak Welsh in 1891. Sadly every census since has shown a decline in Welsh speakers, except for a very small rise in 2001 to 20 per cent, but falling again to 19 per cent in 2011.

O. M. Edwards, a Welsh historian, educationalist and writer, raised many concerns about the recording of Welsh speakers in an article in *Cymru* in August 1891, one being how to define if one could speak English. He knew of locals who could speak a few words in English but were not fluent, but they may have noted that they spoke both languages; five out of six people in a nearby town were monoglot Welsh; a man he knew could understand an English book but could not speak the language due to lack of practice: therefore, was he listed as speaking English as well as Welsh? He gives examples of how he thinks the number of Welsh speakers in the 1891 census was less than shown, and that there were more English speakers. There were also government concerns about the number of Welsh children who were recorded as speaking only Welsh, when English was the compulsory language in all schools. Such considerations should be taken into account when looking at whether a family could speak Welsh, English or both.

A problem that occurred throughout the very Welsh areas of Wales was the fact that the census officers insisted that the census schedules were completed in English, with many householders having great difficulty in understanding them or having to find someone to fill them on their behalf. Welsh schedules were available on request after 1841, but census enumerators had to translate any information on Welsh schedules to English in order to complete the Enumerators' Books, as they were to be in English. From 1871 enumerators were asked to record how many schedules they had completed on behalf of others, due to illiteracy and lack of knowledge of English. Some Welsh-speaking parishes found that the majority of schedules had been completed by the enumerator. This was the case in the Anglesey parish of Llanallgo (RG10/5742) where of ninety-seven schedules, ninety-four were completed in Welsh, and eighty-four of them by the enumerator himself. It was also in 1871 when a 'W' was noted in the first column of the enumerator's book if the original schedule had been completed in Welsh. It is difficult to establish how accurate this was throughout Wales, but if found against a household, it could be of interest that Welsh was spoken within the family. Some enumerators did note if they received Welsh schedules, but others did not, and not all enumerators gave a number for the schedules they completed.

From 1901 the language question was for those aged three years or above, but in the 1891 returns, children under this age – many a few days or months old – can be seen recorded as speaking English, Welsh or both, and as a result would have influenced the statistics obtained. The language statistics do not include the many hundreds of thousands of Welsh speakers who had crossed the border to England and beyond.

Discrepancies in the place of birth are a common problem throughout Wales. The 1841 census asked only whether born in the same county, but from 1851 a specific county, town or parish was requested. However, very often only a county was recorded, or very often 'ditto' was used, inadvertently giving an incorrect birthplace. Variations and translations in place-names caused problems, especially when enumerators were unfamiliar with the Welsh language, often

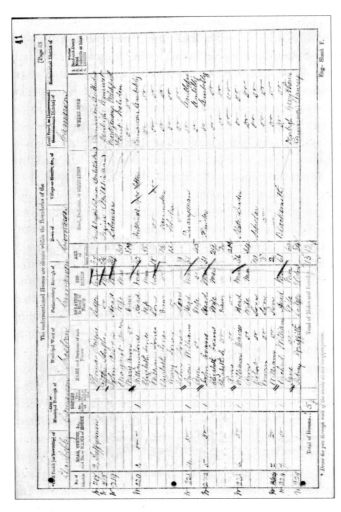

1871 Census, Llanbeblig, Caernarfon (RG/5721/20)

Reproduced with the permission of The National Archives, London, and findmypast.co.uk

Note: This is an example in which the letter 'W' in the first column indicates that a Welsh-language schedule had originally been completed

1881 Census, Aberystwyth (RG11/5445/19/62)

Reproduced with the permission of The National Archives, London, and findmypast.co.uk

Note: This example indicates the various birth-places of the residents of Terrace Road, Aberystwyth

1881 Census, Lledrod Lower, Ceredigion (RG 11/5450)
Reproduced with the permission of The National Archives, London, and findmypost.co.uk
Note: All the houses listed here are now ruins, and the locality on Mynydd Bach, between Trefenter and Bronnant has been entirely depopulated

mishearing and misspelling place-names. Truncation of place-names also causes problems, such as those given only as 'Llanfair', 'Llanfihangel' or 'Llanrhaeadr' as there are numerous place-names throughout Wales with these prefixes. A good gazetteer and the volume *Cofrestri Plwyf Cymru/Parish Registers of Wales* are useful tools for identifying correct places.

The 1911 census differs slightly from previous returns as this is the first census where the schedules completed by the householders have been retained. This allows us to see the handwriting of our ancestors for the first time and any supplementary information or comments made on the schedules are intact, whereas previously these would have been ignored by the enumerators when completing their enumeration books.

In addition to the previous information requested on census forms, the 1911 census asked for information relating to a woman's fertility, asking each married woman the number of years in the present marriage, number of children born alive to the marriage, how many still living and how many have died. Occasionally, this information can be found completed for the husband, widower or widow, and not just a married woman, giving family historians additional information. As was the case of Frances Phillips, a 48-year-old widow, of Pont-rhyd-y-groes, Tregaron, she was noted as having been married for eight years, and having two children, both of whom were alive. The enumerator had subsequently crossed out this information, but it is still visible for us to see. The number of children can also alert historians to otherwise unknown children who had died between the census returns, or to step-children and subsequently to another marriage or relationship.

Occupational information is also more detailed, asking specifically for information about those aged ten years and above – personal occupation; industry or service connected with; whether an employer, worker or own account, and whether working at home. Occasionally additional occupational information can even provide the name of the employer or company. All this information gives a broader picture of how our ancestors lived and contributed to the local community at around the time of the census.

More details were also requested in the 'Infirmity' column, whether 1. Totally deaf or Deaf and Dumb, 2. Totally Blind, 3. Lunatic, 4. Imbecile or Feeble-minded, and also the age at which the infirmity first occurred.

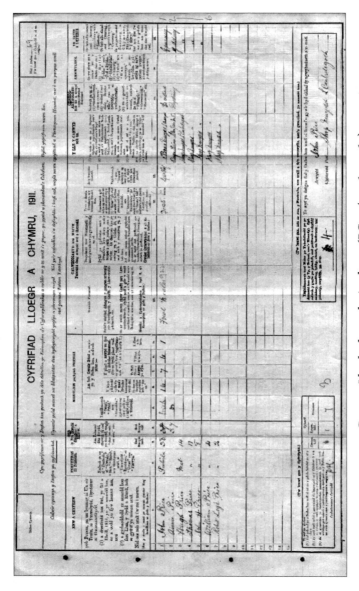

1911 Census, Llanbedr-goch, Anglesey (RG 14/34561, p. 69)
Reproduced with the permission of The National Archives, London, and findmypast.co.uk
Note: This is an example of a Welsh-language form

Householders were given the option to fill in a form in English or Welsh, and many completed the Welsh version. As is the problem across all census returns, the few surnames that a large proportion of the Welsh population share (a product, partly, of these non-Welsh-speaking officials) makes tracing individuals with common names sometimes difficult. Additional information such as house name, occupation and place of birth will often make searching easier, and differentiate between those of the same name and similar age. Looking at other members of the family, especially those with less common forenames, is another way of narrowing down your search. If the census schedule you come across is in Welsh, *Findmypast* have worked with the Association of Family History Societies of Wales to provide translation tables for various fields found on the forms (*http://www.findmypast.co.uk/help-and-advice/knowledge-base/ 1911census#welshtables*).

Other useful translation tables that may be used across all census returns and other Welsh research can be found on the Association website (*http://www.fhswales.org.uk/censuses/Schedules.htm*).

The returns prior to 1911 have been available in microfilm or microfiche format for quite some time, however, with exceptional developments in digitisation over the past few years, consultation of all census returns from 1841 to 1911 has been made much easier by digital images being available through commercial websites by subscription and pay-as-you-go packages. In Wales, due to financial assistance by the Welsh Government, the National Library of Wales, county archive offices and some public libraries are able to offer their users free access to *Findmypast.co.uk* and/or Ancestry Library within their respective offices. Users should be aware that transcriptions created for indexing are not always 100 per cent accurate, therefore, the digital images of the returns should be compared for accuracy. The 1881 census is the only census available free of charge as it has been transcribed and indexed by The Church of Jesus Christ of Latter-day Saints and available through their website (*www.familysearch.org* and *www.findmypast.co.uk*).

Free census information is also available at Freecen (*http://www.freecen.org.uk/*), an online project intending to make all census information free of charge – coverage of Wales is far from complete, however, but worth checking to see if the area you are researching has been transcribed and available online.

Access to numerous transcripts and indexes are also available through the continuous hard work of county family history societies. Their publications lists can be found on their websites, for a full list of societies visit *www.fhswales.org.uk*. Alternatively, many are available in the relevant county archive office and at The National Library of Wales.

Further Reading

Peter Christian and David Annal, *Census: The Expert Guide* (2008)
Jeremy Gibson and Mervyn Medlycott, *Local Census Listings 1522–1930: holdings in the British Isles* (1997)
Ieuan Gwynedd Jones and David Williams (eds.) *The Religious Census of 1851: A Calendar of the Returns*
Edward Higgs, *Making Sense of the Census Revisited: Census Records for England and Wales, 1801–1901 – Handbook for Historical Researchers* (2005)
Stuart A Raymond, *Census 1801–1911: A Guide for the Internet Era* (2009)
Christopher Williams and John Watts-Williams (eds.) *Cofrestri Plwyf Cymru/ Parish Registers of Wales* (2000)
The Religious Census of 1851: A Calendar of the Returns relating to Wales, Volume 1: South Wales; Ieuan Gwynedd Jones, *Volume 2: North Wales* (1976)

11. Estate Papers

David Howell

Large landed estates were to dominate the Welsh countryside from late medieval times down to the turn of the twentieth century. Although the outlying parts of some of the great estates were being sold from the 1870s, sales of landed estates noticeably quickened from 1910 and reached fever pitch after 1918 in response to the ever diminishing status bestowed by landownership within Britain as a whole, but the more so within radical Nonconformist Wales.[1] These landed estates had emerged in the century after 1350 out of the collapse for various reasons – not least the use of the *tir prid* or Welsh mortgage – of the old *gwely* system.[2] Furthermore, the growing adoption from the fifteenth century of the English inheritance system of primogeniture, which saw the eldest son become the sole heir, in place of *cyfran*, which had divided land equally among all male heirs, facilitated the accumulation of large estates. The reign of Henry VI (1422–61), claims John Davies, witnessed the laying of the foundations of many of the landed estates, which would play a crucial role in Welsh politics and society over the following 500 years.[3] These ascendant families would gain further opportunities to enlarge their estates from a clause in the Tudor Act of Union, which, recognising an existing practice in Welsh society, outlawed *cyfran* in favour of primogeniture. They also obtained rich pickings through the acquisition of Crown and monastic lands during the Tudor era. Happily for the Welsh gentry and aristocracy, their support for the Royalist cause in the Civil Wars of the mid-seventeenth century did not result in any drastic breakup of their estates and the extinction of their families.[4]

The large estates grew ever larger over the course of the eighteenth century at the expense of smaller ones. As a consequence of the unusually high incidence of failure of male heirs among the gentry and aristocracy from the late seventeenth into the eighteenth century, certain landed families of all ranks enlarged their properties through marrying heiresses. However, it is not surprising that it was the wealthiest families who attracted the pick of them. A similar advantage was enjoyed by the greater landowners in their possessing the means to purchase land that came onto the market from the late seventeenth into the late eighteenth century, because of the burdensome land tax between 1692 and 1715, low agricultural prices and sluggish rents between the 1660s and the 1750s, and war-time taxation from the 1750s to the 1790s. Even though many small Welsh estates yielding annual incomes of £300 up to £2,000 were to be found dotting the Welsh landscape at the close of the eighteenth century, there was thus a noticeable swallowing up of lesser properties by the 'Leviathans', as Thomas Pennant was to describe them, owners enjoying estates worth £5,000 a year and upwards.[5] Such a consolidation of estates into the ownership of fewer families prompted contemporaries to wistfully observe that the Welsh countryside in the late eighteenth century was bestrewn with 'withering' mansions, those proud old *plasau* ignominiously deserted or else inhabited by mere tenants. For Edmund Hyde Hall, writing about Caernarfonshire at the beginning of the nineteenth century, the process amounted to no less than 'a revolution among country houses'.[6]

No better illustration of the expansion of a Welsh estate from the late seventeenth century through inheritance, marriage and purchase can be provided than that of Wynnstay. In 1675 Sir John Wynn, fifth and last Baronet of the direct Gwydir line, married Jane, heiress of Eyton Evans of Watstay, and upon gaining the estate he re-named it Wynnstay. Sir William Williams, first Baronet (d. 1700), besides inheriting the Chwaen Isaf estate (date unknown) and purchasing Llanforda in 1676 from Edward Lloyd (son of the indebted royalist, Colonel Edward Lloyd), acquired the Glascoed estate through his marriage in 1664 with Margaret, daughter and co-heiress of Watkin Kyffin of Glascoed, Llansilin. Sir William Williams, second Baronet, of

Llanforda, acquired Plas y Ward by virtue of his marriage in 1684 to its heiress, Jane, daughter and co-heiress of Edward Thelwall, and their son, Sir Watkin Williams Wynn, third Baronet, of Llanforda, inherited Wynnstay in 1719 under the will of his cousin, the aforementioned Sir John Wynn, fifth and last Baronet of Gwydir. Upon taking the Baronetcy he assumed the additional surname and arms of Wynn. He married in 1715 Ann, daughter and heiress of Edward Vaughan of Llwydiarth and Llangedwyn, a union which drew into the Wynnstay estate the properties of Glan-llyn, Llwydiarth and Llangedwyn. A huge estate, sprawling mammoth-like across the counties of north Wales, had come into being, producing an income of £19,623 in 1736.[7]

In the following century there would occur a further concentration of landed property; after 1814 small freehold properties of anything up to a hundred acres or so were bought up by neighbouring landed families, so that by 1882, in the words of a contemporary, 'The class of small Welsh owners who were numerous enough 100 years ago is comparatively limited now'.[8] An impression of the dominance of large proprietors in the 1870s is gained from John Bateman's *The Great Landowners of Great Britain and Ireland* (final edition, 1883), which revealed that landed estates of over 1,000 acres occupied 60 per cent of the total area (excluding waste) of Wales. They were in the hands of 571 owners, who constituted a mere 1 per cent of the total owners of land!

The estate-owners in this category were not practical farmers. Apart from a home farm adjacent to the mansion which the owners kept in hand, they let out their estates to tenants, who rented small farms generally covering from 50 to 100 acres or so. The number of tenancies on the largest estates predictably amounted into the hundreds; for example, on the Powis Castle estate in Montgomeryshire there were 960 farms.[9] This system of letting out large estates to tenants is a piece of good fortune for the family historian, for information about an ancestor can sometimes be provided by searching the different kinds of estate records. Such records are housed in the local record offices, in Welsh university libraries and in the National Library of Wales. A useful microfiche resource for discovering the location and contents of estate records throughout the United Kingdom is the Chadwyck-Healey National Inventory of Documentary Sources in the United Kingdom. Details of the types of documents useful to the family historian that can be found in estate records are available at the National Library of Wales

Photograph of Golden Grove, c. 1880, with garden labourers
With the permission of the Carmarthenshire Record Office

website on family history (*http://www.llgc.org.uk*).

It is the records of landed estates from the mid-eighteenth century onwards that are particularly valuable for the family historian, for it was from that time that estate administration became noticeably more efficient with the aim of maximising profits. This trend was mainly apparent on the largest estates, whose owners, adopting a more business-like approach to their properties, had their farms surveyed and valued by specialist surveyors and cartographers. These large estates, unlike their smaller counterparts, were administered by agents who from the mid-eighteenth century were requested, sometimes harangued, to make their accounts and rent books more orderly and regular. The spirit of the time was conveyed in a letter sent in 1756 by John Vaughan, the owner of the Golden Grove estate, Carmarthenshire, to his backsliding chief agent, Lewis Lewis, whose accounts were muddled. Lewis was requested to enter every detail in his rent roll of former tenants, the farms they held, the present tenants of those holdings, the old rents and the 'improved' ones. These various items were to be entered in different columns with Lewis' observations, including the present-day real value of each holding. Vaughan ended waspishly: 'I am surprised you will not do things methodically according to the plan sent you which is the method used in passing accounts before Masters in Chancery, *and with every agent but you.*' (my italics). The hapless Lewis was subsequently demoted to a mere receiver of rents. Such a lowly official as rent receiver was also being urged to make regular entries of rent payments in an account book, as was the case on the Gogerddan estate (Cardiganshire) in the 1740s when part-time bailiffs were requested to record rents they had received more efficiently.[10] If some officials were slow to change their negligent ways, these attempts on the part of large owners to achieve openness, clarity and order in their accounts resulted in a discernible improvement in the standard of administration by the close of the century.

More accurate estate rentals, with the names of tenants occupying particular holdings at a precise date, are especially valuable to the family historian. Some of the largest estates have complete runs of rentals from the eighteenth century onwards. Rentals of landed estates like Wynnstay, Chirk Castle, Powis Castle, Bronwydd, Nanteos, Crosswood, Tredegar Park, Margam and Penrice, Golden Grove, Dynevor, and Picton Castle are available at the National Library of Wales and allow the searcher to trace individual tenancies and their occupants over a long period of time. Thus the main run of Powis Castle estate rentals extends from 1745 down to 1941. The family historian will have to take account of sudden changes in the rent collecting system. To stay with Powis Castle, the estate saw a major re-arrangement in 1779 whereby the different series of rentals obtaining between 1745 and 1779 (series RA-RK) were combined into a single volume for each year (Series RL). Furthermore, in 1780 a series of rentals begins for the paternal and purchased estates of Edward, Lord Clive, in the counties of Salop, Radnor and Montgomery (series RM). This meant that from 1780 to 1927 records of rent-collecting comprise two volumes for every year.[11]

The best-organised series of rentals at the National Library of Wales, however, is that for the Wynnstay estate which boast an unbroken run from the time of the first Baronet, Sir William Williams (d. 1700). Those musty bound volumes for the nineteenth century are heavy to lift but provide fascinating insights (not least the agent's annotations alongside different tenancies) into the fortunes of individual tenants over a run of years. The availability of specific rentals can be best discovered by reference to the volume 'Rentals and Accounts' contained in the Schedule of the Wynnstay Archives, 1980. By describing the rentals twice over, the compilers, A.J. Roberts and G.C.G. Thomas, have eased the labours of the family historian who approaches the rentals in order to discover a known property and to trace it through successive rentals. An analytical list of rentals is provided for the searcher who wishes to discover a particular property, or to find out what property Wynnstay owned in a given parish, or whether a person known to reside in a particular parish was a Wynnstay tenant. In the analytical list, the separate estates or collections which comprised the Wynnstay estate at different periods are isolated and the location of all their extant rentals is provided. Local record offices, too, contain valuable estate rentals, as, for example, those of the Cawdor estate housed at the Carmarthenshire Record Office.

The value of estate rentals for the family historian is further enhanced by the striking continuity of tenancy that existed on many Welsh estates, particularly the large ones. Generations of the same family were to be found holding the same farm, a custom of continuous family succession that persisted even under the yearly tenure that came in from the close of the eighteenth century to replace the old type of tenure for lives or a number of years. Family succession meant a certain amount of indulgence on the part of the landlord, as in allowing a widow to continue in the holding after her husband's decease or, again, permitting bankrupts to remain on their holdings and to let out their grazing lands till they recovered liquidity.[12] The preference for keeping on a member of the same family when a tenancy became vacant, rather than letting the holding to a 'stranger', was conveyed by Sir Watkin Williams Wynn of Wynnstay in a letter to his agent in March 1781.[13] Evidence given before the Welsh Land Commission of the early 1890s again and again drew attention to this continuity of tenancy on the large estates across the whole of Wales; such family succession meant that some families had occupied their tenancies for well over a hundred years. The Hon. W. E. Sackville West, principal agent of the Penrhyn estate, informed the Land Commissioners that certain tenants had claimed that their families had been on the estate for over 200 years.[14] On the Montgomeryshire estates of the Earl of Powis, out of 751 tenancies whose particulars had been gathered for the Commissioners by the agent, seven farms had been held in the same family from 130-140 years, nine from 140-150 years, thirteen from 150-160 years, nine from 200-210 years and seven from 250-400 years![15]

Examples were provided in the evidence submitted before the Land Commission of the length of tenure enjoyed by certain tenant farmers' families on the large estates. The family of Richard Edwards, tenant in the 1890s of Tyn-twll in the parish of Llanarmon Dyffryn Ceiriog, Denbighshire, belonging to Colonel W. Cornwallis West of Ruthin Castle, had occupied that same holding for about 150 years.[16] On the Glan-llyn estate in Merioneth, just one of the many estates belonging to the Wynnstay dynasty, families living in the parish of Llanuwchllyn had lived for generations on the same holdings: the Jones family had lived at Llwyn-gwern for over 350 years, the Williams family at Dwrnudon, 300 years, the Edwards family at Drwys-y-nant, 200 years, the Jones family at Cefn Gwyn, 150 years, the Jones family at Wern, over 300 years, and the Evans family of Tŷ-Coch, 160 years.[17]

Moreover, when changes did occur these were sometimes the consequence of certain tenants moving to larger farms on the same estate and others to smaller ones on that estate to accommodate the changing circumstances of these families.[18] When grown-up children moved off the 'family' holding, for instance, the farmer and his wife would naturally want to take a smaller farm. Often such movement between holdings on a particular estate involved members of the same extended family. David Jenkins, in his admirable study of Welsh rural society, indicates that the farmer was identified in the community primarily by virtue of his belonging to a specific kin group and that an important role of kinship was its facilitating such family movements between different size holdings.[19] The landlord willingly acquiesced in this arrangement. (The same urge on the part of families to cluster in close proximity once again saw landlords allowing different members of the same family to hold farms on their estate; this was the case on the Wynnstay estate and, again, on the Crosswood estate where, in the 1890s, the number of tenants' sons who also held farms was fourteen – out of a total of 138 tenancies.[20] Again, in runs of poor seasons when farming was even more difficult than usual, the Wynnstay family and perhaps others allowed struggling tenants to go to smaller farms on the estate. Thus a few Wynnstay tenants who failed in the harsh years at the close of the seventeenth century were sometimes allowed to move to a smaller holding on the estate, an indulgence again in operation in the 1820s. For example, in 1692 Edward ap Richard, having grown poor and unable to work a £10-holding in Maenan, was removed to a smaller farm.[21]

It will be apparent that the rentals contained in these large estate records can be of immense use to the family historian. Of course, previous research will have been necessary in order to establish a connection between a particular farm and a landed estate. If we know what unit of land a person occupied at the time of the tithe legislation in the 1830s then, by consulting the tithe maps, it will be possible to discover which estate owned it. Having once established a link between a person and a farm on a certain estate, then the estate rentals may well yield valuable information, for the long run of such rentals on many of the large estates will enable the searcher to quickly identify the holding and the name of the occupier in a particular year. By using this source the family historian will thus have been able to link the man or woman concerned to a particular farm so that he or she can be distinguished from others of the same name in the parish or district. The yearly run of rentals will then further allow the searcher to find out when the tenant first entered the farm, who he or she succeeded, and also when he or she left and who followed as tenant. As stressed, the custom of continuous family succession to farms may well enable the searcher to discover the names of his subjects, when they came and left, presumably quitting when they died. As the National Library of Wales website on family history rightly claims, rentals may be especially valuable in revealing a death or change of abode when a name disappears from a series of rentals.

Perhaps of greater value to the family historian than even estate rentals are manorial records. Indeed, one informed commentator has asserted that manorial records are the most helpful group of genealogical records after parish registers and wills.[22] They are mainly to be found within the estate records as manors often belonged to great estates. Many landowners were lords of a private manor or of several such manors. It has to be borne in mind, however, that the manorial system was absent in the area of the old Principality of 'Welsh' Wales. The richest manorial records exist for Montgomeryshire and are to be found mainly with the Wynnstay and Powis Castle estate records. There are also considerable amounts of manorial records relating to Glamorgan and Monmouthshire and these are located primarily in the Badminton, Bute and Tredegar estate records.[23] Further west in Carmarthenshire, the Golden Grove estate possessed as many as twenty-five manors in the mid-eighteenth century.[24] An index has been compiled of the manors and manorial records of Wales and can be consulted online via the website of the Historical Manuscripts Commission. It may also be searched on computer at the National Library of Wales in the South Reading Room.

Information about family history and genealogy can be gleaned from the various kinds of manorial records that survive, namely, court rolls and books, jury lists, suit rolls, lists of residents, lists of tenants, presentments of petty constables, rentals, rent rolls, and manorial surveys.[25] Of particular value are the manor court rolls which provide information about the business transacted at the courts baron and leet, including land transfers between one manorial tenant and another. Here we see the value of manorial records as 'linkage' records between generations; a sole instance of a surrender and admission at a manor court, where property was transferred between members of a family, will enable the searcher to establish a pedigree of two or three generations.[26] Moreover, the court rolls can furnish a great deal of vital genealogical information for the period before the commencement of parish registers. For example, genealogical information contained in the Pennard Manor Court Book, 1673–1701, is especially helpful to those wishing to trace their ancestors in the district of Gower, given the fact that the surviving parish registers for Pennard do not start until 1743.[27]

Helen Watt has made use of surrenders and admissions at the manor court of Neath Ultra and Cilybebyll, Glamorgan, in order to demonstrate the kind of genealogical information that can be obtained. One of her examples indicates four generations of the Francis family of the parish of Cadoxton-juxta-Neath. Following the death of Robert Francis, yeoman, on 26 October 1801, his widow, Elizabeth, was admitted as tenant for the rest of her natural life and, after her decease, their two sons, Robert and Owen, were admitted as tenants in common in 1822. (In this manor where copyhold of inheritance operated, on the death of a tenant the property was divided between male heirs and, as in the case of Elizabeth, a widow became entitled to the property for the rest of her life.) Robert the elder, whose will was made on 3 March 1827, married Elizabeth, and they had four children, Daniel, William, Robert and Mary. The said Robert, the third son, was followed in the property by his son, Owen. In this particular case, wills were recorded in the surrenders and admissions thereby affording a helpful aid, but a family tree can be compiled even from surrenders and admissions where wills are not included.[28] The aforementioned Pennard Manor Court Book can similarly yield useful genealogical data for the compilation of family trees. For instance, on 20 April 1692 Rebecca Bowen, widow, was presented as tenant of copyhold lands in the Fee of Trewyddfa during her widowhood as successor of her deceased husband, George, who, in turn we learn from the Manor Court Book, had come into the property upon the death of his father John Bowen, esquire. However, at a later Court Baron held on 24 May 1694 it was decreed that the said Rebecca Bowen was to forfeit her estate because of her recent marriage to Robert Millar, a doctor of physic, and that John Bowen, gentleman infant, was to become tenant in her stead.[29]

Besides 'linkage' records, manorial records also contain 'location' records, all-important in helping the searcher to discover the place where his or her ancestors lived. It is important for the searcher to appreciate, however, that manorial records are but one source among many that can assist in connecting a certain individual to a particular property in a manor; others include directories, land tax returns and estate rentals. But manorial records themselves, such as dated lists of names, can reveal that forebears lived in a particular manor at a certain date. These lists of names are to be found in various kinds of court papers, including suit rolls, jury lists, lists of tenants and returns of petty constables. An example of manorial records containing a jury list is a document in the Cawdor/Vaughan estate collection at Carmarthenshire Record Office entitled: 'A true list of all the names of the landlords, tenements and tenants within the parish of Abernant. May 1, 1767' from whose names the jury of the manor of Elvet, Carmarthenshire, could be selected.[30] Here, importantly, the family historian has access to names, a particular location and date. Other manorial records, too, such as surveys and rent rolls, may also provide evidence of 'location'. Manorial surveys generally give information about the land held by each tenant; for the manor of Pennard there exists a partial survey of 1583, the Cromwellian survey of 1650 and Gabriel Powell's survey of the entire lordship of Gower compiled in 1764.[31] Rentals of Chief Rents owed to a manorial lord, like estate rentals, similarly enable the searcher to identify a person with a particular place. The Wynnstay estate records thus contain an excellent run of Chief Rents of the manor of Cyfeiliog in Montgomeryshire

A True List of the names of the Resident and noncresidents freeholders
Of the parish of Conwyl Elvett Returned by Evan John petty
Constable

Resident

Thos Evans llwyn Conwyl	Gentlman
John Evans Trafol pwll	Gentlman
Humphrey Howells Ciloach y bunda	Gentlman
David Lewis pant lwe dog	Gentlman
Griffith Evan Nant y fgwek	Gentlman
Thomas Williams trodarren	Gentlman
David Thomas nant y fenn	Gentlman
Thomas Griffith nant y Clawdd	Gentlman
Lewis Griffith nant y Clawdd	Gentlman
David Howells trod y rhiw	Gentlman
Evan David nant Coch	Gentlman
David Thomas pant y ffynon	Gentlman
Jane Griffith pant y ffynon	

Noncresidents

William Rees Uethrmol	Gentlman
Olbart Davis and Borge oakley nant	Undigaed Gentlman
Thomas Bothcase penfol Cary	Gentlman
Robert morgan pen rhiw renis	Gentlman
Jooys Rice Widow nant Gwyn	
David mathias Clyn y bigail	Gentlman
Bruffot Lewis nant Grenis	

List of inhabitants and freemen of Cynwyl Elfed, recorded by
Evan John, 'Petty Constable' [Cawdor Vaughan 64/6611]
With the permission of the Carmarthenshire Record Office

183

payable to the owner of the Wynnstay estate; tenants' names and the tenements they held in different parishes and townships are all contained in these lists of Chief Rents, so that a particular person can be identified quite quickly.[32]

Once the manor wherein an ancestor resided has been traced from 'location' records, the searcher can then move on to consult the 'linkage' records of that vicinity, like, for example, parish registers and manorial admissions and surrenders, in order to obtain a pedigree.[33] This mention of parish registers must serve as one more reminder that manorial records can best be employed in determining a person's ancestry when used in conjunction with other sources relating to the district under scrutiny.

Estate records include other helpful types of document for the family historian. Thus leases for lives and those for ninety-nine years, determinable upon three lives, can provide extra information about those families named as holding particular farms in the estate rentals. Such long leases were to remain popular in south Wales down to the close of the eighteenth century whereas by that time they had been replaced in the north by yearly tenure. Leases for lives contain the names of the lives in the two- or three-life lease, and these, conveniently for the family historian, were usually the wife of the first life and the children or other close family members. Helpful for the family historian was the practice on some of the large estates of drawing up schedules of leases wherein details of old leases are provided. For example, the Powis Castle estate papers at the National Library of Wales contain a list of old leases within the lordship of Mechain pertaining to the eighteenth century. Again, the Cawdor/Vaughan estate records include an 'Old Rental' covering the parishes of St Ishmaels, Llangyndeyrn and Cydweli, which reveals details of early eighteenth-century leases, including the names of the lives.[34] As an illustration of the useful information for the family historian that is contained in long leases, one of the leases granted by the Powis Castle family to a tenant in the lordship of Mechain can be cited. In November 1730 Richard Charles was granted a lease for ninety-nine years if his children, John, Humphrey and Mary, should live that long, of a tenement within the township of Bodyddan, which had formerly been in the possession of Lewis Evans.[35]

Estate surveys can also be helpful to the searcher intent on tracing his or her family history. Once again, such surveys provide a name (of

The Bulkeley family, Beaumaris church

the tenant of a farm), a date and a location (in the form of a named holding), the three crucial pieces of information required by the family historian. Here, we can usefully remind ourselves of the improvements being carried out in the late eighteenth century in the management of landed estates, and an important starting point was the surveying and mapping of an estate's farms[36] and other income-yielding possessions like coal pits, lead mines and timber resources. Examples of such surveys are those made of the Caerhun estate in Caernarfonshire and Anglesey in 1774, and of the Greenhill estate in Pembrokeshire in 1778.[37] Resembling the estate survey are the 'particulars' of estates about to be put up for sale. One such document is housed in the Pembrokeshire County Library at Haverfordwest entitled 'Particulars of the Llanstinan, Martel and Ford Estates in Pembrokeshire' drawn up in the early 1780s and containing a list of the farms in their respective parishes, the tenants' names, the rents and the duration of the leases.

Details about landowners themselves, as distinct from tenant farmers, can be found in the estate papers in the form of the 'Abstract of Title' of a landowner to a particular property he or she had acquired. The title deed provides details of the land, like the name of the previous owner, the date of transfer and the precise location. An example can be found among the papers of the Haverfordwest solicitors, Williams and

Poster advertising sale of part of Mabws estate,
Llanrhystud, in 1918

Williams, dated 1816, which, relates to 'The Abstract of Title of Sir John
Owen, Bart., to the Ford estate in Haycastle parish, Pembrokeshire, for
the perusal of W. E. Tucker, Esq., the purchaser'.[38]

There is less information in the estate papers about the landless
groups in the community. Nevertheless, lists of employees, male and
female, hired by a gentleman's family to work either as servants within
the family mansion or as servants and labourers on the home farm, can
be of use to the family historian. As so often with regard to estate
records, it was the large estate owners who kept records of this
workforce, lists that name individual servants and labourers, and that
specify their precise tasks and wages. Account books of servants' wages

186

paid by the year are to be found in a number of estate collections. Among the Wynnstay papers at the National Library of Wales there is a document entitled 'Llangedwin servants' wages for one year due 1 May 1747'.[39] A particularly good run of servants' wages is to be found in the Mostyn estate collection housed at the library of Bangor University entitled 'Account Book of Servants' Wages at Mostyn, 1737–1782'.[40] Not only are individual names and type of employment detailed, but the fact that some servants remained in service over a run of years enables the family historian to keep a particular individual in focus for a short period of time. Although individuals are named in these lists as working at specific locations, the fact that they were not associated with a specific location on a one-to-one basis, as was a farmer with a particular tenement, means that any attempt at tracking them down and then, perhaps, tracing them over a run of years, is a more difficult task, particularly when confronted within a Welsh context with commonality of surnames.

It is clear that estate records can be of value to the family historian in assisting him or her to construct a family tree. Their data, used in conjunction with other types of document like parish registers and land tax returns, are particularly valuable for the years before the Census Enumerators' returns starting in 1841. Moreover, the information provided in landowners' correspondence with their agents on a range of issues like, for example, the state of farming, the not infrequent hardship endured by tenants and labourers, food riots, and disturbances at parliamentary and more local elections, is helpful in allowing the family historian and others to learn of the conditions and circumstances under which earlier generations lived, and this is particularly so before the days of the nineteenth-century newspapers and parliamentary papers.

NOTES

1. John Davies, 'The End of the Great Estates and the Rise of Freehold Farming in Wales', *WHR*, vol. 7, no. 2 (1974), 186–212
2. John Davies, *A History of Wales* (Penguin, 1994), 188–90. This study is a brilliant overview of the whole sweep of Wales' past.
3. Davies, *A History of Wales*, 208
4. David W. Howell, 'Landlords and Estate Management in Wales', in Joan Thirsk (ed.), *The Agrarian History of England and Wales, vol. V, ii, 1640–1750; Agrarian Change* (1985), 254–58
5. P. R. Roberts, 'The decline of the Welsh squires in the eighteenth century', *NLWJ*, 13 (1963–4); M. Humphreys, *The Crisis of Community: Montgomeryshire Society 1680–1815* (1996), 100 ff; P. Jenkins, 'The demographic decline of the landed gentry in the eighteenth century: a south Wales study', *WHR*, ii (1982-3), 31–49
6. Edmund Hyde Hall, *A Description of Caernarfonshire (1809–1811)*, (Caernarfon, 1952), cited in Glyn Parry, 'Stability and Change in mid-eighteenth century Caernarvonshire' (unpublished MA thesis, University of Wales, 1978), 27
7. NLW, *Schedule of Wynnstay Archives*, 1980, vol. i: Rentals and Accounts; Roberts, 'The decline of the Welsh squires', p. 163
8. Royal Commission on Agriculture, Parliamentary Papers, xv (1882), *Report*, 7
9. Royal Commission on Land in Wales and Monmouthshire (hereafter RCLWM), vol. iv, Q. 66, 174
10. David W. Howell, *Patriarchs and Parasites: the Gentry of South-West Wales in the Eighteenth Century* (1986), 57–8
11. NLW, *Powis Castle Rentals, Catalogue*, Introduction
12. RCLWM, vol. i, Q. 16,832 and vol. iii, Q. 40,249
13. NLW, Wynnstay MS, 124, fo. 397
14. RCLWM, vol. i, Q 11,968
15. *Ibid.*, vol. iv, Q. 66,174
16. *Ibid.*, vol. iv, Q. 55,321
17. *Ibid.*, vol. iv, Q. 70,030
18. *Ibid.*, vol. i, Q. 8, 169: evidence of Richard John Lloyd Price of Rhiwlas
19. David Jenkins, *The Agricultural Community of South-west Wales at the turn of the Twentieth Century* (1971), 176–7
20. RCLWM, vol. i, Q. 8,186 and vol. iii, Q. 49,044: John Gibson in his *Agriculture in Wales* (London, 1879), p. 5, observed how through intermarriage of families, some Welsh estates were virtually in the occupation of one extended family, landlords putting up 'with the losses and inconveniences of a low' rather than 'rudely' break up these 'clans'
21. NLW, Wynnstay MS. R8, rental 1670–93; David W. Howell, *Land and People in Nineteenth-Century Wales* (1978), 54
22. D. Steel, *Discovering Your Family History* (revised edition, 1986), 98, cited by Helen Watt, *Welsh Manors and their Records* (2000), 132
23. National Library of Wales website on family history: *http://www.llgc.org.uk*
24. F. Jones, 'The Vaughans of Golden Grove', *Transactions of the Cymmrodorion Society* (1964), 189
25. Watt., *Welsh Manors and their Records*, 117-19; *The Pennard Manor Court Book, 1673–1701* (South Wales Record Society, 2000), Introduction by Joanna Martin, p. ix
26. Watt, *Welsh Manors and their Records*, 132; Martin, Introduction, p. x.
27. Martin, Introduction, p. x, and p. xxxiii, fn. 3
28. Watt, *Welsh Manors and their Records*, 135–6

29 *The Pennard Manor Court Book*, 71 and 77
30 Carmarthenshire Record Office, Cawdor/Vaughan MSS, box 64/6,611
31 Martin, Introduction, p. ix; *Welsh Manors and their Records*, 133
32 NLW, Wynnstay R76: 'WWW Rental, 1821'
33 Watt, *Welsh Manors and their Records*, 133
34 NLW, Powis Castle MS.16,753; Carmarthenshire RO, Cawdor/Vaughan MSS, box 103/8,057
35 NLW, Powis Castle MS.16,753
36 M. C. S. Evans, 'The Pioneers of Estate Mapping in Carmarthenshire', *The Carmarthenshire Antiquary*, xiii (1977), 52–64
37 NLWMS 4,703F; Pembrokeshire County Library, Haverfordwest, Survey of the Greenhill Estate
38 NLW, Williams and Williams MS. 4,637
39 NLW, Wynnstay rental 1745–47
40 Bangor University Library, Mostyn MSS. 6,508 and 6,509

12. Maritime Sources

William Troughton

If you are fortunate enough to have ancestors who went to sea in the age of Victoria then you are very fortunate. Today the bureaucracy that must have been the bane of sea-captains in the nineteenth century provides a rich and easily accessible source of information. For many people the first port of call will be family folklore that links an individual to one or more ships. Frequently seamen, master mariners in particular, named their houses after ships on which they served. The coastal village of Llanon in Ceredigion, for example, has numerous houses whose names reflect the maritime past of the area. Examples include Convoy, Salop and Eagle-eyed. Churchyards in maritime communities also contain graves of departed seamen and memorials to local men lost at sea, very often with the name of their vessel.

Local record offices are now the home for most Shipping Registers. Kept at ports of registry around the coast of Wales these registers record the ownership of vessels. Usually a vessel was divided into sixty-four shares, which would be owned by numerous members of a community.

Lloyds Register of Shipping and the Mercantile Navy List (MNL) will give the port of registry of a vessel. Details such as a ship's size, age and port of registry are common to both, but the MNL includes smaller vessels, even fishing boats, and gives more detail. Lloyds Register for the nineteenth century is available in the National Library of Wales, at the National Museum of Wales and at some local record offices. A complete set of the MNL is to be found in the Guildhall Library, London

Aerial photograph of Cardiff Docks taken in 1929 by Aerofilms.
This is the present-day site of the Wales Millennium Centre
and the Welsh Assembly building
©Crown Copyright: RCAHMW: Aerofilms Collection

and issues from 1913 onwards at the National Library of Wales. A short cut now available is the CLIP database compiled from these two sources (see *http://www.crewlist.org.uk*). This will in most cases give a link to a digitised version of one of the above publications.

Once equipped with the port of registry of a ship the next step is to track down the crew agreements. From 1747, masters or owners of merchant ships were required to keep and file a Muster Roll giving details of the number of crewmen and the ships' voyages. These lists, which were kept as a result of the Act for the Relief of Disabled Seamen 1747, were filed with the Seamen's Fund Receivers at the ports of arrival. The musters are found in 6994 boxes in The National Archives at Kew, reference BT98. They cover a number of ports and various dates from 1747 to 1853. Following the 1835 Merchant Shipping Act, Crew Lists and other documents were filed with the Register Office of Merchant Seamen and these, up to 1860, now form part of Agreements and Crew List (BT98). These name the captain and crew and list their ages, place of birth, name of the vessel last served on and (with the exception of the captain), their wages. Dates and places of discharge are also given. There are two types of agreement. For vessels engaged

List of ships (Shipping Register), 1824–1832
With the permission of Ceredigion Archives

Agreement and account of crew, 10 February 1876
With the permission of Ceredigion Archives

in the home trade, such as coasters and fishing vessels operating in UK coastal waters, or from the UK to North European and Baltic ports, agreements were usually for a six-month period and record the ports visited as well as details of the crew. Foreign Trade agreements do not formally list ports visited but give a general voyage description with dates. These were usually for the duration of a voyage rather than for any fixed period of time. Frequently overseas voyages can be reconstructed from consular stamps on the reverse of the agreements and from amendments to the crew list. Any amendment had to be made in the presence of the British Consul.

For example, voyages of the Aberystwyth-registered brigantine *J Llewellyn* to Port Alfred in South Africa, St Lucia and to Newfoundland during the 1870s have been reconstructed from her crew agreements. Through reading up on the ports of call and consultation with local record offices it has been possible to determine the nature of the cargoes she carried. These included general cargo, salt, copper ore and sugar. She was a small vessel, and the members of her crew were predominantly well-behaved. Agreements for some larger vessels show they rarely left port without leaving at least one crew-member behind in either a hospital or prison. *Caroline Spooner*, another and much larger Aberystwyth vessel, seems to have liberally distributed crewmen of numerous nationalities around the prisons and hospitals of Australia and South America over a number of years.

Today, agreements for the dates 1863–1913 are held in local record offices pertaining to the ports of registry. In Wales these are Aberystwyth, Beaumaris, Caernarfon, Cardiff, Cardigan, Carmarthen, Chepstow, Llanelli, Milford Haven, Newport and Swansea. The only exceptions are Aberystwyth and Cardigan, held at the National Library of Wales and Pembrokeshire Record Office respectively. In addition, all crew agreements for years ending in '5' are held at the National Maritime Museum, Greenwich, London. Many, many Welsh sailors served at one time on Liverpool-registered vessels. Some agreements for Liverpool-registered vessels are held at the Liverpool Record Office. The Maritime History Archive at the Memorial University of Newfoundland, Canada (*http://www.mun.ca/mha/index.php*) now holds most crew lists from 1863–1938 and 1951–1976. Those for the intervening years are held by the General Register and Record Office of Shipping and Seamen, Cardiff. Many crew agreements for Welsh ports

Captain and crew of the steamer Glanhafren,
registered in Aberystwyth, at Helva, Spain, in 1894
Note: This ship had a number of associations with Aberystwyth

Aberdyfi, c.1925

Vessels at Nefyn, Llŷn

have now been transcribed and the details readily found on the Welsh Mariners database (*www.welshmariners.org.uk*). This useful website is the beginnings of an index to the men, women and their vessels which will allow family and local historians the opportunity to research their maritime past.

Movements of larger vessels can frequently be traced through Lloyds List, a newspaper specialising in shipping movements. No complete run is to be had in Wales though the National Library of Wales holds facsimile copies for the years 1741 to 1826. Gwynedd Archives hold copies for much of the later half of the nineteenth century. Again the Guildhall Library in London has a complete run. Years up to 1826 are now also available online through both Google and the Hathi Trust (*www.hathi trust.org*).

If your ancestor rose to the exalted rank of Master Mariner then his career will be even easier to trace. Once again it is the Guildhall Library in London that will be of interest. Amongst the papers passed to the Guildhall Library by Lloyd's of London are 'Captains' Registers', which detail the careers of masters and mates of merchant ships who held masters' certificates. As well as personal details they contain records of service for all vessels making the tracking of an individual career straightforward. For further details of these registers see *www.cityoflondon.gov.uk/Corporation/leisure_heritage/libraries_ archives_museums_galleries/city_london_libraries/guildhall+library +guides.htm*

The digital age is fast changing and more and more information is now becoming available online. It is always worth looking at developments on the above mentioned websites to see what further information may now be at your fingertips.

13. MAPS

D. Huw Owen

Guides to the sources available for Welsh family and community historians have emphasised the importance of various types of cartographic evidence compiled over an extended period of time.[1] Wales had been represented on a number of medieval manuscript maps, and it is probable that Gerald of Wales had produced a map to accompany the text of his volumes *Itinerarium Kambriae* and his *Descriptio Kambriae*, issued after his tour of Wales in 1188: the map was described soon after it has been destroyed by fire in 1694.[2] Examples of extant medieval maps featuring Wales include Matthew Paris' map of the British Isles (1250); the *Mappa Mundi* (c.1290), housed at Hereford Cathedral Church, which had placed Great Britain on the edge of the world, with the Dee and Severn rivers separating Wales from England, Snowdon occupying the space for north Wales, and the references to Conway and Caernarfon castles of key significance with regard to dating the map; and the Gough Map (c.1375), which indicated the route from London to Pembrokeshire.[3]

A considerable improvement in terms of technique and accuracy may be observed in the printed maps published in the sixteenth century. The earliest printed map to denote Wales as a separate country was Humphrey Llwyd's *Cambriae Typus* (1573), which was published by Abraham Ortelius in Antwerp. A prominent Renaissance scholar, Llwyd was a native of Denbigh, one of the major towns of sixteenth-century Wales, and his background probably explains the improved delineation of the coast and rivers of north Wales in his map of Wales. The names of the traditional Welsh kingdoms, such as *Deheubartia* (Deheubarth) and *Venoditia* (Gwynedd), were presented, and also those of towns, in a bilingual format, including *Abertyvi/Cardigan; Abergwayn/Fyscard*; and *Abertawy/Swansey*. On the whole towns were accurately located, and errors or inconsistencies could possibly be explained by the employment of foreign artists or engravers.

Political and military considerations were responsible for Christopher Saxton's topographical survey of 1573–8, which resulted in the publication of his atlas, comprising maps of the counties of England and Wales (1579); the large scale wall-map of England and Wales (1583); and also the proof-map of Wales dated 1580. The outline of the latter represented a considerable improvement on that depicted on previous maps of Wales, and provided for the first time the correct representation of Anglesey, St Bride's Bay and the Llŷn and Gower peninsulas. The location of a large number of the towns and villages of Wales was also presented in this map.[4]

Saxton's county maps were published in William Camden's volume, *Britannia* (1607), whose Latin text was translated into English by Philemon Holland in 1610. The only exception among the maps of Wales was the map of Pembrokeshire by the antiquarian George Owen of Henllys, which had been engraved by William Kip. This map was based upon a far more detailed map compiled by him in 1602, depicting rivers and roads, and also bridges, parks and wooded areas, and the symbols representing high ground, such as the Preseli mountains, were far more accurate than those included on Saxton's maps.[5] In 1611 John Speed published his atlas, *Theatre of the Empire of Great Britain*, and in addition to his maps of Wales, and the Welsh shires, he also presented sixteen town-views, one for each one of the four episcopal centres, and the predominant town in twelve shires, containing a key for the names of streets and the main buildings: Monmouthshire was included among the shires of England and not of Wales.[6]

A number of the roads of Wales were shown on the strip-maps in John Ogilby's volume, *Britannia, Volume the First* (1675), and also in Robert Morden's set of playing-cards (1676): more roads were added by Robert Morden on his maps published in the volume *Britannia*, edited by Edmund Gibson (1695), that is the volume which included sections on Wales by Edward Lhuyd.[7] Many of these maps, such as those which

John Speed, Carmarthenshire (1611)
With the permission of the Carmarthenshire Record Office

199

were presented in *Britannia*, formed part of general collections which included maps of other areas in Wales and England. Attention was focused on specific localities by some map-makers, and notable examples include the maps of the shires of Denbigh and Flint by William Williams (1720), south Wales by Emanuel Bowen (1729), north Wales by John Evans (1799), Glamorgan by George Yates (1799) and Cardiganshire by Joseph Singer (1803). The Welsh hydrographer Lewis Morris' survey of the coast from Llandudno to Milford Haven was published in 1748 as *Plans of Harbours, Bars, Bays and Roads in St George's Channel*, and, re-issued by his son William in 1800-01, this work was extended to incorporate the entire coast of Wales.[8]

Many maps in this period were associated with parliamentary measures. They include enclosure maps, which, with an accompanying schedule formed part of an enclosure award compiled by a commissioner appointed under the terms of an Act of Parliament to conduct a survey of the ownership of land in open fields and of rights over the commons. They generally date from c.1800 to c.1890, with most prepared after 1840, and are normally housed in county record offices. Details were often provided of boundaries, rights of way and the ownership of land and size of holdings in the new allotments.[9]

Plans relating to the construction of canals and railways, and prepared following parliamentary orders, were often kept among Quarter Session records, and again are preserved at county record offices. These are frequently valuable sources for local studies, but yet one must be aware that a number were later substantially modified, and several proposed projects were never undertaken. However, there was a considerable increase in the railway lines built in Wales during the period 1845–50, and the collection of railway plans held at the National Library of Wales dates mainly from 1860 to 1900.[10]

A direct result of the Tithe Commutation Act, 1836, was the production of maps and schedules by surveyors appointed by Tithe Commissioners for each tithe district in Wales and England during the period 1840-1845. The maps often represent the earliest surviving large-scale maps of a locality, and the schedule or apportionment provided the names of the landowners and their tenants, the extent and land use of each field. Three copies of each map and schedule were prepared: one copy was kept by the parish clerk, the second was sent to the diocesan registry and the third to the office of the Tithe

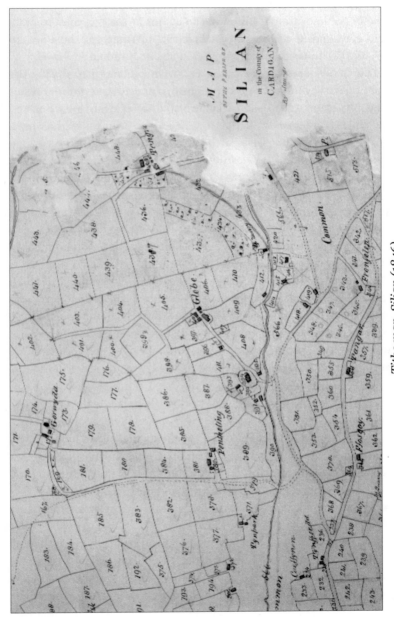

Tithe map, Silian (1846)
With the permission of Ceredigion Archives

Commissioners in London. Some examples of the first copy continue to be kept in the parish, but most have been transferred to a county record office or to the National Library. The copies in the diocesan registry have been deposited at the National Library of Wales, and those sent to the Tithe Commissioners are preserved at The National Archives.[11]

The same repository also houses the maps compiled during the valuation survey undertaken between 1910 and 1915 as a direct result of the Finance Act (1910), and also the National Farm Survey of England and Wales, undertaken in 1941–3. The term 'Domesday' has been applied to the two surveys, with the valuation described as 'Lloyd George's Domesday of Landownership', and the National Farm Survey as a 'second Domesday Survey'. The Valuation Office Field Books named the owners and tenants of the properties whose condition and use was occasionally recorded, and which may be identified on the accompanying Ordnance Survey map sheets. Whilst these Field Books are kept at The National Archives, working maps and valuation books were occasionally placed in county record offices.[12]

Manuscript maps of farms and estates, containing detailed topographical information, were prepared by professional surveyors commissioned by landowners seeking to define the boundaries of their property. They also presented those distinctive features of the rural landscape, such as lanes and tracks, fords, bridges and ferries, often overlooked by the compilers of the engraved maps of the individual shires. Thomas Lewis was one of the most productive estate map-makers in west Wales, and has been described as 'the doyen of West Wales mappers'.[13] An estate map was occasionally accompanied by a book of reference listing the names of tenants, fields and holdings, or, more frequently, by a summary terrier on the map itself to supplement the details presented cartographically. The value of this source for local studies was emphasised by a renowned archivist who commented that 'well-drawn, detailed and accurate estate maps are the greatest treasure for the local historian.'[14]

Collections of estate maps, ranging chronologically from the late sixteenth century to the late-nineteenth century, consist of single manuscript sheets depicting an individual property, or a large volume containing the mapping of the lands of an extensive estate, comprising several farms. The earliest known dated example of a planned mapped estate survey (or estate atlas) in Wales and England is the survey of the manors of Crickhowell and Tretower (1587). This is housed at the National Library of Wales, as also is Thomas Hornor's *Plan of Rheola* (1815), an outstanding example of a large, detailed and artistically coloured estate map.[15] The late seventeenth-century map of Dynant, in the parish of Llan-non, part of the Cynghordy collection at the Carmarthenshire Archive Service, is the earliest estate map to denote the county's industrial sites, marked as 'cole-workes'.[16] The collections of the West Glamorgan Archive Service include maps of the Gnoll Estate, Neath, produced by B. Jones, c.1750, and by Paul Padley, 1801.[17]

A map forming part of a collection of estate maps may possibly be described as a 'panorama' or 'prospect', presented artistically and combining elements of a map and a landscape picture. The two brothers, Paul and Thomas Sandby served with the army in Scotland in the period after the Jacobite Rebellion, 1745, and Paul Sandby later became one of the significant artists induced to visit Wales during the period when travel to the European continent became difficult because of the war waged against France.[18] The association of the military activity in Scotland with the production of maps and visual surveys, together with the preparations for waging war with France, formed part of the background to the establishment of the Ordnance Survey in 1791.

The main objective of the Survey was to produce a map, on a scale of 1 inch to the mile, of Great Britain. The preparatory work involved the production of drawings by surveyors, on scales of 2, 3 and 6 inches to the mile. The original drawings are housed in The National Archives, but photocopies of the 2-inch to the mile drawings of Wales, produced between 1809 and 1836, are preserved at the National Library of Wales. The first series of 1-inch maps for Wales, published in the period 1819–1842, was followed by other series, and the Seventh Series for Great Britain was completed in 1961. A succession of revised series of maps on larger scales, including maps at 6" and 25" to the mile, were published at regular intervals during the second half of the nineteenth century and first half of the twentieth century, Fields and individual buildings in rural areas are shown on the 6" maps, and the 25" maps recorded every building, even in the towns, and the name of every field, administrative boundary and ancient monument.

Detailed plans were also published of the main towns, including plans on the scale of 1/500 or 10.56 foot to one mile. The first National Grid 1:10,560 (6":1 mile) scale maps were published in 1946 (and

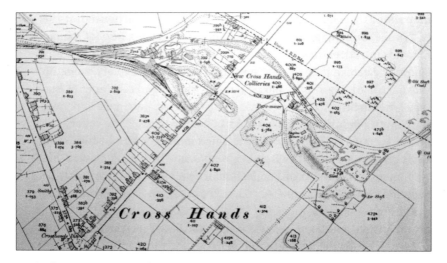

Ordnance Survey 25" map, Carmarthenshire Sheet, XLVIII 5 (1906)
Note the references to the colliery and the engine house

Part of the New Cross Hands Colliery, the site shown on the Ordnance Survey map above

Part of the A48 dual carriageway near the site of the colliery shown on the Ordnance Survey map above

metricated to 1:10,000 in 1969), and the National Grid 1:2,500 (25":1mile) scale maps were published in 1948. The 1:25,000 (2":1 mile) map was introduced in 1945, and was continued by the *Pathfinder* and *Outdoor Leisure* map series, and then the *Explorer* series on the 1:25,000 scale (4 cm:1 km, or 2½" to the mile), and the *Landranger* series on the 1.50 000 scale (2cm:1km, or 1¼" to the mile).[19]

Paper copies of the large scale 1:2,500 and 1:1,250 maps were published for the last time during the last decade of the twentieth century. Today, a variety of sophisticated high-tech measuring equipment is utilised to gather data, including state-of-the-art satellite technology, theodolite 'total stations', lasers to measure distances, and aerial photography. Constantly updated information is available to subscribers who may access the data via the *OS getamap* digital service.[20] The practically-instantaneous accessibility of this mapping represents a considerable enhancement in the provision for family and community historians in Wales, and the continuing popularity of the *Explorer* and *Landranger* series of paper maps confirms the view that 'maps are among the most visually attractive and most frequently consulted categories of public records'.[21]

NOTES

1   W. B. Stephens, *Sources for English Local History* (1981), 30, for statement that maps and plans 'must be regarded as the chief single type of source for the study of the local topography and they are of course of value to the local historian for the pursuance of many other topics too'; Brian Paul Hindle, *Maps for local history* (1989) for details of various maps relevant for local history studies
2   Gerald of Wales, *The Journey Through Wales/The Description of Wales*, trans. Lewis Thorpe (2004)
3   P. D. A. Harvey, *Mappa Mundi* (1996); Ian Jack, *Medieval Wales* (1972), 215–7
4   Olwen Caradog Evans, *Maps of Wales and Welsh Cartographers* (1964); D. Huw Owen, *Early Printed Maps of Wales* (1996); D. P. M. Michael, *The Mapping of Monmouthshire* (1985)
5   B. G. Charles, *George Owen of Henllys, a Welsh Elizabethan* (1973)
6   *The Counties of Britain* by John Speed, ed. Nigel Nicolson (1988)
7   William Camden, *Camden's Wales*, trans. Edward Lhuyd, introduction by Gwyn Walters, set and printed by Terrence James (1984)
8   Olwen Caradoc Egans, *Marine plans and charts of Wales* (1969)
9   John Chapman, *A Guide to Parliamentary Enclosures in Wales* (1992); Roger J. P. Kain, John Chapman and Richard R. Oliver, *The Enclosure Maps of England and Wales, 1595–1918* (2004)
10   Frazer Henderson, *The Engineers and Architects of Wales* (1991), 55, 57, 59 for list of railway plans and sections prepared by Henry Robertson and Benjamin

Piercy and held at the National Library of Wales

11 Roger J. P. Kain and Hugh C. Prince, *Tithe Surveys for Historians* (2000); Roger J. P. Kain and Richard R. Oliver, *The Tithe Maps of England and Wales* (1995); Robert Davies, *The Tithe Maps of Wales, a Guide to the Tithe Maps in the National Library of Wales* (1997)

12 Geraldine Beech and Rose Mitchell, *Maps for Family and Local Historians* (2004)

13 Michael C. S. Evans, 'The pioneers of estate mapping in Carmarthenshire', *The Carmarthenshire Antiquary*, XIII (1977), 56

14 F. G. Emmison, *Archives and Local History* (1974), 62

15 Estate maps of Wales, 1600–1836: exhibition catalogue (National Library of Wales) (1982); Pamela and Martin Redwood, *Estate Maps, the Crickhowell Area, 1587 and 1760* (2006)

16 Evans, *Pioneers of estate mapping*, 55; Carmarthenshire Record Office, Cynghordy, 355

17 Hilary M. Thomas, *A catalogue of Glamorgan estate maps* (1992), 67, 69, and 68 for reproduction of part of the *c*.1750 map

18 See also p.208

19 J. B. Harley and C. W. Phillips, *The Historian's Guide to Ordnance Survey Maps* (1964); J. B. Harley, *Ordnance Survey Maps: A Descriptive Manual* (1975); Richard Oliver, *Ordnance Survey Maps, a concise guide for historians* (2005)

20 Further information on all the Ordnance Survey products is available on the website: *www.ordnancesurvey.co.uk*

21 Geraldine Beech and Rose Mitchell, *Maps for Family and Local Historians* (2004), Preface, vii

14. Pictures

D. Huw Owen

Visual collections, including topographical prints, drawings and paintings, together with portraits, present valuable information for the family and community historian. The earliest portraits of Welsh persons include those housed at the National Museum of Wales, such as the one of William Herbert, 1st Earl of Pembroke by an unknown artist of the Netherlandish School (c.1560-5); Adriaen van Cronenburgh's *Katheryn of Berain*, known as 'The Mother of Wales' because of her connections with many important Welsh families as a result of her four marriages, c.1568; and the 'British School' double portrait of Sir Thomas Mansel and his wife Jane, c.1625. Portraits safeguarded at other institutions include those of the Gogerddan, Clennenau and Garthewin families, and various individuals preserved at the National Library of Wales; and the Golden Grove family at the Carmarthen Museum. Over 4,000 portraits located in Welsh country houses were recorded in John Steegman's *A Survey of Portraits in Welsh Houses* (1957, 1962), and include portraits of the Jones and Boothby families in Fonmon Castle; the Mansel, Talbot and Methuen Campbell families in Penrice Castle, Gower; and the Wynne-Finch family at Y Foelas/Voelas, near Pentrefoelas, Denbighshire. Steegman's work was updated by the survey of portraits held by individuals, families and institutions in Wales organised by the National Library of Wales in the 1980s.

In the seventeenth century, landowners commissioned pictures of their houses and lands, in the form of bird's eye views, and examples include the four pictures of the Dinefwr estate, near Llandeilo, and now housed at Newton House, owned by the National Trust and situated in Dinefwr Park. Several topographical print volumes were produced by Johannes Kip in the late seventeenth century, and a fine example is his print of Chepstow castle in the *Britannia Illustrated* volume. In the early eighteenth century the brothers Samuel and Nathaniel Buck were prolific engravers, responsible for views of castles, monasteries, abbeys and other antiquities, and also panoramic town views. Richard Wilson (1713–82), born at Penegoes, has been described as 'the father of British landscape painting' and he was also a gifted portrait artist. Examples of his work include *Llys Peris and Dolbadarn Castle*, and his self-portrait at the National Museum of Wales; and *Pembroke Castle* and his portrait of the sea-captain Captain Walter Griffith, at the National Library of Wales. One of the many artists influenced by him was his pupil, Thomas Jones, Pencerrig, Llanelwedd (1742–1803) who painted views of the estate and gardens of Hafod, Ceredigion, whilst visiting the home of Thomas Johnes before 1786.

Wales was 'discovered' by many leading artists, who presented idealistic views of the country in the late eighteenth century and early nineteenth century at a time of an intense interest in the 'romantic' and 'picturesque' and when the war with France restricted travelling to the continent. J. M. W. Turner (1775–1851) visited Wales on several occasions, and was inspired by the mountains of Snowdonia, historical sites such as Tintern Abbey and Dolbadarn castle and the industrial landscape of south Wales: paintings of Aberdulais Mill and the Cyfarthfa ironworks are among his more important works. Drawings produced by other artists attracted to Wales include *Valle Crucis Abbey* and the view of the copperworks in Neath by Paul Sandby, acclaimed as 'the father' of English watercolour painting: reference has already been made in Chapter 13 to his military activities in Scotland. Visits made by other artists resulted in the extensive collections of watercolours drawn by Samuel Hieronymous Grimm, Sir Richard Colt Hoare, Thomas Rowlandson, John 'Warwick' Smith and Julius Caesar Ibbetson. The latter two produced striking images of Parys Mountain, Anglesey, following their visits to the site of the copper mine. Thomas Pennant, Downing, in Flintshire, arranged the preparation of detailed watercolour views of sites in Wales by Moses Griffith (1747–1819) and John Ingleby (1749–1808), including many churches and country

Moses Griffith, Snowdonia

houses, which were published in Pennant's volumes, *Tours in Wales* (1778 and 1781).

An increasing amount of attention was focused on industrial developments, and images of the ironworks of Cyfarthfa and Penydarren appeared among the engravings of J. G. Wood in his *Rivers of Wales* (1813). Also, Edward Pugh's collection of aquatints in his *Cambria Depicta* (1816) included pictures of the copper mine of Mynydd Parys. George Orleans Delamotte's volume of drawings, housed at the West Glamorgan Archive Service, was compiled in the period c.1816–1835, and contained views of several localities in south Wales, including those of Swansea, Briton Ferry, and the Vale of Neath. As a result of the patronage provided by the Glamorgan gentry Thomas Hornor produced watercolour drawings, including one of the tinplate works at Ynysgerwn, near Aberdulais; panoramic maps, such as his plan of Rheolau, c.1815; and a number of large albums. At approximately the same time, Penry Williams (1800–85), a native of Merthyr Tydfil, had produced a picture of the Merthyr riot, 1816, together with several industrial scenes, including those of the Cyfarthfa ironworks for their owner, William Crawshay II.

The Cyfarthfa ironworks had been purchased by his grandfather, Richard Crawshay, who had been portrayed c.1800 by Richard Wilson.

At approximately the same time Henry Thomson had produced a portrait of Richard Pennant, the founder of the Bethesda slate quarries. Industrialists therefore followed the trend set by gentry families of acting as patrons of the leading contemporary artists. The career of Sir Watkin Williams Wynn, the most influential landowner in eighteenth-century Wales, has been discussed above in Chapter 11, and among the numerous portraits of him, two were produced by Thomas Hudson, the foremost portrait artist of his day. Thomas Gainsborough, the renowned artist, produced a portrait of Thomas Pennant who had also, when a child, been the subject of a portrait attributed to Joseph Highmore. Family members of privileged patrons were the sitters for many portraits, but those housed at Erddig, the National Trust property near Wrexham, include portraits of servants at the country house, in addition to members of the Yorke family. Six members of Philip Yorke's staff were portrayed by John Walters, Denbigh, between 1791 and 1796, including the blacksmiths William Williams and Edward Prince, the keeper Jack Henshaw, and the maid Jane Ebrell. W. J. Chapman was commissioned by Francis Crawshay to portray seventeen workers in the tinplate works at Treforest and the Cyfarthfa ironworks. Their names were provided and the portraits also included the equipment used by the workers, such as the dynamite sticks carried over his shoulder by the quarryman Thomas Francis and the dividers of the mechanic, Rees Davies, Hirwaun.

Hugh Hughes, the artisan painter (1790–1863), was responsible for many portraits, including those of Methodist leaders and their families, who belonged to the middle class at that time emerging in Wales in the early nineteenth century. This tradition was continued a generation later by William Roos (1808–78), and portraits of gentry patrons by the two artists were exceptions to the ones usually associated with them. The patronage-pattern in relation to portrait artists was transformed by those developments which resulted in the increasing popularity of photographs, and especially the *cartes de visites* after 1860 (see Chapter 15). A significant local publication of this period was the volume of prints by Charles Norris, *Etchings of Tenby* (1812). Hugh Hughes presented views of Wales in his collection of wood engravings, *Beauties of Wales* (1823), and an image of the ideal Welsh home in his *Y Gegin Gymreig* [*cegin*: kitchen]. Engravings of industrial scenes were published in Henry Gastineau's *South Wales Illustrated* (c. 1830–5).

The Royal Oak, Hotel, Betws-y-coed, an important centre for artists

In 1834 details of the distinctive Welsh dress were published by Lady Llanover, with the clothes favoured by her based upon those worn by women in rural areas in that period. John Cambrian Rowland's book of drawings (1849–50) also presented images of peasant clothes, and these were reproduced in extremely-popular engravings.

The Revs. E. Pryce Owen, vicar of Wellington, Shropshire (1823–40), and John Parker (1798–1860), rector of Llanmerewig, Montgomeryshire and vicar of Llanyblodwel, Shropshire (1798–1860), were two prominent artists/clerics in the first half of the nineteenth century. The latter was responsible for an extensive collection of views, especially of Snowdonia, pictures of flowers and also architectural drawings and details of items in churches, dating from c.1818 until 1860. Betws-y-coed developed into a centre for artists, largely because of the activities of David Cox (1783–1859) and Clarence Whaite (1828–1912), who both visited the area regularly, with Whaite settling there c.1870. Two extremely-influential oil paintings produced by them were *The Welsh Funeral* by David Cox in 1848, and *To the Cold Earth* by Clarence Whaite in 1865. Also associated with the artists' 'colony' at Betws-y-coed was Samuel Maurice Jones (1853–1932), who contributed pictures of the homes of prominent Welshmen to the journal, *Cymru* from 1891, and then to *Cartrefi Cymru* [*cartrefi*:

homes] (1896), which, edited by O. M. Edwards, was one of the most popular volumes of the period. Many Welsh persons also treasured the widely-distributed prints of the picture of the congregation in Salem chapel, Cefncymerau, painted in 1908 by Sydney Curnow Vosper, and considered to be one of the most characteristic images of Wales ever produced.

Several artists were associated with one of the rapidly-growing commercial and industrial towns. William Watkeys was a prolific portrait-artist in Swansea, as also was Cleopas Harris and his son George Frederick (1856–1924) at Merthyr Tydfil. James Flewitt Mullock (1818–92), who was very active in Newport, had influential contacts with local landowners, and a number of his pictures may be viewed at the Newport Museum and Art Gallery. Several local pictures by Alfred Worthington (1835–1925), a native of Kent who had settled in Aberystwyth, are housed at the town's Ceredigion Museum. T. H. Thomas, 'Arlunydd Penygarn' (1839–1915), was a prominent member of a group that organised exhibitions at Cardiff, by the end of the nineteenth century the largest town in Wales, and which succeeded in establishing the National Museum of Wales at Cardiff in 1907. A number of his works are housed at the Museum, including an oil painting of women working on the coal tips of south Wales, and drawings of various industrial scenes, including tinplate works at Treforest and coalminers working underground. The pictures of Carey Morris (1882–1968) included studies of Welsh weavers and fisherwomen at Llangwm. The mountains of Wales continued to appeal to artists and notable landscape pictures were drawn by James Dickson Innes (1887–1914) and Augustus John (1870–1961). In approximately the same period, before the First World War, important portraits were produced by Margaret Lindsey Williams (1888–1960) and Christopher Williams (1873–1934), and striking sculptures by William Goscombe John (1860–1952), including those of Daniel Owen (1902), T. E. Ellis (1903) and Lewis Edwards (1911).

David Jones (1895–1874) produced landscapes of the area to the north of Abergavenny in the 1920s when he was a member of the community which had established itself at Capel y Ffin, and also of Caldey Island whilst he was staying in a monastery on the island. Cedric Morris, Charles Burton, Arthur Giardelli, Esther Grainger, Heinz Koppel and Ernest Zobole are associated with artistic activities organised in the industrial valleys of south Wales in the 1930s and 1940s by Settlements formed at Dowlais and Pontypridd. The docks of Swansea and Cardiff were featured in the works of Ceri Richards (1903–71) and so also were the daily tasks undertaken by workers at the tinplate works in Gowerton where his father had been employed. Various aspects of the living and working conditions of coal miners were presented by a number of artists, including George Chapman, Nicholas Evans, Vincent Evans, Archie Griffiths, Josef Herman, Denys Short and Evan Walters.

Two artists from England who made a significant contribution by creating notable landscape pictures were Graham Sutherland (1903–92) in Pembrokeshire, and John Piper (1903–92) in north Wales: the latter artist also produced a number of significant images of Welsh religious buildings. Harry Hughes Williams (1892–1953) was responsible for landscapes of Anglesey during the period before and after the Second World War, with a series illustrating windmills and haystacks. Rural life and the birds of the island were illustrated by Charles Tunnicliff (1901–79), and the seascapes of the coast of Anglesey, together with landscapes of the Snowdonia mountain range and portraits of local inhabitants were among the most important pictures of Kyffin Williams (1918–2006), who had been born on Anglesey and created most of his work at his home on the island. The experience of living in Deiniolen explains the emphasis on the landscape of the slate-quarrying areas of Gwynedd in the pictures of Peter Prendergast (1946–2007). His memories of rural south Ceredigion represented a most significant influence on the works of John Elwyn (1916–97); and Will Roberts (1907–2000) was inspired by his visits to Ty'n y Waun farm, near Neath, in addition to his experience of working with Josef Herman (1911–2000) in a coal-mining community.

In the late twentieth century and first decade of the twenty-first century various areas of Wales were the subjects of landscape pictures by numerous artists, including Donald McIntyre and Gwilym Prichard. Attention was drawn to the mountains and coast of north Wales by Keith Bowen, Rob Piercy, William Selwyn and David Woodford; Anglesey by Keith Andrew; Nefyn and the Llŷn peninsula by Emrys Parry; the Banwy valley in Montgomeryshire by Eleri Mills; and Pembrokeshire by John Knapp-Fisher and David Tress. David

Carpanini and Valerie Ganz concentrated on industrial communities in south Wales; Falcon Hildred's watercolour drawings have recorded industrial buildings and landscapes; Aneurin Jones, reared in the Usk valley, farmers and the rural community; farm buildings, barns and sheds are featured in the works of Ogwyn Davies; and chapels in the textile works of Cefyn Burgess. Settlements in several areas of Wales have been presented by Christopher Hall, and many prominent Welsh figures have been sitters for the portraits produced by David Griffiths. In addition to these artists, a number of others, including Iwan Bala, Shani Rhys James and Mary Lloyd Jones, have emphasised the influence exerted upon them by the landscape and people of Wales, and their works again emphasise the value of visual images for family and community history studies.

Further reading

David Griffiths, *Portreadau/Portraits* (2002)
Anthony Jones, *Painting the dragon* (2000)
Paul Joyner (ed.), *Dolbadarn*, (1990); *Artists in Wales , c.1740–c.1851* (1997); Paul Joyner (ed.), *Will Roberts, RCA* (2001)
Peter Lord, *Hugh Hughes: 1790–1863* (1990); *The Francis Crawshay worker portraits* (1996); *Clarence Whaite and the Welsh art world* (1998); *The Visual Culture of Wales, Industrial Society* (1998); *The Visual Culture of Wales, Imaging the Nation* (2000); *The Visual Culture of Wales, Medieval Vision* (2003); *The Meaning of Pictures* (2009); *Winifred Coombe Tennant* (2007); *Between Two Worlds*, ed. Peter Lord (2011); *Relationships with Pictures* (2013)
Robert Meyrick, *George Chapman* (1992); *John Elwyn* (2000); *Gwilym Pritchard* (2001); 'Famous among the Barns: The Cardiganshire Landscapes of John Elwyn', *Ceredigion*, xiv, 2 (2002), 89–104; *Christopher Williams* (2012); D. Meredith (ed.), *Bro a Bywyd Kyffin Williams, his life, his land* (2007)
George Orleans Delamotte, A South Wales Sketch Book, c.1816–1835, ed. Bernard Morris (2007)
Barry Plummer (ed.), *Evan Walters* (2011)
Glyn Rhys, *A Celtic Canvas: the Life, Works and Times of Carey Morris, 1882–1968* (2013)
Thomas Jones (1742–1803), ed. Ann Sumner, Greg Smith (2003)
Peter Wakelin, *Worktown: the drawings of Falcon Hildred* (2012)
D. P. Webley, *Cast to the Winds, The Life and Work of Penry Williams* (1997)
Tal Williams, *Salem* (1998)

Note

Access to pictures in public collections throughout Wales has recently been enhanced by the *Your Paintings* website (*ww w.bbc.co.uk/arts/yourpaintings/*). This has resulted from a joint initiative between participating institutions; the BBC; and the Public Catalogue Foundation, a registered charity established to create and make available, by the provision of core data, a complete record of the United Kingdom's collections of oil, tempera and acrylic paintings. A total of 212,000 paintings have been photographed and put on the website; this sum includes 12,500 paintings from 195 Welsh institutions, with over 1,950 photographs of oil paintings from the collection of the National Library of Wales.

15. Photographs and Postcards

William Troughton

Whether from the back of a drawer in their own house or from a cupboard in the home of a relative every family historian will at some point be presented with an accumulation of photographs and postcards.

Very many of these will be anonymous portraits of family and friends. It is also inevitable that the mists of time will confuse the identity of some sitters and rob others of their identity. There is no time like the present to write lightly (in pencil) a caption on the reverse of your own family photographs and prevent the cycle repeating itself.

Even though at first glance a bundle of old and anonymous photographs may seem of little use there is a great deal that can be gleaned from them to interpret the lives of the sitters.

Photography dates back to 1839 but it was another two decades before photography was available to other than the most prosperous citizens. Early processes were expensive and time-consuming, and the results fragile.

Amateur photography existed in this period as a country-house pastime, as exemplified by John Dillwyn Llewellyn and his circle of friends. Their work can be seen on the excellent National Library of Wales website.

Commercial portrait photography in this era was confined to daguerreotypes and the later ambrotypes and ferrotypes. Each produced a single image which was presented in a 'jewel case' to protect the image and add an air of exclusivity to the proceedings. Ambrotypes were both cheaper to produce and due to various innovations cheaper to present than daguerreotypes. Ferrotypes, photographs printed on a thin sheet of steel were cheaper still. In 1839 William Henry Fox Talbot had also announced his invention of the negative/positive process, but it was not until refinements took place in the late 1850s that portraits could be produced inexpensively and en masse using his process. *Slaters Trades Directory* for 1858 does not record any 'photographic artists' in either Swansea or Cardiff. A decade later they could boast eleven and nine respectively, whilst Caernarfon and Merthyr Tudful each supported five. Smaller towns such as Haverfordwest, Mold and Ruabon each had two commercial photographers in 1868.

Ambrotypes and daguerreotypes are frequently confused but easy to tell apart. Daguerrotypes are very metallic and silvery, almost mirror-like, in appearance and the image very fragile. Ambrotypes lack the metallic sheen and on close inspection the image can be seen to be almost transparent. Ambrotypes frequently survive as single sheets of glass with a faint ghostly image. Placing them on a black background transforms them, and what appeared as a faint image will present itself as a clear and lucid portrait. Ferrotypes in a jewel case can be told apart from ambrotypes by its flatter image. Occasional rust spots on the face of the photograph and a lack of transparency also serve to distinguish ferrotypes from ambrotypes.

Cartes de visite heralded the true popularisation of photography. A *carte de visite* is a small paper photograph printed from a glass negative and mounted on a piece of card usually 10.2 x 6.4cm in size. From 1860 these were produced in their millions. There is little evidence to suggest that they were ever used as true 'calling cards' but were instead given to family and friends and collected. This is the format frequently found in collections of family photographs. Many were kept in leather-bound albums with ornate brass clasps. These would be looked through by the family on a Sunday afternoon. *Cartes de visites* of scenery, royalty, politicians, bishops and other prominent persons were sold commercially and collected. Albums that have survived provide a precious and unwitting record of the political, social and religious framework of their compilers. Although the format remained in vogue for the next forty years changes in clothing, the style of the *cartes* themselves and the pose of the sitters can all help date the images to within a few years. Knowledge of a particular family can help date the photographs as many were taken to mark special occasions in one's life – coming of age, engagement, first job might all be reasons for a visit to a photographer's studio.

Dating *cartes de visite* is relatively simple, in theory at least. As a broad rule of thumb the closer the camera to the subject the later in the century the photograph was taken. Early cameras had poor lenses that did not flatter the sitter. Portraits from the 1860s tended to be full length, usually in a simple setting. During the 1870s and 1880s three-quarter length and half-length poses became the norm and by the 1890s a vignette of head and shoulders was the fashion for individual portraits. Most *cartes de visite* of male sitters tried to emphasise a sense of authority and self-reliance. Women were usually portrayed in calm, demure poses.

There are many pointers for dating photographs in the hairstyle and clothing of sitters in Victorian portraits. This is especially true of female sitters. Here a book such as *Victorian Dress in Photographs* by Madeleine Ginsberg can be invaluable. However, it should be pointed out that the latest trends in fashion could take some time to reach the provinces and could stay in vogue for far longer in less cosmopolitan rural Wales than in urban centres. A particular style of clothing is therefore best regarded as a 'no earlier than ...' rather than 'no later than ...'

The reverse of a *carte de visite* can often reveal as much about the date of a photograph as the front. Most *cartes de visite* give the name and address of the photographer. Reference to contemporary Trades Directories or newspapers can frequently pin down a photographer to particular premises for a relatively short period of time. For example J. L. Berry, an Aberdare photographer, is listed as being at 1 Market Street in directories from 1875–1880; at 43 Cardiff Street in 1884–1891 and at 47 Commercial Street from 1895–1912. It is quite possible that a search through local newspapers of the time could further refine the dates above. On the other hand, Alfred Betts, a Merthyr Tudful photographer, occupied the same premises at 94 High Street from at least 1868 until 1903.

As with most things, the style of *cartes de visite* also had trends and fashions. In the 1860s the card tended to be fairly thin, the corners square and the reverse plain with just the photographer's name and address, perhaps within a shield. By the 1870s a thicker card, rounded corners and information covering the entire back were the order of the day. The 1880s saw the use of more elaborate designs using coloured cards and inks. By the early 1890s angels, cherubs, hanging baskets and all manner of decoration were to be seen. The last years of the century (and of the *carte de visite*) saw a return to plainer designs on pastel-coloured board.

Cabinet cards are larger versions of *cartes de visite*, usually measuring 16.7 x 11 cm. They usually have the photographer's imprint and exhibit similar styles of decorative artwork on the reverse to *cartes de visite*. They started to gain acceptance in the 1870s, eclipsing *cartes de visite* by the 1880s. They were still available until the early 1920s. Many *cartes de visite*, cabinet cards and other forms of studio portraits were the work of local high street photographers, people such as D. C. Harries of Llandeilo, P. B. Abery of Builth Wells, and William Harwood in Cricieth. Every town had at least one photographic studio in the late nineteenth century and the first half of the twentieth. Local photographers tended to combine portraiture with supplying views of their locality. John Thomas was born in Wales but opened a studio in Liverpool. He chose to travel far more widely around north and mid Wales during the 1870s to 1890s than his contemporaries. He specialised in taking individual and group portraits, local scenes and Welsh celebrities of the day, many of them ministers of religion. His collection is preserved in the National Library of Wales and can be viewed on their excellent website. Where negatives and prints of photographers such as these have survived in archive offices, museums or establishments such as the National Library of Wales you can be sure to find many photographic gems. It is the work of many of these photographers that provides the backbone for so many books of views of localities across Britain, such as those published by Chalford Publishing and S B Publications.

One other photographer of particular note is Geoff Charles. He too criss-crossed north and mid Wales, working for North Wales Newspapers as a photo-journalist for nearly fifty years. His archive of 120,000 photographs, indexed and catalogued, is in the National Library of Wales. Many are also available to view on their website.

The careers of many of these photographers are now being re-visited

The Pontypridd bridges

with a number of books, including three on the work of Geoff Charles by Ioan Roberts, a volume on D. C. Harries by Iestyn Hughes, and most recently a volume by I. M. Jones on the work of John Thomas.

Amongst any bundle of family photographs there are likely to be at least a few picture postcards. Although postcards are highly ephemeral objects and the vast majority have been destroyed (estimates suggest 3–5 per cent of Edwardian postcards now survive), those that have survived can tell us much about their owners. Just like *cartes de visite* postcards were collected and put in albums. The contents of these albums often reveal much. They will contain cards sent by friends and family, views of favourite places, and again may reveal political, social or religious loyalties.

Plain postcards were introduced in Britain in 1870. These had to be purchased at the post office and had a stamp printed, not stuck on. The address was written on the front, the message on the reverse. Because the postage on a card was half the cost of posting a letter they rapidly attained popularity. September 1 1894 saw the withdrawal of the restriction that the stamp had to be pre-printed on the card by the Inland Revenue Dept. People were now free to stick an ordinary half-penny stamp on a privately-produced postcard. Manufacturers quickly began to emulate pictorial postcards to be had in Europe, especially Germany, and by 1900 postcard collecting was becoming popular in Britain, helped by an increase in the size of cards allowed, first of all to the 'Court' size in 1895 and secondly, in 1899, to what we regard as the normal size, 3.5 ins by 5.5 ins. The final stage in the evolution of the

Lisburne Arms, Pont-rhyd-y-groes, c.1910

postcard was the introduction of the 'divided back' in 1902. This allowed both message and address to be written on the same side leaving the entire reverse free for the illustration. It also ushered in the Golden Age of postcards.

It is difficult for us today to imagine how popular postcards were. Postcards were readily available everywhere, often sold in packets of six or twelve and carried in handbag or pocket ready to dash out a message that today would be the subject of a phone call, email or text message. The Post Office in Britain handled 866 million postcards during 1909, or put another way, 22 cards for every man, woman and child in the country. The Post Office in Aberystwyth handled 24,000 postcards in a week in August 1903. All manner of themes were covered – art, politics, current affairs, celebrities, social history, humour and of course topographical views. Added to this was an efficient postal service, which in cities delivered post up to six times a day. It quickly became a craze amongst young ladies to collect postcards. Human nature being what it is young men were of course obliged to indulge this craze.

Amongst the first companies to produce postcards of Wales were James Valentine of Dundee and Francis Frith of Reigate. Both companies were founded by men who had been involved in photography since the 1850s and had been engaged in selling

Salmon fishing

photographs of views throughout Britain. Consequently they were both well placed to produce and distribute postcards. The earliest picture postcard of Wales the author is aware of was published by Raphael Tuck and Co. in 1894. The card is of Snowdon Summit and was sold near the summit. How many were sold in the first year is a matter for conjecture, especially as the mountain railway was not completed until the following year!

Not far behind these national companies were regional publishers, that is, those companies and photographers who specialised in views of a particular area. *Landscape, Portrait and Fine Art Photographers* of Llandrindod are one of the earliest examples. The company produced about six hundred different postcards from *c.*1903–*c.*1909, mainly of views throughout Wales, but also several series of Welsh MPs and cartoons. Ernest Bush from Cardiff also falls into this category. He diligently recorded the pit villages, collieries, docks, civic buildings and bustling streets of south Wales. His cards are much sought after today. He died at the relatively young age of fifty-four in 1930, having published hundreds of different views of south Wales.

Although responsible for fewer quantities of cards than national or regional publishers, local postcard publishers produced by far and away the most interesting topographical cards. The advent of photographic emulsions coated on thicker papers from 1904 onwards allowed local photographers to produce postcards of every manner of local event and

Tresaith, Ceredigion, postally used 1906

view. The flexibility of the system allowed them to print out as many or as few as were required within hours of the event having taken place. These postcards, known as 'Real Photographic', record in detail views and events of the pre-First World War era. No town or village was too small to have a local photographer to record the local chapel, post office, public house, Sunday School trip, football team or carnival. Seaside resorts were especially well served. As an example north Ceredigion was served by E. G. Crudge (Tregaron and Pontrhydygroes), C. H. Dierks (Aberaeron, Llanon and Llanrhystud), J. Meurig Edwards (Bow Street), E. O. Jones (Talybont and Taliesin), Williams (Borth), and E. R. Gyde, William Jenkins, Lewis Y Mart, Pickfords (all Aberystwyth). Many of their cards would have been produced in very small quantities indeed.

E. R. Gyde is a prime example of a seaside photographer. He had a shop and studio in Pier Street, Aberystwyth. One of his specialities was to take photographs of groups of holidaymakers on pleasure boats, charabancs or carriages. These photographs would be printed as postcards and then placed in the shop window to be sold to the sitters. This was a common practice in most holiday resorts. William Jenkins on the other hand purchased a licence each year from the local council. He would then patrol the beach at Aberystwyth with his camera and heavy wooden tripod. Hanging from his tripod were two buckets, one containing developer, the other fixer. On finding a customer on the beach he would photograph them there and then, plunge the exposed plate into the developer for the required length of time, then into the fixer. Armed with a sheet of postcard-sized photographic paper he would then produce a contact print from the negative using the available daylight. This would then be immersed in the developer and fixer. A quick shake to remove any excess drops of fixer, perhaps a wipe on his jacket sleeve, and your postcard was ready! Like many photographers William Jenkins was kept busy during the First World War years photographing servicemen in uniform. It is a tribute to his craftsmanship that so many of his beach photos survive.

Whereas today we rely on newspapers and television to relay pictures of important events to us prior to the First World War this role was also served by the postcard. Even national newspapers carried only occasional illustrations as the process involved was time-consuming and expensive. Real photographic postcards bridged this gap. When an explosion at the Universal Pit, Senghenydd, killed 439 men in October 1913, a Glasgow photographer named Benton rushed to the scene and published a series of twenty-five real photographic cards showing scenes on the surface. This may seem bizarre by the standards of the present day but these are also the exact same images you would expect to see on television if a similar event happened today. Any event considered newsworthy was likely to have had cards produced, including motor-car accidents, carnivals, shipwrecks, Sunday school outings, fires and even a typhoid outbreak in Lincoln in 1905. These items are not easy to find, but it can be very rewarding to find postcards of events that your ancestors may have witnessed first-hand.

A phenomenon as popular as the postcard naturally attracted the attention of advertisers who gave cards away with their products, whether soap, dog food or cocoa. In the case of hotels postcards were left in guest rooms. Railway companies were particularly adept at exploiting the medium and sold numerous series, often at low prices. London and North Western Railways published nearly 1000 different postcards and claimed to have sold 11 million cards by 1914.

Just as quickly as the postcard had gained its popularity, so did it fall from grace. The main reasons for this were an increase in postage to one penny in 1919 and the increasing availability (and novelty) of the telephone. However, it remained a standard practice amongst many

Tal-y-llyn lake, c.1910

developing and printing houses to offer customers prints on postcard backs until at least the 1940s.

Just as the *carte de visite*, cabinet card and postcard made *photographs* available to ordinary people, the invention of the Kodak Brownie made *photography* accessible to the masses. Early Brownies came loaded with film. After exposure the whole camera had to be returned to Kodak for the film to be extracted – 'you press the button, we do the rest'. The camera was then returned to its owner loaded up with film. This invention heralded the era of the snapshot and the snapshot album. The Kodak price list for 1904 lists forty-seven different types of album, indicating how rapidly the new genre took hold. Albums rapidly filled up with groups posed outside the front door, holidays to the seaside, days out, picnics in the garden, weddings and any number of special occasions. The more affluent may have photographs of valiant motorists struggling to complete their journey. More effort seems to have been put into these early snapshots than those of today, perhaps reflecting the meticulous methods of the professional studio photographer. Strangely, nearly every snapshot album from this era seems to have a photo of a person or group on a bridge.

Colour photography became affordable from the 1960s, since when most snapshots have been in colour. Early colour photos often have a magenta cast, the result of dyes used breaking down at different rates.

Aberystwyth promenade, postally used 1921

This fading can occur in photographs and slides stored in the dark. Fortunately the photographs can be re-created using software such as Photoshop.

Having discovered a horde of family photographs it is natural to want to care for and display them in the best possible way. This is a subject on which much has been written. A starting point would be the websites of specialist companies such as Secol (*www.secol.co.uk*), Conservation Resources (*www.conservationresources.com*) and Conservation by Design (*www.conservation-by-design.co.uk*). All sell suitable archival storage materials, as well as giving much useful advice on their websites.

Digital photography is now the dominant medium for the family archive photographs of tomorrow. But a word of caution – how safe is this new medium? What happens if your computer crashes? Are your files backed up? What is the shelf life of your photo CDs? These are all problems that didn't tax our ancestors, but need addressing sooner rather than later if records of the present generation are to be as well preserved as those from previous centuries.

Further Reading

R. Iestyn Hughes, *D. C. Harries, A Collection of Photographs* (1996)

Iwan Meical Jones, *Hen Ffordd Cymreig o Fyw/A Welsh Way of Life – John Thomas Photographs* (2008)

Ioan Roberts, *Cymru Geoff Charles* (2006); *Cefn Gwlad Geoff Charles* (2006); *Eisteddfodau Geoff Charles* (2007)

William Troughton, *Aberystwyth Harbour – An Illustrated History* (1997); *Ceredigion Shipwrecks* (2006)

16. Houses and Landscapes: Sources at RCAHMW, Aberystwyth

Richard Suggett

This chapter considers houses and their landscape contexts as sources in their own right for local history. The historian with mud on his or her boots will eventually need to visit unfamiliar archives, especially the National Monuments Record of Wales (NMRW: the public archive of the Royal Commission on the Ancient and Historical Monuments of Wales), and the regional Sites and Monuments Records curated by the four archaeological trusts in Wales. The Royal Commission occupies a functional building in Aberystwyth, once shared with the Inland Revenue, but researchers should not be deterred from calling at Plas Crug! The NMRW is a national archive, part of the public service, and must be the first port of call for the house and landscape detective. At the very least, the National Monuments Record can usually supply historic mapping and aerial photography of a house and its environs; if one is lucky, the NMRW can supply much more. Those seeking to understand the structural history of a house and to place it in its architectural context will very probably need professional advice at some point. However, be warned! It is important to consult those with the appropriate architectural expertise. One must also expect to pay the standard rate of remuneration (currently around £200 a day). However, with persistence and a little luck the house detective can make a great deal of headway using the free resources of the NMRW and other specialist archives.

There is not as yet a 'one-stop shop' for the researcher who wants to search the various sites and monuments records in Wales. Thorough researchers will want to consult the searchable databases of both the Royal Commission (Coflein: *www.coflein.gov.uk*) and the regional Welsh Archaeological Trusts (Archwilio: *www.archwilio.org.uk*), much as the shopper may need to visit several supermarkets. However, it needs to be appreciated that Coflein alone has online images of sites and an all-Wales map-based search facility. In an attempt to provide a one-stop shop, RCAHMW hosts the Historic Wales Portal (*www.historicwales.gov.uk*), a map-enabled portal that allows the simultaneous searching of hundreds of thousands of records relating to archaeological monuments, historic buildings and artefacts held by different organisations across Wales: the National Monuments Record of Wales, the archaeology collection of Amgueddfa Cymru – National Museum Wales, the historic environment records of the Archaeological Trusts, and Cadw's descriptions of scheduled ancient monuments and listed buildings.

Houses

We are fortunate in having a large stock of historic houses in Wales. An estimate of the number of Tudor houses suggests that more than 1,000 survive as standing structures, and there are many more seventeenth- and eighteenth-century houses. This is a large resource, but undoubtedly there are still more discoveries to be made. The Royal Commission routinely comes across hitherto unknown medieval houses during its emergency recording programme.

Peter Smith's *Houses of the Welsh Countryside* (revised edition, 1975; 2nd enlarged edition, 1988) is a wonderful guide to these houses which summarises much information collected by the Royal Commission. It is indispensable for the house historian, commanding a high price in the second-hand market, but is now available as an e-book.[1] *Houses of the Welsh Countryside* is an encyclopaedic and superbly illustrated overview of vernacular houses in Wales with many reconstruction drawings. The evidence is presented in a series of over fifty distribution maps of key architectural features, each provided with a list of sites. The same site may have features recorded on several maps. The sites are indexed according to historic counties and identified by grid reference. The second edition has additional sites and a supplementary index arranged according to the same principles. Even if a house isn't listed in *Houses of the Welsh Countryside*, readers can soon discover the historic features that one would expect to find in a house of regional type. The bilingual volume, *Introducing Houses of the Welsh Countryside: Cyflwyno Cartrefi Cefn Gwlad Cymru* (RCAHMW and Y Lolfa, 2010), based on the S4C television series, attempts to introduce a new audience to Peter Smith's book and conveys the excitement of discovering the distinctive features of vernacular houses in Wales.

Peter Smith's all-Wales overview is complemented by the Royal Commission's published *Inventory* volumes for the historic counties, notable Anglesey (1937) and Caernarvonshire I-III (1956, 1960, 1964), and by several thematic volumes. The Alder County Inventories cover all types of monuments but RCAHMW has published detailed regional studies of houses in Glamorgan (1988) and Radnorshire (2005), historically stone and timber building areas respectively. Eurwyn Wiliam's *The Welsh Cottage* (2010), deals in part with clay buildings. In addition, there are scholarly studies of houses in Monmouthshire and Breconshire. The innovative study of *Monmouthshire Houses* by Lord Raglan and Sir Cyril Fox, published in three volumes (1951–54), has been republished by Merton Priory Press. The houses of Breconshire have received valuable attention from John Smith and Stanley Jones, but their study extends over seven parts in *Brycheiniog* between 1963–72 and re-publication as a single volume is long overdue. In addition, one must mention the study of *Old Gower Farmhouses and their Families* by Bernard Morris (1998), and Peter Smith's overviews of houses specially written for the county histories of Merioneth and Cardiganshire. Successive volumes of *A Bibliography of Vernacular Architecture* issued by the Vernacular Architecture Group, and now available online (*archaeologydataservice.ac.uk/archives/ view/vagbiblio*), provide details of further regional and local studies, but is commendably wide-ranging with sections on building types, construction and materials, and the economic and social contexts.

In addition, Cadw's community resurveys provide descriptions of many thousands of listed buildings. These include numerous houses, especially many eighteenth- and nineteenth-century farmhouses of traditional type which do not figure much in the regional studies noted above. The list descriptions compiled over several decades (mainly 1980s–90s) are variable in scope. The best have detailed exterior and interior descriptions, a justification for the listing, and note relevant sources. The community re-surveys are surprisingly difficult to consult outside reference libraries and planning offices, but a full set is kept in the NMRW with the amendments (additions and occasional deletions) regularly issued by Cadw. Cadw's database of listed and scheduled buildings is available online through the Historic Wales Portal hosted by RCAHMW.

Finally one must highlight the extraordinary achievement of the *Buildings of Wales* series of 'Pevsners', now published by Yale University Press. The series now covers the whole of Wales in seven regional volumes. Historic houses in numerous communities are succinctly described, and each volume has a survey of building types with bibliography.

In combination, these printed and online sources are a huge resource for the building historian, but more material remains unpublished. If a house is mentioned in one of the published sources noted above, there is a every chance that there will be additional information in the Royal Commission's archive. There are numerous unpublished assessments of buildings, with plans and photographs, relating to every district of Wales, especially those counties that have *Inventory* volumes. The fieldworkers for RCAHMW's thematic volumes on Glamorgan and Radnorshire aimed to visit every historic farmstead, but only a relatively small proportion of historic houses that were investigated were selected for publication.

A properly-considered architectural assessment of a house will provide a narrative in its own right. A surprising number of houses have a continuous structural history from the late-medieval period to the present. If one is lucky a house will have evidence for an open hall of late-medieval date; the open hall will have been modified in the sixteenth and seventeenth centuries with the building of the chimney, the insertion of ceilings, and the replacement of timber walls by stone; and in the eighteenth and nineteenth centuries the building will have been modified to create a conventional 'modern' plan. Examples of this characteristic development are given in *Houses and History in the March of Wales* (RCAHMW, 2005).

An architectural narrative for a house can be peopled only through the documentation. A number of very useful guides to compiling documentary house histories are available in the National Library of Wales and in the county record offices. Deeds and leases can provide a chain of ownership and occupation; wills and inventories may survive for those who have lived in a house. If one is exceptionally lucky, a probate inventory will list the contents of named rooms.

Sooner or later the house detective will want to establish the date or dates (generally a house has several phases) of a house. Date inscriptions are not numerous (many are listed in *Houses of the Welsh Countryside*) but stylistic considerations will allow the broad dating of a house. However, the technique of tree-ring dating now permits (assuming the timber is suitable) the accurate dating of historic timbers. If full sapwood survives (as it does surprisingly often) the year of felling can be established and sometimes even the season of felling. Assuming that a structural timber has not been reused, the year of felling is a good guide to the date of construction, since timber was generally used green and allowed to season in situ. Thus The Old Vicarage, Berriew, Montgomeryshire, has a date inscription of 1616 on the porch, dating the completion of the house; tree-ring dating has shown that the timber used to build the vicarage was felled in 1615.

It is certainly true that tree-ring dating has transformed our understanding of building chronology in Wales. The buildings usually selected for tree-ring dating are medieval in origin. The date range of medieval houses of the open hall type is uncertain, but we now know that most medieval houses in Wales date from after 1400. The earliest identified house is Hafodygarreg in Breconshire, built from timber felled in 1402. The majority of early houses are cruck-framed, like Hafodygarreg, and many hundreds of cruck-framed houses survive in Wales. Given the documentary references to substantial houses in Wales before 1400, there are probably some fourteenth-century houses waiting to be identified.

'How old is this house?' is a fundamental question which tree-ring dating can often answer. However, tree-ring dating is an expert service that has to be paid for. A reasonable estimate for dating a single phase is around £750, but of course a house may well have two or three phases. So far some 250 buildings have been dated throughout Wales, many by the Royal Commission, but there is considerable scope for partnerships with local groups and historical societies. In particular, the North-west Wales Dendrochronology Project has collaborated with RCAHMW to date and interpret a range of important and representative houses. The group, now renamed the Dating Old Welsh Houses project, is dedicated to finding out more about the older houses (generally pre-1700) in Anglesey, Caernarfonshire, Merioneth, and further afield. The group has compiled some exemplary house histories. Several are now available in edited form on the People's Collection Wales website with illustrations, including the remarkable Gwastadannas, a cruck-framed house tree-ring dated 1506 with documentation extending back to 1508.

A list of all tree-ring dated sites in Wales up to 2003 has been compiled,[2] and further Welsh tree-ring dates are reported annually in the journal, *Vernacular Architecture*. The Vernacular Architecture Group has a web site listing all dates published in the journal, which is arranged by historic counties (*http://archaeologydataservice.ac.uk/archives/view/vag_dendro/*). There are five tree-ring dating laboratories and all have worked in Wales. The Oxford Dendrochronology Laboratory has done most work in Wales and maintains a website summarising their results (*http://www.oxford-dendrolab.com/dated_buildings_uk.asp*). The highly-regarded laboratory based at the Department of Archaeology in Lampeter has the advantage of being based in Wales.

Landscapes and Deserted Settlements

It is important to study a house in its landscape context. Fifty years after Hoskins published *The Making of the English Landscape*, the historic landscape is readily regarded as a primary historical resource with archaeological and architectural features, boundaries, and an inheritance of place-names that can be used to track the history of agriculture and settlement. Historical landscape studies have long roots in Wales. The earlier studies of tenure by A. N. Palmer and others are still useful but rather neglected. Much information about settlement and land use was depicted on William Rees' magnificent and rather maddening map of *South Wales and the border in the fourteenth century by William Rees* (1933). These map sheets are magnificent because Rees has plotted on the O.S. base map information derived from his first-hand trawl of primary sources in the Public Record Office, and they are maddening because references are not provided for the numerous annotations. Nevertheless, they provide an indispensable framework for the landscape researcher. One must also mention David Williams' *Atlas of Cistercian Lands in Wales* (1990) which plots and describes the extensive lands of the Welsh Cistercians and their granges.

Garden archaeology has been an exciting relatively recent development which links houses and landscapes. Elizabeth Whittle's *Historic Gardens of Wales* (1992) provides an all-Wales overview of parks and gardens but there are numerous studies of individual gardens and a few regional studies, notably Caroline Palmer's *Historic Parks and Gardens in Ceredigion* (2004). *Gerddi*, the Journal of the Welsh Historic Gardens Trust, is a guide to current research on gardens and designed landscape. Outstanding sites (about 400) are described in Cadw/ICOMOS's *Register of Parks and Gardens of Special Historic Interest* (six parts completed in 2002), but the dedicated garden historian will need to consult RCAHMW's online database Coflein, as well as the national database of parks, gardens, and designed green spaces in the UK, supported by the Heritage Lottery Fund and developed by the Parks and Gardens Data Partnership (*http://www.parksandgardens.org*).

There have been some recent brave attempts at 'landscape characterisation', in which the archaeologist or historical geographer draws out the distinctiveness and historical character of a region. In England this has resulted in eight very useful regional studies that make up the series *England's Landscape* published by Collins and English Heritage. Some have relevance for Welsh studies, including Della Hooke's *The West Midlands* (2006). In Wales a different course has been pursued. Here specific landscapes rather than regions have been selected for their historical and social interest. The results are rather tucked away in Cadw's 'Register of Landscapes of Historic Interest' (1998, 2001). Thirty-six landscapes of 'outstanding historic interest' have been designated as well as fifty-eight 'special historic landscapes'. This is a top-down exercise which is barely known outside professional bodies. The register entries are professional assessments of the historic landscape, and they are additionally useful because they provide a guide to the relevant literature including some case studies. These registers do not have any statutory force but they may inform the planning process. The register entries are brief but a few detailed landscape studies have emerged. Special mention must be made of Kenneth Murphy's *Upland Ceredigion: Historic Landscape Characterisation* (Archaeoleg

Tŷ-draw, Llanarmon, Mynydd Mawr: the cruck frame of a derelict house in Denbighshire, photograph taken in 2003
© Crown Copyright: RCAHMW

Cambria Archaeology Report 1999), and Stephen Rippon's *The Gwent Levels: the evolution of a wetland landscape* (1996).

Much archaeological effort has been expended recently in systematic archaeological survey of the Welsh uplands. This work has been sponsored by RCAHMW through the Uplands Initiative (*Menter yr Uwchdiroedd*) and the results are available on Coflein. The survey work is rapid but it is the first step in documenting the physical remains of settlement in the uplands. An overview of the project is provided by *The Archaeology of the Welsh Uplands* (RCAHMW, 2003). Most surveys remain unpublished; however, David Leighton's wide-ranging *The Western Brecon Beacons: The Archaeology of Mynydd Du and Fforest Fawr* (RCAHMW, 2012) and *Mynydd Hiraethog: The Denbigh Moors* (RCAHMW, 2011) by Robert J. Silvester *et al* have appeared.

Some thematic studies have emerged from uplands archaeology. The most significant is the study of deserted medieval settlements funded by Cadw and carried out by the four archaeological trusts. An overview of recent work has been edited by Kathryn Roberts, *Lost Farmsteads: deserted rural settlements in Wales* (CBA Research Report 148, 2006). The editor makes the point that much of upland Wales is characterised by abundant evidence for abandoned houses and farmsteads that show that areas now regarded as marginal once

235

supported many farms. The volume explores the evidence for deserted settlements region by region. An impressive number of platforms, longhouses, and long-huts have been identified from Glamorgan-Gwent, Gwynedd (624), Clwyd-Powys (1139), Dyfed (624), in addition to uncertain site types. General themes include problems of dating, definition and use, including transhumance. An interesting contribution by Bob Silvester analyses the 1587 Badminton estate maps for Crickhowell and Tretower and shows that over one-third of the known settlements in 1587 have disappeared without trace.

The deserted rural settlements project has accumulated much data but interpretation has lagged behind the accumulation of evidence. Archaeological exploration has been limited, and in some respects analysis has not greatly advanced since Lawrence Butler's account of 'The Study of Deserted Medieval Settlements in Wales (to 1968)' in *Deserted Medieval Villages*, edited by Maurice Beresford and John G. Hurst (1971). This has the merit of a gazetteer of selected sites and a select bibliography, which includes some useful case-studies. More case-studies of deserted settlement are needed which combine accurate survey with an analysis of the available documentation. In this respect, the Lampeter/RCAHMW study of Troedyrhiw, Ceredigion, is exemplary (by A. Fleming and Louise Barker in *Post Medieval Archaeology*, Vol. 42 (2008), pp. 261–90). The later-medieval settlement of several farms within a Cistercian grange includes a spectacular barn-like 'bercary' or sheepcote for the sheep of the grange, but the settlement has now been consolidated into a single farmstead.

Very occasionally circumstances allow a total record of a site which combines archaeological and architectural recording with tree-ring dating. The total record of Tyddyn Llwydion, a derelict upland house at Pennant Melangell, allowed the reconstruction of a peasant hallhouse which was built from timber felled in 1554. The absence of any sixteenth-century documentation for Tyddyn Llwydion serves to emphasize that in many cases a medieval house is the primary surviving historic record. Other higher-status medieval houses can be linked to documentary sources, although there are often sources (poetry and pedigrees) that do not have an exact counterpart outside Wales. The published total record of Tŷ-mawr, Castle Caereinion, a lavish timber hall of high status, tree-ring dated 1460, includes a reconstruction of the social context of the hall.[3]

Resources at the Royal Commission

Sooner or later the serious researcher will need to visit the Royal Commission's offices at Plas-crug. The NMRW is open on weekdays between 10.00 a.m.–4.30 p.m. Callers are advised to phone (01970 621200) or e-mail (*nmr.wales@rcahmw.gov.uk*) in advance of their visit. Expert staff will guide enquirers through the relevant sources.

Coflein

Preliminary searching of the Royal Commission's holdings can be made remotely through Coflein, the Royal Commission's online database. Coflein is essentially an index to RCAHMW's holdings. Coflein, like all databases, has its quirks. It is certainly not comprehensive but it is continually enhanced. It has the advantage of having a sophisticated map-based search system. Sites appear as red dots on an Ordnance Survey base map, and information spots indicated by 'pins' can be interrogated. Alternatively, text-based searches can be undertaken, although name searching can be problematic because of variant place-name spellings. Searching by kilometre square will however bring up all records within the area and relevant records can easily be identified. The text of the record will usually give a short description and list archival holdings. Again, it should be emphasised that the information on Coflein is not comprehensive; researchers will need to consult site files and other records that lie behind a database entry.

Site Files

The core collections are the site files arranged by OS quarter sheet (rather than parish) and divided into archaeological, domestic, defensive, and industrial sites. These site files contain an utter miscellany of information, sometimes tantalisingly short and sometimes almost overwhelmingly detailed. The fullest files are those which include the fieldwork for the Inventory volumes: Anglesey, Caernarvonshire, Glamorgan, Radnorshire. However, every county has useful files although the early parish files for Denbighshire and Flintshire have become separated from the main collections and are now in exile in Flintshire Record Office.

RCAHMW's archive is site-based rather than collection-based. In other words sites are assigned a NPRN (national site identifier number) and information is cross-referenced to the NPRN on Coflein from various collections. There is a guide to the National Monuments Record of Wales (1998) supplemented by Gareth Edwards' 'Highlights from the National Monuments Record' (*Archaeology in Wales* 45, 2005). The historic or special collections are surprisingly varied, and the following collections may be noted: a small collection of sale catalogues (derived from the National Society of Auctioneers), including some not available in the NLW; the Rev. Rokeby's albums of black and white photographs of railway stations and halts throughout Wales; the Gresham and Hemp parish files for Caernarfonshire and Merioneth; Arthur Chater's Cardiganshire photos which include black and white photographs of Cardiganshire buildings and other monuments, with an important sub-set on monumental inscriptions; the Vernon Hughes localities collection – an unlisted miscellany of guides, notes and press cuttings arranged according to towns and villages throughout Wales. There is an enormous collection of plans which are cross-referenced to sites on Coflein. In addition to RCAHMW's own drawings, the NMRW is fortunate to have the Welsh School of Architecture's project drawings of historic buildings. The Emergency Recording Collection is a continually growing series of plans as existing and other information relating to listed buildings which have been received by the Royal Commission because of its statutory role as consultee in applications for listed building consent that involve demolition.

There are historic photographs in abundance, many taken by professional photographers. The Royal Commission's centenary volume, *Hidden Histories* (RCAHMW, 2008) reproduced a good range of this illustrative material. A selection of photographs of interiors with commentary has been published as *Inside Welsh Homes: Y Tu Mewn i Gartrefi Cymru* (RCAHMW, 2012).

Ordnance Survey Maps
Those interested in the historic landscape will want to consult historic maps. The various editions of the Ordnance Survey six-inch and twenty-five inch county series maps can now be consulted online at the Royal Commission's offices. A guide to the different series and conventions of these maps is provided by J. B. Harley's *Ordnance Survey Maps: a Descriptive Manual* (1975). It should be noted that there seems to have been a progressive loss of information (place-names, minor features) in the various editions of the county series maps. Comparing different

editions of a map is an interesting exercise and can be done online. Special mention must be made of the Royal Commission's unique collection of 25" proof maps. These maps show the changes between first and second editions, with features omitted from the second edition outlined in blue. These engraved maps are a delight, printed on special paper, and signed by the surveyors who were often military men. There isn't complete coverage of Wales: maps relating to some counties (e.g. Montgomeryshire) have been destroyed. However, the collection includes some large-scale maps which were prepared for publication but were never issued, presumably because they covered tracts of uninhabited upland Wales.

Aerial Photography

Those studying the landscape will need to consult the Royal Commission's unique collection of aerial photographs. The Royal Commission is constantly adding to its collections through a flying programme. Several books have been published by the Royal Commission which are both an introduction to aerial photography and to historic landscape interpretation. In order of publication they are Chris Musson's *Wales from the Air* (1994) and *Snowdonia from the Air* (1996); Toby Driver's, *Pembrokeshire from the Air* (2007), and the large format *Historic Wales from the Air* (2012) by Toby Driver and Oliver Davis. These books explain the usefulness of aerial photographs for interpreting historic settlements.

The Royal Commission's collection of aerial photographs is arranged in five main groups and in combination covers most of Wales. A distinction is made between 'vertical' photographs (taken looking straight down from a survey aircraft) and 'oblique' photographs (taken looking out of a light aircraft). The vertical photographs are high-quality black-and-white prints which show large areas. The oblique photographs are low-altitude photographs showing sites in more detail.

There are five main collections:

1. Royal Air Force collection of vertical photographs, 1945–65 (170,000 6' x 6' prints).
2. The Ordnance Survey collection of vertical photographs, 1962 onwards. Some 84,000 9' x 9' prints.
3. Historic Collections, some specifically taken for archaeological

purposes, including the pioneering archaeological photography by Cambridge University.
4. Royal Commission's own oblique photographs of archaeological sites from 1986. These include many colour images.
5. The Aerofilms Historic Collection.

Special mention must be made of the Aerofilms Collection as a major visual resource that has only recently become publicly available. It was purchased by English Heritage in partnership with the Welsh and Scottish Royal Commissions. It is by far the best and most complete collection of commercial oblique aerial photography, with well over a million images, some reproduced as postcards and as illustrations for books and magazines, but mostly never published. The core of the collection is Aerofilms' own archive, but this archive eventually absorbed the smaller archives of some competitors. Its chronological and geographical coverage is superb, covering most communities in the British Isles (as well as parts of the Empire) for much of the twentieth century from the end of World War I to the end of the century. The emphasis is on landscape and settlements but some events are also covered (including, for example, great sporting events like the 1928 cup final). It is clear that the collection is an extraordinary visual record of the changing face of Britain. The prints and negatives are in process of conservation and will be steadily indexed. The aim is to have nearly 100,000 images online by 2014. At present the finding aids to the collection are a series of rather fragile print albums arranged topographically by place-name (mainly towns and villages) within the historic (pre-1974) counties. However these albums have prints of only a fraction of the estimated 80,000 negatives relating to Wales.

Appendix:

Nannerth-ganol: a case study[4]
NPRN 81416

The longhouse, combining dwelling and cowhouse in a single range, is often regarded as the quintessentially Welsh upland house. Iorwerth Peate coined the term 'longhouse' and he discovered Nannerth-ganol, near Rhayader, which still occupies a prominent place in the literature as a classic longhouse.

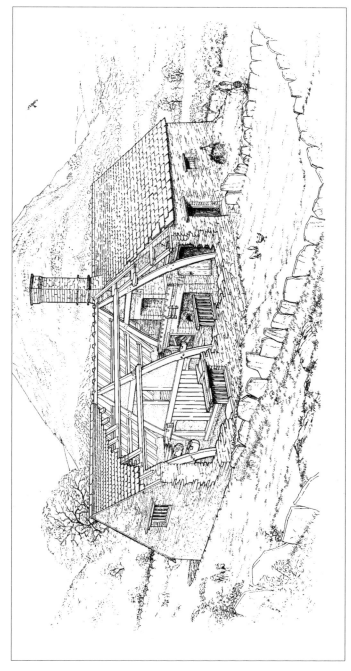

Cutaway drawing of Nannerth-ganol, Radnorshire, showing the cruck-trussed longhouse after the fireplace had been inserted in the late sixteenth century

© Crown Copyright: RCAHMW

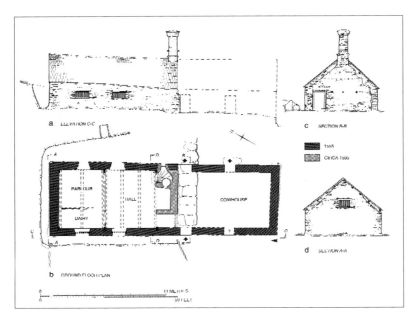

Reconstructed plan and elevations of Nannerth-ganol,
from Richard Suggett, Houses and History
in the March of Wales, Radnorshire, 1400–1800
© Crown Copyright: RCAHMW

The Royal Commission's survey of Radnorshire houses provided the opportunity to reassess the house and place it in its historical context. The cutaway drawing by Geoff Ward shows the essential features of the house. Nannerth-ganol was a substantial stone-built range with thick walls and an intercommunicating house and cowhouse that could be secured from the inside. The house is cruck-framed and these great arched timbers, still smoke-blackened in places, belong to the first building phase. Later, a fireplace was inserted against the cruck. The unusually tall and slender chimney expressed the pride of the owner of Nannerth-ganol in his new, heated house.

This homestead, it must be emphasised, was not a poor man's house. The builder of Nannerth-ganol could probably have afforded to build a house of a different type if he had wanted to. The longhouse needs to be understood in terms of its historical context, but who built it and when was it built?

Dendrochronology has now established that the timber used for the cruck-trusses was felled in the mid sixteenth century: building work was well under way in spring 1556, and a construction date towards the end of the sixteenth century would be reasonable for the inserted fireplace.

242

Documents show that Nannerth-ganol was held on a long lease by Bedo (or Maredudd) ap Steven whose sons were indicted in 1557 at the Radnorshire great sessions on three separate counts of cattle stealing: Thomas as principal and Edward as accessory. They failed to answer the charges and were outlawed. Both must have 'fled to the woods' and were able to return only when a general pardon was declared at the beginning of Elizabeth's reign. Nannerth-ganol was still a newly-built house when Thomas and Edward returned to plead their pardons and to be bailed for their future good behaviour.

Nannerth-ganol, before its restoration
© Crown Copyright: RCAHMW

It is extraordinary that these accusations of cattle theft should have coincided so closely with the construction of Nannerth-ganol. Cattle theft was a risky but obvious short cut to capital accumulation and it may be, of course, that it helped to finance the large, professionally-built house-and-byre homestead. The capacious and secure cowhouse of a longhouse might be used not only to safeguard cattle but also to conceal them. The exact circumstances at Nannerth-ganol are not recoverable but it is clear that the longhouse has to be understood

Nannerth-ganol, after its restoration
© Crown Copyright: RCAHMW

in part in relation to a pastoral economy in which cattle rustling was common.

Longhouses were the products of particular historical circumstances. They offered additional security for over-wintered stock in areas prone to livestock theft. Indictments for cattle theft actually increase during the second half of the sixteenth century, reaching a peak at the beginning of the seventeenth century. The house-and-byre homestead may be understood as a prudent response to these conditions.

NOTES

1 Now all the Royal Commission's out-of-print titles can be accessed via our website and viewed through Google Books. Most importantly, those published over fifty years ago are free to download, while those published later are available for purchase from Google Play.
2 Richard Suggett, 'Dendrochronology: Progress and Prospects' in C. Stephen Briggs (ed.), *Towards a Research Agenda for Welsh Archaeology* (2003), 153–69
3 W. J. Britnell and R. Suggett, 'A sixteenth-century peasant hallhouse in Powys: survey and excavation of Tyddyn Llwydion, Pennant Melangell, Montgomeryshire', *Archaeological Journal*, vol. 159 (2003); 'Ty-Mawr, Castle Caereinion', [a special volume of] *The Montgomeryshire Collections*, vol. 89 (2001)
4 Taken from RCAHMW's centenary volume *Hidden Histories* (2008). Further details in *Houses and History in the March of Wales: Radnorshire, 1400–1800* (RCAHMW, 2005)

17. Identifying Place-names in Historic Records

Richard Morgan

There can be very few historians who have not at some time been faced by difficulties in the correct identification of place-names, whether they are attempting to edit original manuscripts or simply collecting evidence. The importance of this can, of course, be critical to the reliability of any discussions and conclusions based on that work. Many historians – especially those who use early and medieval sources – will have encountered errors of identification in both printed and digitised texts and indexes. Unfamiliarity with a particular geographical area, together with differences between the spelling recorded in historical sources and those in modern sources of reference such as modern maps, can often prove troublesome for the historian. Making the link between these forms, and fixing on the correct identification, can prove to be a formidable challenge even to those with lengthy experience in historical research and writing.

In attempting to solve this problem, historians have traditionally relied on older histories and antiquarian compilations, directories, gazetteers such as that of the Ordnance Survey, and older historical maps. This task used to require frequent visits to reference libraries and archives repositories but the arrival of digital technology has greatly reduced our dependence on this manner of research. The Ordnance Survey website (*www.ordnancesurvey.co.uk/oswebsite*), for example, now possesses a searchable gazetteer with grid references, postcodes and modern locational maps covering the whole of the United Kingdom. Other gazetteers such as Bartholomew's 1887 and Goring's *Imperial Gazetteer 1870–2* are now accessible (*www.visionofbritain.org.uk*) and Mackenzie's *Comprehensive Gazetteer 1895* is at (*www.origins.net*), a subscription site. Traditional works of reference such as Samuel Lewis' *Topographical Dictionary* (fourth edition 1849) can be accessed at (*www.british-history.ac.uk/place*). These have been supplemented by the appearance of a number of out-of-date publications on CD and a rapid growth of online websites offering access, for example, to historical directories (notably that sponsored by the University of Leicester), maps (old and new), and rare out-of-print historical publications. Many can be identified simply through search engines such as Google. Some of these sources, such as the older editions of the Ordnance Survey maps and plans at (*www.old-maps.co.uk*), and the digital images of the Ordnance Survey two-inch scale drawings on the British Library website, are especially valuable. A critical look at a few of these websites appears at the end of this article.

If research has been eased, digital technology has not, by any means, solved all of the problems of identifying historical place-names; we still need to understand the nature of place-names and the way in which they were coined and developed if we are to avoid errors. A basic knowledge of the ways in which place-names might be rendered in manuscripts together with Welsh mutations can prove a useful aid in the analysis and identification of unfamiliar written forms. Older place-names were not, after all, fixed in print in the manner of modern place-names. That may not have been of critical importance in informal correspondence, for example, but it often posed great problems for anyone attempting to make a formal written record. The clerks and administrators who compiled such records – lists of manorial tenants with their rents and obligations, tax schedules, descriptions of property and boundary lines, estate surveys and maps, parish registers of baptisms, marriages and burials, and similar compilations – all had to attempt to render a particular place-name (or personal-name) in a form recognisable to both their contemporaries and successors. The fundamental difficulty was that early administrators worked without a comprehensively agreed orthography. Both written Welsh and English, and most languages in western and central Europe, are based on the Roman alphabet – one better suited to classical Latin than any other

Land Assessment Tax, Miskin Hundred, 1791 (LTA 5/17)
Courtesy of Glamorgan Archives
Note: A number of names in this document remind us of present-day place-names in the Rhondda Valley, such as Blaenclydach, Bodrhingallt, Gelli, Ystrad, Llwynypia, Nant-y-gwyddon and Pen-y-graig.

language. The alphabet lacked (and indeed still lacks) sufficient consonants and vowels to adequately represent the range of sounds of modern Welsh and English. The importance of acquiring a more consistent and flexible alphabet was not widely appreciated until the arrival of printing and, certainly in the case of English, there was little inclination to formalise and standardise received manuscript forms of both common words and proper names. The inadequacy of the Roman alphabet was partly compensated in some languages by the use of diacritical marks and signs to indicate, for example, the position of irregular stress and long vowels – as in modern Welsh Llandybïe, Llandygái, Caersŵs and Llandyfân – and especially by the use of digraphs, i.e. doubling certain letters to represent particular sounds. Welsh-speakers are all familiar with *ll* as in *llall* [ɬaɬ], *dd* [ð], *rh* and *vv*, *w* ('double-u') which were not employed in this way in classical Latin, but there were other ways in which these particular sounds might be represented in script; *ll* may appear as *lh*, *dd* as dh, δ or ∂, and *rh* as *rr*. Some of these inconsistencies survived down to the eighteenth century in the orthography of educated scholars such as Edward Lhuyd (1660?–1709) who himself used the additional forms *Llwyd* and *Lloyd* even for his own surname.

If Welsh clerks were inconsistent in their methods, then it is little wonder that English and Anglo-Norman clerks often floundered in attempting to render the unfamiliar sounds and stresses of Welsh in a form which was consistently recognisable for their own administrations. Their attempts to do so can vary considerably from one written source to another but may sometimes be predicted or 'decoded'; *llan*, for example, might also appear as *lan* or *thlan, ddu* as *thee* or *dee*, and *foel* as *voil* or *voyl*, and so forth. Irregularities often appeared when copies were made. Words might be misread, mistranslated, accidentally omitted or misdivided and then so irregularly written that the modern historian or editor will misread and misprint them yet again. One common example is where clerks or editors have mis-associated initial *De-* in place-names such as Defynnog and Degannwy with Latin and French *de* 'of, from' to produce forms such as *de Vennok* and *de Ganneu*. An indexer may record these names as *Vennok* and *Ganneu* without any attempt at identification or, worse still, misidentify them. Some letters or combinations of letters were especially prone to mistranscription and misreading, particularly *t* and *c*, long *s* and *f*, and the 'minims' *u, n, nn, m* and *mm*. Problems were often made worse when clerks used contracted or abbreviated forms, particularly when they were writing in Latin and English, often to save paper or parchment or speed their work. Particular sounds such as 'er' or 'ar' were often represented by loops extended over the top of preceding letters; a contracted form might be indicated by scribal marks such as a bar over an alphabetical letter; and an abbreviated form could be distinguished by a suspension mark, particularly an apostrophe. Llanfihangel, for example, might appear contracted as *Lañihangel* but *Card'* could represent some form of *Cardigan* or *Cardiff*. Anyone intent on understanding these historical sources has to be prepared to be aware of these practices.

Place-names which occur in isolation in original manuscripts can be especially difficult to identify but in the majority of historical documents there is generally some clue to geographical location. If the place-names are found, for example, among the records of a particular lordship, diocese or county, it is possible that they can be identified by comparing the order of their occurrence in the records with modern gazetteers or maps, particularly if one or more places is recognisable. A good example of this is *Llandethauk* recorded in 1353 as a rectory possessing a chapelry called *Pendyn*. The latter can be identified easily with Pendine, co. Carmarthen, which helps us to identify *Llandethauk* with Llandawke (Llan-dawg in its regular Welsh form), near Llanddowror, co. Carmarthen. Llandawke/Llan-dawg is simply a contracted form of an earlier Llandyddog or Llandyddawg, 'church of Tyddog *or* Tyddawg'. In this particular case, identification has not merely added to the historian's stockpile but helped explain the meaning of the actual place-name which had hitherto confounded expert analysis. Its next occurrence seems to be *Llandauke* in 1513 when the place-name had already contracted.

When a place-name occurs without such clues they can sometimes be identified by their chronological and general historical setting. Place-names in chronicles, can prove especially difficult in this respect. Several versions of the Welsh chronicles, for example, contain mentions of a castle (*Weidgrut, yr Wydgruc*) captured in 1263 by Gruffudd ap Gwenwynwyn (died 1286), a lord of Powys. The castle was once misidentified with Yr Wyddgrug (Mold), co. Flint, largely on the basis of the similarity of this place-name with Gwyddgrug. A closer look at its chronological sequence in the chronicles and contemporary documents, coupled with our knowledge of Gruffudd's uneasy relationship with his English neighbours in Shropshire at that period, helps us to identify it as a lost name for a ruinous castle at Nantcriba near Forden, two miles from the modern border between Wales and England. Yr Wyddgrug, co. Flint, itself was once interpreted by many prominent Welsh scholars as 'tomb mound' in reference to a cairn on top of the castle mound but it is best interpreted as 'high, prominent hill (or mound)' with gŵydd in the sense 'prominent', qualifying *crug*, duplicating the meaning of the French name *Monthaut*, 'high mound', which became modern *Mold*. The belief that Mold and *Yr Wyddgrug* meant much the same thing dates at least as far back as Nicholas Carlisle's *Topographical Dictionary* (1811) yet the close association between the names and castle mounds was overlooked by many later historians. There is another example of the name in Gwyddgrug (SN4635), Carmarthenshire, that possesses a small castle mound close to Castell farm.

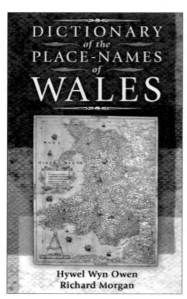

DICTIONARY
of the
PLACE-NAMES
of
WALES

Hywel Wyn Owen
Richard Morgan

Cover of Dictionary of the Place-names of Wales *(Hywel Wyn Owen and Richard Morgan (2008)*

Welsh historians who deal with early records will already be fully aware that their written sources are likely to be written not only in Welsh and English but also in other languages such as Latin and French. This has to be borne in mind whenever we attempt to make place-name identifications. Most of us are familiar with places which have Welsh and English names and, generally speaking, it is usually not too difficult to find them on modern maps, in histories and in place-name dictionaries such as the *Dictionary of the Place-names of Wales* (Llandysul, 2007). To take an example, all Welsh historians are likely to know that Tyddewi and St David's refer to the same place in Pembrokeshire but histories and dictionaries will also supply an earlier name *Mynyw*, with a latinised form Menevia, which do not survive as spoken forms but which occur frequently in historic manuscripts. Some of these dual place-names are relatively easy to identify in records when their variant forms are very similar, such as Beaumaris/*Biwmares*, derived from a French name meaning 'beautiful marsh', found latinised as *Bellus Mariscus*. Similarly, early recorded forms of Flint include the French form *Le Chaillou*, both names referring to the hard rock on which the medieval castle is constructed. Names like these can be found in modern histories but it is important to stress that sometimes historic forms can only be identified by personal research of original records and by questioning accepted opinion.

A good example of this is *Alretone*, recorded in the Shropshire part of Domesday Book 1086 in a large manor straddling the border between Wales and England. This was long misidentified with Cause, in Shropshire, which was the location of the main manorial castle, but a straightforward examination of the evidence shows that *Alretone* is identical in meaning to Trewern, in Montgomeryshire, a few miles away from Cause. The Domesday place-name consists of Old English *alra* and *tūn*, answering respectively to Welsh *gwern* and *tref*, both meaning 'farm or settlement near alder-trees', i.e. in a wet place where this particular species thrives. Various manuscript forms of *Alretone* survive down to the end of the thirteenth century but the name is now lost.

Not all dual place-names, however, will match each other in meaning; Northop ('north valley', etc), Flintshire, is *Llaneurgain* in Welsh, referring to the church dedication. Most intriguing are a small number of place-names such as Granston, Pembrokeshire, and Bonvilston, Glamorgan, which respectively bear the distinct Welsh place-names *Treopert* (*tref* and *Robert*) and *Tresimwn*, but referring, in all likelihood, to Robert le Grand and Simon de Bonville, their medieval tenants.

If scrutinising the documentary and geographical context fails to help with identification, then it may be worth looking at any recognisable elements within the place-name. The best glossaries are accessible in the *Dictionary of the Place-names of Wales* and B. G. Charles' *The Place-names of Pembrokeshire* (1992) with a useful discussion of topographical elements in D. Geraint Lewis' *Y Llyfr Enwau* (cited below). Until recent years, the study of place-names in Wales has lagged behind that in England, and has typically relied on uncoordinated specialist research, sometimes not easily accessible to

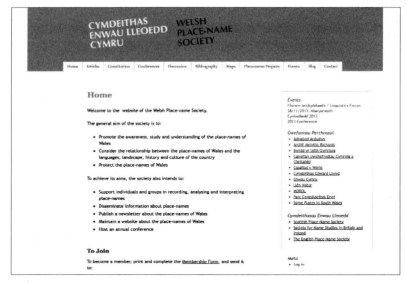

Website: Welsh Place-name Society

local historians, or written in technical language. Happily, the establishment of *Cymdeithas Enwau Lleoedd Cymru*/Welsh Place-name Society in 2011 is set to change matters (see below in 'Printed sources and websites') and will in due course assist non-specialists through its lectures and newsletter.

Most Welsh local and family historians will already be aware that English place-names are concentrated in south Pembrokeshire, Gower, the Vale of Glamorgan, along the border with England – especially in Flintshire, and in early boroughs established by Anglo-Normans but there are a few examples such as *Ferwig*, near Cardigan, and Newborough/*Niwbwrch*, Anglesey, in areas which were, and are, predominantly Welsh-speaking. Some Welsh and English words also have distinct geographical distributions. Welsh *ton* (unploughed land) is more common in south Wales, especially south-east Wales (Tongwynlais, Tonyrefail, and Tonypandy), while *pelan* (hillock) (Cwmbelan, Montgomeryshire) and *bod* are more common in north Wales (Bodedern, Anglesey; Botwnnog co. Caernarfon; and Bodelwyddan, Denbighshire). Similarly, Old English *hōc* (spit of land between streams) is more common in Pembrokeshire and *hop* (remote settlement in marshes or a valley) and (small valley) is more common along the border with England. Regional elements of this nature and dialectal variations in spelling are especially prominent in topographical and field-names. In north and mid Wales, for example, a 'hay meadow' may appear in written sources as *gweirglodd*, but in south-east Wales as *gweirlod*, *gwyrlod* and *gworlod*.

Persistence and experience will solve many problems encountered in place-name identification and will highlight the sorts of influences which the Welsh and English languages had upon each other. Welsh-speakers will easily recognise the relationship, for example, between names such as Glandŵr, Glamorgan, and its anglicised form, Landore, which derives directly from the mutated form *Landŵr* caused by prepositions such as *i* 'to' and *o* 'from'. Assimilation and re-interpretation are more difficult matters and often require extensive research and local knowledge. Mutated *glan*, as in Landore was notably prone to confusion with *llan*, hence Llanbradach (from *Glanbradach*), Glamorgan, but *llan* might also have displaced *nant* ('valley' or 'stream') as in Llancarfan (earlier *Nantcarfan* from its location next to a stream called Carfan), *llannerch* (Llanhedrick, in the former Welsh-speaking part of south-west Shropshire, with an Old English personal-name *Ēdred*), *llyn* (Pontllanfraith, Monmouthshire) and *llwyn* (Llanhaylow, Radnorshire, with a personal name *Hoedlyw*). Variations and irregularities of this nature are often dismissed as corruptions but are best regarded as re-interpretations. That is the proper way of explaining manuscript forms such as *Liveoaks* for Llwyfos, Monmouthshire; both names have meaning, even if this is properly a place where 'elm-trees' (*llwyf*) were abundant, not 'oak-trees'.

A few place-names generated an extraordinary variety of manuscript spellings, sometimes difficult to identify when they occur in isolation, and often bearing the marks of re-interpretation; Llan-y-bri, Carmarthenshire, for example, appears Latinised as *Moraburia* 1419, misinterpreted as *ll. fair y byri* c.1566 (as if it contained Llanfair, 'church of Mary'), and anglicised as *Morbulchurch* 1567, *Morbichurche* 1586, *Marblechurche* 1602, *Marble Church otherwise Lanibree* 1716, *Llan y Bri* 1753, and *Llan-y-bre* 1831. The place-name translates as 'church of (man called) Morbri' but there is an obvious misassociation here with English 'marble'. Confusions of this nature are generally associated with English influence but the opposite is also fairly common; many place-names along the border such as Gwersyllt

(?'Wērsige's hill' probably containing an Old English personal-name and *hyll*), co. Denbigh, and Prestatyn ('farm of the priests'), co. Flint, are of English origin despite their Welsh appearance. There are examples, too, of Welsh-language place-names which have been changed in this way by *Welsh*-speakers; Llanfihangel Orarth, with a personal-name Orarth, is now Llanfihangel-ar-arth as if were a 'church of St Michael on a ridge', and Pontardulais, cos. Carmarthen and Glamorgan, is now formalised as Pontarddulais though it has been shown that it is in origin a contracted form of *Pontaberdulais*, 'bridge near mouth of the river Dulais'. Llanvetherine, a village and parish in co. Monmouth, appears in Welsh gazetteers in the standard spelling Llanwytherin, 'church of (man called) Gwytherin', but this form can almost be regarded as an affectation since a number of historic forms such as *Lanvetherin* 1348 and *ll. fetherin* c.1590–1 (in a Welsh-language source), suggest that it had developed into *Llanfetherin*; there was, in addition, a local dialect form *Llanafferin(g)* or *Llanyfferin(g)* recorded in the sixteenth century.

Printed sources and websites

All guides and sources of reference have their weaknesses and most deal with modern forms rather than historic forms and are, generally speaking, of more value to the geographer than the historian. Many too are Anglocentric and make little allowance for the Welsh language which is central to the task of correctly identifying historic place-names in Wales. Some older printed sources will remain important for the foreseeable future; the most notable are Melville Richards's, *Welsh Administrative and Territorial Units* (1969) and Elwyn Davies' *Rhestr o enwau lleoedd* (Caerdydd 1967; reprinted in paperback in 1996). Richards' list is particularly valuable because it relates place-names to ancient and modern pre-1974 administrative divisions, although he sometimes made too little allowance for the need to cross-refer modern forms in widespread use with what he regarded (nearly always correctly) as the proper standard Welsh form. Whatever one might think of the merits of forms such as Kerry (for Ceri or Llanfihangel-yng-Ngheri), Montgomeryshire, and Llantilio Pertholey (for Llandeilo Bertholau), Monmouthshire, these forms can prove useful to those attempting to identify place-name forms in historic records and because they are still current on Ordnance Survey maps. Much of *Welsh*

Administrative and Territorial Units has now been superseded by D. Geraint Lewis' *Y Llyfr Enwau. Enwau'r Wlad. A check-list of Welsh place-names* (Llandysul 2007). Lewis gives priority to 'orthographically accepted' forms of Welsh names which means that the main body of the text has no entries for non-Welsh and anglicised names such as Buckley, Haverfordwest, Holyhead, Lisvane and Ilston. These are identified by way of an index cross-referring them to Bwcle, Hwlffordd, Caergybi, Llys-faen and Llanilltud Gŵyr – not to everyone's satisfaction if they are writing in English – but Lewis makes up for this by including topographical names, Ordnance Survey grid references, short translations of individual names, and maps of administrative divisions. There are inevitably a few errors in a work of this scale and some places are unfortunately missing; readers will find no mention of the historic parishes of Hyssington in Montgomeryshire, Caldicot and Hadnock in Monmouthshire, and the old civil parish of Bettisfield (either in its English form or Welsh form Llysbedydd), Flintshire.

The greatest weakness of *Welsh Administrative and Territorial Units* is that Richards related many place-names to civil parishes (abolished in 1974) rather than historic parishes whose boundaries were often different. He also omitted the National Grid references recorded by Elwyn Davies. Some early printings of Ordnance Survey maps show parish boundaries but they were omitted from the facsimiles of the first series of the one-inch scale maps published by David and Charles and digitised in *Vision of Britain*. Thankfully, this problem has now been overcome by the online six-inch scale maps Ordnance Survey maps (first edition c.1880) reproduced on *www.old-maps.co.uk*, and by *Historic Parishes of England and Wales. An Electronic Map of Boundaries before 1850* by Roger J.P. Kain and Richard R. Oliver (Colchester History Data Service 2001), published with two CDs and a gazetteer. The Kain and Oliver CDs are especially valuable since they provide images of the one-inch scale Ordnance Survey maps printed in the 1940s on which the ancient parish boundaries can be shown or removed by computer key.

Electronic reproductions of maps are not only important guides in the identification of place-names but an historical resource in their own right. Undoubtedly, the most valuable are the coloured, two-inch scale facsimiles of the original Ordnance Survey field sketches produced in the early nineteenth century during surveying for the first edition one-inch scale maps. These are accessible at *www.collectbritain.co.uk/ collections* on The British Library website 'Collect Britain. View whole collection' file. Facsimiles of the sketches were once accessible only at major libraries and some archives repositories but the online sketches have facilities for zoom and printing which could previously only be obtained by photography. The drawings were difficult to use when they first appeared online in 2007 because some possess odd descriptions such as 'Baulit' for Builth. On many drawings too, 'north' is not always at the top of the sheet and they frequently cover very irregular areas defined by the original map surveyors – often areas between large rivers and major highways – rather than the old County and later National Grid grid patterns seen in Ordnance Survey maps and plans. These problems have now been resolved by geo-referencing, i.e. making digital links between locations on the drawings and modern maps; by the addition of a compass wheel (which can be turned on screen); and by a facility enabling imposition of the sketch on Google Earth. The detail of some place-names is occasionally obscured by the use of hachuring and colour wash (used to indicate the shape of the landscape) and by the poor physical condition of some of the sketches – very evident, for example, in that for 'Caernarvon'. Fortunately, these problems can usually be overcome by using the zoom facility. Spellings of place-names on the original sketches are often irregular as one would expect for the period when they were produced. Evidently more work needs to be done on the 'search facility'. In order to identify the relevant drawings for Llanelli and Conwy, for example, one has to search under the obsolete forms 'Llanelly' and 'Conway'.

Richards' outstanding legacy – and one invaluable in the identification of place-names – is his place-name archive, Cronfa Ddata Enwau Lleoedd Archif Melville Richards, Canolfan Bedwyr, University of Wales Bangor, now online (*bangor.ac.uk/amr*) and (*www.e-gymraeg.org/enwaucymru/chwilio*) which can be searched by head-name, parish, form, date, county and source. As the introduction to the website stresses, Richards' archive was 'never intended to be an exhaustive collection of the place-names of Wales' but it remains the single, most important source for Welsh place-name history. Richards, however, died in 1973 and his archive is in need of extension to include the very large number of printed and archival sources which have appeared since that time. A few problems can occasionally make place-name identification on the website difficult. A search for obsolete historic forms such as *Pola, Marblechurch* (mentioned above) and *Newbridge*, Glamorgan, will not produce any references to Welshpool, Llan-y-bri and Pontypridd; there are also some odd omissions such as Glynogwr (which has displaced Llandyfodwg misspelt 'Llandyfedwg'), Glamorgan; and, inevitably, recent coinages such as Cil-y-coed (for Caldicot, Monmouthshire) which have no historic base. One of the greatest weaknesses is the absence of cross-referencing, such as Porthaethwy with Menai Bridge, Anglesey.

Printed publications which have appeared before and after 1973 are best identified through online indexes of major local libraries, university libraries, and the National Library of Wales, Aberystwyth, but a number of useful websites providing bibliographies can be found on the internet such as (*www.earlymodernweb.org.uk/embiblios/emwales.bib.htm*). Archival collections in Wales held in the National Library of Wales and local archives repositories are best identified at collection level from *www.archivesnetworkwales.org.uk* – a bilingual site – and by way of individual repositories. Most new archival accessions now appear on this database and older accessions are gradually being added. Many of the original catalogues to Welsh archives collections in the National Library of Wales (*www.llgc.org.uk*) before 1999 are accessible online. Local archives repositories are rapidly digitising their older lists for online access. University holdings are best searched through *archiveshub.ac.uk* and their individual websites.

The proliferation of historical websites on the internet is legion and it is no exaggeration to state that 'definitive' lists are obsolete almost as soon as they are completed. Useful updates of websites can, however, be found in *The Local Historian* or simply by keeping a careful eye on media news. Some of the flaws evident in printed sources are, unfortunately, repeated in some historical and geographical databases and websites. Their reliability is very variable but their greatest advantage over printed sources is that they can be corrected and expanded with relatively few problems. All of the websites need to be used critically but the most reliable sites are those established by universities, most historical societies, major libraries and archives repositories. The following list makes no pretence of being exhaustive:

www.visionofbritain.org.uk

The website of the Great Britain Historical Geographical Information System (GBHGIS) developed by the University of Portsmouth and funded by the National Lottery. The site was originally focused on historical statistics but is now constructing a descriptive gazetteer incorporating Melville Richards' *Welsh Administrative and Territorial Units* (1969), Bartholomew's *Gazetteer of the British Isles* (Edinburgh 1887), and Goring's *Imperial Gazetteer of England and Wales* (1870-2), together with transcripts taken from William Camden's *Vision of Britain* 1610, Daniel Defoe's *Tour* 1724-7, George Borrow's *Wild Wales* 1862, and Gerald of Wales.

http://homepage.ntlworld.com/geogdata/ngw/

The National Gazetteer of Wales (last updated in 2001) comprises lists of place-names, national grid reference, local authority area, and alternative versions of place-names 'commonly encountered since the start of the twentieth century'. The gazetteer is particularly useful to anyone who has identified a particular place-name and wishes to cross-refer it to modern administrative divisions. Some errors are perpetuated: Newbridge (= *Trecelyn*), Monmouth, is given the Welsh form '*Cefn Bychan*' (following the Ordnance Survey) which properly applies to Newbridge (*Cefnbychan*) near Wrexham, Denbighshire; and Fonmon, co. Glamorgan, is given the Welsh form *Ffon-mon*, when historical sources favour *Ffwn-mwn, Ffwl-mwn* and *Ffwl-y-mwn*.

www.gazetteer.co.uk

Established by the Association of British Counties and advertised as an 'exhaustive Place Name Index to Great Britain' includes 'Notes for Historians and Genealogists' containing useful advice on the definition of modern administrative areas and the identification of Welsh counties since 1536. The gazetteer does, however, have omissions such as Llanerch Banna (= Penley), Flintshire, and has a small number of spelling errors such as 'Abergwyngiegyn' for Abergwyngregyn, Caernarfonshire. Its greatest weakness is that it has not attempted to link standard Welsh and English names.

www.historicaldirectories.org.uk

'A digital library of local and trade directories for England and Wales from 1750 to 1919' established by the University of Leicester. The database can be searched and although the information contained in it is of primary interest to family and modern historians, it is valuable for its local content to all historians.

www.genuki.org.uk

This includes 'county pages' and possesses a searchable database of places in the 1891 census. It is based on Tallis' *Topographical Dictionary of England and Wales* (with county maps) 1860, transcripts of gazetteers, the Ordnance Survey Landranger maps, 1891 census, and the National Gazetteer of Wales. This omits many Welsh forms and fails to identify many places such as Bodaeoch, Montgomeryshire, Cenol, Breconshire; Clegyrog, Anglesey; and Cil-march, Carmarthenshire, easily identifiable in *Welsh Administrative and Territorial Units*.

www.ancestry.co.uk and *www.findmypast.co.uk*

These sites contain huge databases and indexes which draw on a wide range of historic sources such as indexes of births, marriages and deaths, wills and census returns in the United Kingdom and worldwide. The databases are primarily used by family historians and modern social historians but are indispensable to anyone studying modern place-names, such as the numerous new names which appeared in Welsh industrial areas in the nineteenth century. Data is accessible from both sites by subscription. Welsh libraries and archives repositories generally offer free access to one or both of these.

www.digital.documents.co.uk

The website of Archaeology UK (described as 'used by Field Archaeologists and Family Historians') which contains an archaeological sites index. Of particular value is the 'UK Placename Finder' file (/archi/placename) which can be searched by place-name element and by combinations of letters. This is of potential value to the historian attempting to identify places in original manuscripts of which only fragments of words may be confidently read. This file provides a four-figure grid reference and free links to modern street maps and aerial photographs. The website also has a geo-referenced database, accessible by payment, which links individual place-names to the National Grid and Ordnance Survey 'eastings' and 'northings'. Precise information on archaeological sites has to be purchased by subscription.

www.wales.ac.uk/en/CentreforAdvancedWelshCelticStudies
The website of the Centre for Advanced Welsh and Celtic Studies, National Library of Wales, Aberystwyth. The centre has engaged a leading place-names scholar to plan and attract funding for a major research project on the place-names of Wales, and is assembling an electronic guide to existing research and resources.

www.cymdeithasenwaulleoeddcymru.org
The website of Cymdeithas Enwau Lleoedd Cymru/Welsh Place-name Society. The society's primary aim is to further the study of place-names in Wales through its conferences and newsletter but also provides a useful link with other websites and organisations with related interests, reading lists, discussion groups, and local projects.

www.snsbi.org.uk
The website of the Society for Name Studies in Britain and Ireland, with the primary aim of furthering the study of place-names and personal-names. Its newsletter contains regular notices of publications, current research and related websites.

18. Folk Poetry as a Source for Local Historians

Tegwyn Jones

Although the balladmongers, the writers of '*tribannu*' (triplets) and other varieties of folk poetry were not in the business of providing convenient sources for students of local and social history, nevertheless their copious outpourings serve as a mine of information that we may well take advantage of today. It has been fashionable among literary critics to maintain that the material produced by these rhymesters has but little literary merit, street ballads especially, and that any value that may attach to them lies in whatever light they may throw on the everyday life and social customs of their day. This, however, is not the entire truth, but this is the aspect that will be explored in the following observations.

Of the various forms of folk verse that exist, street ballads are almost certainly amongst the most common, and the richest for those who seek to trace the history of their area and family, particularly with regard to the eighteenth and nineteenth centuries. Collections of such ballads, varying in number and importance, are to be found in several public institutions in Wales – and at least one in London. But the principal venue to aim for by any researcher in this field is the National Library of Wales at Aberystwyth, home not only to its own large collection, but also copies on film of important collections elsewhere, especially that of

Cover of Tegwyn Jones, Abel Jones, Bardd Crwst *(1989) and cover of Tegwyn Jones,* Hen Faledi Ffair *[Old Fair Ballads] (1970)*

the Library of the University of Bangor. There is a database of the nineteenth-century ballads in the National Library which facilitates access to their contents.

After Thomas Jones the Almanacker, a native of Corwen in Meirioneth, had moved his printing press from London to Shrewsbury in 1695, to be followed shortly to that town by a number of other printers, it became clear that there was a considerable demand in Wales for reading material of all kinds, and the most popular medium for disseminating such material were ballad sheets. They were sung and sold in fairs and markets – indeed anywhere in fact where people gathered together – and their contents reflected all life's situations and experiences. While the poets of the eighteenth century strove to re-establish the classical tradition, and the poets of the following century sought eisteddfodic glory, the ballad authors and singers (not necessarily the same people) were pleased to provide material about the real world around them, much of it based on their own experiences. The title, or prose introduction – sometimes of great length – at the beginning of the ballad, is frequently rich in place and personal names, and can easily be the starting point for the history of a parish or a particular person.

It would be impossible in a short article such as this to encompass

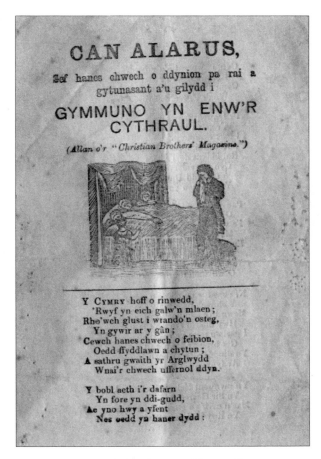

CAN ALARUS,

Sef hanes chwech o ddynion pa rai a gytunasant a'u gilydd i

GYMMUNO YN ENW'R CYTHRAUL.

(*Allan o'r "Christian Brothers' Magazine."*)

Y CYMRY hoff o rinwedd,
'Rwyf yn eich galw'n mlaen ;
Rhe'wch glust i wrando'n osteg,
Yn gywir ar y gân ;
Cewch hanes chwech o feibion,
Oedd ffyddlawn a chytun ;
A sathru gwaith yr Arglwydd
W nai'r chwech uffernol ddyn.

Y bobl aeth i'r dafarn
Yn fore yn ddi-gudd,
Ac yno hwy a yfent
Nes oedd yn haner dydd :

Cân Alarus *[Mournful Song]*

the varied topics that are touched on in the ballads. Foreign wars are mentioned, together with the county militias who went to fight in them. Skirmishes and local disturbances, such as those associated with the Merthyr Riots of 1831, and the Rebecca Riots and the Chartists in the 1840s, are recorded by the balladists, as well as floods, storms, shipwrecks, drought and destructive fires. Industrial accidents in coalmines and quarries figure large, as do more domestic occurances. The coming of the railways is celebrated, and the beginnings of human cremation is recorded. All of which are peppered with place and personal names. Here one can but seek to draw attention to a few topics

Cân Newydd ... *[New song of a conversation between a man and a woman]*

only, in the hope that this will emphasize the importance of this particular source.

A topic that appealed greatly to ballad writers and singers was murder, which usually assured them of good sales. As the nineteenth century progressed, it became possible to read more about events such as murder in newspapers and in the news columns to be found in the denominational journals, but before their day the ordinary folk of town and country relied upon the balladeer for all the gory details, and he would not be slow in meeting the demand. Many murders committed in Wales in the eighteenth century would have been long forgotten had they not been recorded in contemporary ballads. Two examples of such ballads are number 433 and 535 in *A Bibliography of Welsh Ballads* published between 1908 and 1911 by J. H. Davies. The former records the murder of Mary Lloyd by John Benjamin in Llangeitho, Ceredigion, in April 1792, and how the murderer was hanged and his severed head paraded on a stake through the streets of Cardigan where the execution took place; and the latter tells the tale of the murder of Humphrey Jenkins in 1772 by a manservant and two female servants at Nantstalwyn, a remote farm in Breconshire. The life of one of the maidservants was spared when she agreed to testify against the other two. The manservant managed to make his escape, but the remaining maidservant was burnt at the stake near the town of Brecon. These are examples of ballads which record two occurences that could be profitably researched in the Court of Great Sessions records in the National Library, where possibly one could find the names of witnesses together with their evidence, which in turn would throw light on the everyday life on a lonely, isolated farm in the mountains of Breconshire, or in a rural village in Ceredigion. It is well to remember also that the offence did not necessarily have to be as serious as murder to merit being brought before that court. A ballad about a thief sentenced to be transported could also have background knowledge in the records pertaining to it.

Another abundant body of ballads is that which records the vast number of coal-pit disasters which occurred during the eighteenth century and particularly during the following century. The earliest of these is of an accident that occurred in 1758 at the Wern-fraith colliery in the parish of Llangatwg near Neath where seventeen men and boys perished. It was penned by Ben Simon of Abergwili, a diligent and important transcriber of manuscripts, who wrote, among other things, an eulogy on the death of the renowned educational reformer, Griffith Jones of Llanddowror. Not being a native of the area where the accident occurred, he tells his audience how he went about gathering the information and details that he required. Just like a newspaper reporter of today he went to interview the landlord of the *Bull* at Neath, who himself had lost a brother in the accident:

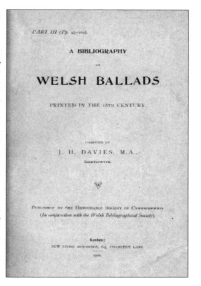

Title page, J. H. Davies,
A Bibliography of Welsh
Ballads, Part III (*1910*)

> *Dymma'r hanes fel y cefais,*
> *Pan y Cenais hyn ar goedd,*
> *Oddiwrth Forgan Harri gwiwlan,*
> *A fu'n datgan fel yr oedd.*
> *Yn Llun y Tarw or Hewl newydd,*
> *Yngwych gaerydd Castell Nedd,*
> *Brawd i'r cynta Enwais yma,*
> *Lle roedd Cyrchfa rhai Sy'w Bedd.*

[Here is the story as I was given it and as I have sung it publicly, by Morgan Harri who related things as they happened. This at the Sign of the Bull in the new Road within the bounds of Neath, a brother of the first that I name here, [and landlord] of the haunt of some who are now in their graves.]

This tavern, to many of those who died was their usual meeting place, and the result is an important ballad from the point of view of local knowledge, and that in a period when to follow the story in a local newspaper would not have been possible.

As well as the 'professional' ballad singers such as Ywain Meirion, Richard Williams (*Dic Dywyll*, 'Blind Dick'), Levi Gibbon, Dafydd Jones, Llanybydder, Abel Jones (*Bardd Crwst*), and many others in the nineteenth century who would garner some of their information from newspaper reports, other more local rhymesters would compose their ballads without having recourse to such a source, but offering eyewitness evidence instead. One of these was Archibald Skym, Dyffryn, who wrote of an accident in his locality of Pontyberem in 1852 when twenty-six miners were drowned. An intinerant ballad singer and seller could hardly be expected in a case such as this to name each and every one of those who died, but this is what Skym did, together with details that could be of importance to anyone researching his family tree in this particular part of the country:

> *Roedd John mab David Harry lon*
> *A'i frawd bach Davi,*
> *Oedd gynne'n gwenu*
> *Ond nawr yn tewi.*

[There was John son of David Harry / And his little brother Davy, / Who a while ago was smiling / But is now silent.]

A similar local note is struck in a ballad by William Jones, Cerrigllwydion, about the death of 12 men in 1852 following an explosion in a coal pit in Port Talbot. He also lists them by name – possibly men well known to him – occasionally adding the name of an abode:

> *Yn eu plith roedd Walter Morgan,*
> *Hopkin William Tylefedwan.*

[Among them were Walter Morgan, / Hopkin William of Tylefedwan]

As well as the 'professional' ballad singers therefore, who turned these sad events into a source of meagre income, there were others who derived their information from the horse's mouth, so to speak, who recorded their reactions in doggerel which was then published in pamphlet form. Further information that may be garnered and which should interest the historian is the fact that the proceeds in such cases would not of necessity be pocketed by the author. Following a major pit disaster in Aber-carn, Gwent in 1878, the *South Wales Daily News* referred to a 'local poet', Edward Jones, who had written a poem about the event (more than likely a leaflet ballad) which was now being printed, it is reported, 'and will be sold for the benefit of the sufferers, as well as the widows and orphans of the killed'. Between the lines, as it were, it is possible occasionally to catch a glimpse of the customs associated with coalfield tragedies, as for example the suspension of work in other pits of the area, so that the miners there could help in the rescue work.

As to customs, the ballads are a rich depository of information pertaining to these, which in turn throw a valuable light on the everyday life of the Welsh rural society in the eighteenth and nineteenth centuries. Women, according to the ballads again, would enjoy nothing more than to gather together of an afternoon to drink tea and to put the world to right. Occasionally something stronger would be added to the tea – usually brandy – and the conversation would proceed at an even livelier pace. One balladeer at least, evesdropped – so he maintains – on the conversation at one of these meetings, and found that the topic under discussion was how these ladies could purchase various items of clothing and headgear unbeknown to their husbands. Is there not useful information in lines such as these?

> *Pan fo arnoch chwi neu finne*
> *Eisie Pâr o Gappie gore:*
> *Rhaid cael hanner Llath o Fyslin,*
> *A phedwar Swllt yw'r Pris cyffredin.*
> *Am Gadach gwyn rhoi Coron Arian,*
> *A chwe Swllt am Gadach Sidan;*
> *Sei'swllt rhwng yr Hwd a'r Cnottyn,*
> *Saith a chwech yr Het a'r Trimmin;*
> *Ac ni wisgir wedi hynny,*

Ond o'r Ysgwydd ar i fyny,
Fe wyr pawb a deimlo ronyn
Mai Darn go fach yw hyn o'r Corphyn.

[When you or I require a pair of best caps, half a yard of muslin is required, usually costing four shillings. For a white kerchief, a silver crown, and six shillings for a silk kerchief: Seven shillings for the hood and knot, seven shillings and sixpence for the hat and trimmings; and that dresses only from the shoulder up, Anyone who knows anything will be aware that this is only a small part of the body].

In the occasional ballad there will be a brief portrait of a worker or craftsman at his task, and although these were usually named persons, their likes were to be found in every rural village and parish throughout Wales. One Richard Parry (bardic name '*Athroysgol*' ('Schoolteacher')) in a ballad of his, praised Edward Jones of Hollywell, a castrator or gelder of renown:

Ni bydd niwed ar yr un a dorro,
A ddel yn ddilys dan ei ddwylo,
Cweiriwr Cyffyle gore sy' i'w gael,
Mae'r gair iddo'n bendant er moliant a mael.

[There will be no damage to the one brought to be gelded by him. The finest gelder of a horse available, that is the reputation which he certainly has, for which let him be praised.]

When not actually pursuing his activity as a gelder, he and his friend Robert Roberts had a fine reputation as sawyers as well:

Yn Llifio Coed mawrion yn burion eu bri,
Ni bu'n ddiball wyllys moi gwell ar Bwll-lli,
Yn rhwugo mwy rhagor na nemmor mor fflwch,
Frathiadau drwy Geingciau yn drecha ymhob trwch,
Pob Scwinsin a Gwnin fel rhiddin dâ i raen,
Y Derw Côch cadarn a blygan o'u blaen.

[For sawing timber in a saw-pit they could never be bettered.

Ripping and biting abundantly through branches however thick, always having the upper hand. Timber of every description, even the Scarlet Oak, gives way before them.]

A valuable member of the rural society in the eighteenth century and following centuries – and no doubt before that as well – was the female 'doctor' or healer with her knowledge of all kinds of beneficial plants and roots. One of these was the wife of a Richard Parry (we are not given her Christian name) of Tal-y-bont near Caernarfon, who was lamented in a ballad by the renowned Ellis Roberts (Elis y Cowper, Ellis the Cooper):

> *Meddyges gynfforddus ir clwyfus a'r cla'*
> *P'le gwelir un 'rawron mor dirion a da?*
> *Mae colled am dani i dylodi drwy'r wlad*
> *Un rwydded yn rhoddi 'Luseni e'r lleshad.*

[A capable doctor for the wounded and the sick, where shall we now find her equal? Her loss is felt by the poor far and wide, one who dispensed her charity so freely for the common good.]

She is described as one who provided medicine and salve to the poor and needy. Indeed, says the author, 'many were the personal favours I received'. The evidence for the existence of such women is scanty, and to have a whole ballad dedicated to one of them is of some importance.

A well-known character to be found at a fair or market, as mentioned earlier, was the ballad-singer himself (and sometimes herself), and it is not difficult to imagine the hardship that his or her itinerant life-style involved. Some among them were blind, others lame or semi-crippled, who traversed the rough roads and tracks of the countryside, often in the depth of winter, as they sought to eke out a living. But that was not all, as a ballad seller called William Jones tells us in a ballad he wrote after attending a fair in Wrexham. There, being engaged in his work, he was set upon by two youths whose intention was, he says 'to hinder my market':

> *Ar Ffair Fawrth Dudd Mercher, ar ol haner mi ai henwae,*
> *Daeth ataf wrth ein Dydd, dau leidr Baladae,*
> *Ond Drwg oedd i buchedd, Rhoi Tar ar fy mochae*

Da heudde'r Ddau gostog gael drwg am i castie.
Mae yma ryw rocsiach, ar gyfer Tref Wrexham
Yn llawn o genfigen, a gwenwyn a fagan.

[On the Tuesday of the March Fair, after mid-day there came to me in broad daylight two ballad thieves, whose conduct was bad, they put tar on my cheeks. The two churls deserve punishment for that cast. There are some dregs around the town of Wrexham, full of jealousy, breeding malice.]

Was it only in Wrexham that such violent youths were to be encountered, or was this baiting of ballad sellers something that was witnessed from time to time in other localities? It is a dark picture that is drawn by Thomas Evans of Cefn-y-coed, near Merthyr, of the goings on in the fairs and markets of Wales, in a ballad he published on the subject around 1780. He is highly critical of all those who attend such gatherings, maintaining that deceit and lies rule the roost there:

Ar ddyddiau ffair a marchnad ein bwriad fydd yn llawn
I ddala ar bob nwyfe rhyw brisiau uchel iawn;
A chanmol 'nifel 'nafus wrth ystlys clawdd neu berth,
Nes twyllo'r prynwr mwynlan roi arian mwy na'i werth.

[On market days and fair days our intention will be to extract very high prices for all our wares; And to praise an unsound animal beside some bank or hedge, so that the innocent buyer parts with more money than the animal is worth.]

This is a valuable ballad, full of information as to the customs associated with buying and selling in these important centres of trading in villages and towns throughout Wales.

As in the case of the ballads, hundreds of which were published between the beginning of the nineteenth century and the beginning of the twentieth, valuable material for the local and social historian is to be found also in other forms of the common muse. The four line Glamorgan Triplets (*Tribannau Morgannwg*) are a particularly fruitful source of information to anyone interested in the history of that part of south Wales, while the wealth of '*penillion telyn*' (individual verses sung to a harp accompaniment), and other rustic verses of all kinds, are replete with references to places and to people, many of the latter being named and described as they plied a trade or followed a hobby:

> Sal Timoth am chwedleua,
> Siôn Brydydd am bysgota,
> A Nani'r 'Stag' am gadw stŵr,
> Dai'r hatwr am ffureta.

> [Sal Timoth for gossiping, Siôn the Poet for fishing, And Nancy of the 'Stag' for causing a disturbance, Dai the Hatter for ferreting.]

A ballad referred to above has the author lamenting the passing of a female herbalist, and the fact that many 'tribannau' also refer to similar characters emphasises their importance in a society where no doctor was available, or his services expensive:

> Bûm droeon yn fy ngwely
> Yn fawr fy mhoen a'm cyni,
> Rwy'n credu'n wir mai marw wnawn
> Onibai am ddawn merch Pegi.

> [I have been often in my bed in great pain and distress, Indeed I beleive I would have died were it not for the skills of Peggy's daughter.]

This particular woman tended to the needs of the sick and infirm in the *Rhydri* (Rudrey) area of Cardiff. Another of her kind who is similarly praised in verse came from Pen-coed near Bridgend, and this time we have her name in full:

> Er cymaint oedd fy mhoena
> A cholli cwsg wythnosa,
> Anghofia'i byth mai Mari Tarr
> Rodd eli ar 'y nghlwyfa.

> Gan ddirwyn yn ddiachwyn
> Bob nos at dân y gegin

I wella'r po'n â'i bysedd chwim
Heb ofyn dim yn echwyn.

[In spite of all my pains, and weeks-long loss of sleep, I will never forget that it was Mary Tarr who applied balm to my wounds. Without complaint she would come each night to the kitchen fire, to relieve the pain with her busy fingers, and asking for nothing in return.]

Interesting facts may be gleaned from these *'tribannau'* about ploughmen and their oxen, about reapers of hay and corn − often by name − in a period when their craftsmanship was much admired, and when there was a substantial demand for their labours in the Glamorgan valleys before industrialization arrived. It was not always that these workmen were best pleased by the fare set before them by a farmer's wife. A well-known composer of *'tribannau'*, Tomos Hywel Llywelyn, after he had partaken of a watery broth set before him at Cwmsaerbren Farm in the Rhondda Valley, after a hard morning's reaping, wrote the following *'triban'*:

Tae'n hela blwyddyn gyfan
Heb fwrw glaw yn unman,
Fe ffindir dŵr gan ferch y diawl
I grochan cawl Cwmsaerbran.

[If for a whole year it did not rain at all, this daughter of the devil would still find water for the broth cauldron at Cwmsaerbren.]

Local beliefs and omens are sometimes enshrined in simple verse:

Pan welir pen Moegeila
Yn gwisgo clog y bora,
Odid fawr cyn canol dydd
Bydd ar 'grudd hi ddagra.

[When Moegeila's head wears a cloak in the morning, there is little doubt that before mid-day there will be tears on its cheeks.]

Mention is also made in these verses of various games and pastimes

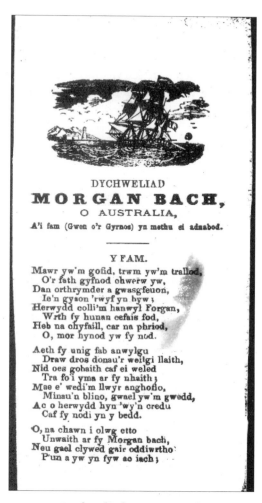

Dychweliad Morgan Bach
[Return of Morgan Bach from Australia]

such as '*y stôl ganddo*' or '*ieir a'r cedny*' (a board game, 'fox and geese', 'a very ancient innocent game, once most popular on the hills of Glamorgan', according to Cadrawd (Thomas Christopher Evans (1846-1918)). One '*triban*' refers to '*wara wic / Wrth gefan Picadili*', that is, 'playing wick' (? a tag game) behind the Piccadilly tavern in Caerffili. A ballad written by one E. Jones, 'Clerk of Hope' (in Flintshire), describes in some detail a game called 'Prisonbars' played in this instance in 1791 between a group of young men from the parish of Halkyn in Flintshire, and of the parish of Shotwick, just across the English border. An interesting feature here is the use made of English in a Welsh ballad. It appears that the Welshmen were the victors on the day, and several of them are named. 'We will play for no more', declare the defeated English players,

> God preserve us our lives,
> We wish that we were at home with our Wives.

A suitable opportunity perhaps to research this particular game which seems to have been very popular, in Flintshire at least, in the eighteenth century.

Occasionally a glimpse is caught of a forgotten custom. A poor or elderly widow, or the mother of a large family, in search of firewood for cooking or heating her cottage, would sometimes remove wooden stakes or other stout items of fencing from local hedges, thereby creating gaps through which the farmer's sheep or cattle could wander away and be lost. One such poor pilferer is indentified in two triplets that have survived:

> *Mi glywais i gan rywun*
> *I Pali dynnu polyn*
> *O'r adwy gaeais i â drain*
> *Yng ngodre Gwaunyfelin.*

> *Mi brofaf i bod Pali*
> *Drwy'r parthau'n plico'r perthi*
> *A'i bath nid oes drwy'r byd yn bod*
> *I lusgo co'd i losgi.*

[I was told by someone that Pali removed a pole from the gap which I had closed with some thorns below Gwaunyfelin. / I will prove that Pali throughout this neighbourhood plucks at hedges, and that there is no one like her for dragging away wood to be burnt.]

Her full name was Pali Siôn Aubery, and the case brought against her is recorded in a journal called *Y Beirniad* iv. (1863), 206-7.

Today, many a conversation revolves around, and many columns of print are dedicated to, the vexed question of the inward influx of people, mainly from England, to all parts of Wales. On a much smaller scale, this also bothered at least one '*triban*' author who commented upon the arrival and settlement of some Caribbean families to a village near Neath:

> *Peth od ym Mhentreclwyda' –*
> *Mae'r tai yn wyn fel eira,*
> *Ac ar bob drws mor ddu â'r glo*
> *Mae hewcyn o Jamaica.*

> [A strange thing in Pentreclwyda' – the houses are all as white as snow, and on every doorstep, as black as coal, is a fellow from Jamaica.]

Another burning issue of our day is the siting of enormous wind-farms which can now be seen on many a Welsh horizon. At least one doggerel verse refers to windmills of another age, and of a far less conspicuous nature. Here some Anglesey mills are listed, together with the author's opinion:

> *Melin Llynnon sydd yn llamu,*
> *Pant-y-gwŷdd sy'n ateb iddi,*
> *Felin Borth a'r Felin Adda –*
> *Llannerch-y-medd sy'n malu ora'.*

> [Llynnon Mill is rotating, Pant-y-gwŷdd responds to her, Borth Mill and Adda Mill, it is Llannerch-y-medd mill that grinds the best.]

The local fairs would be a popular destination for all, and it is not surprising that they are frequently mentioned in folk poetry of every kind, especially in the ballads. 'Who started the fair at Llanllyfni?' is a question posed by one verse:

Pwy ddechreuodd Ffair Llanllyfni?
Daniel Pugh a Daniel Parry,
Pwy oedd y capten ar y rheini?
John Bach Teiliwr wedi meddwi.

[Who started the fair at Llanllyfni? Daniel Pugh and Daniel Parry. Who was their captain? Little John the Tailor under the influence of drink.]

Would any record of these local characters have survived were it not for this verse? And might it be a starting point whereby a search could be made for them in newspapers and other local sources? It appears that Llandaff Fair in Glamorgan had an unenviable reputation:

Y mae Llandaf hynafol
Yn ddinas fach esgobol,
Ond rhaid im dystio, ar fy nghair,
Mae yno ffair uffernol.

[Ancient Llandaff is a small episcopal city, but I must testify upon my word that it has the most dreadful fair.]

Which is partly explained, perhaps, in another 'triban':

Paid byth â mynd ar amnaid
I fysg ymladdwyr diriaid
Yn Ffair Llandaf; oddi yno cyrch
Wa'th gwŷr Pen-tyrch yw'r diawliaid.

[Don't ever go, should you be invited, into the midst of the wretched brawlers in Llandaff Fair; for the scoundrels are the men of Pen-tyrch.]

It would be interesting to hear the whole story.

As to the ballads and other forms of folk poetry mentioned above, one wonders how much information remains hidden in those that would be of value to those with a mind to uncovering the history of various localities and the people who once lived and worked there. Only diligent and dedicated research will show.

Notes

The National Library's Database of Ballads is to be found at
httb://isys.llgc.org.uk
See also *Cronfa Baledi: Mynegai Cyfrifiadurol i Faledi'r Ddeunawfed Ganrif*
(Peredur Glyn Davies, E. Wynn James a Peredur Lynch) at *www.e-gymraeg.org/cronfabaledi*

19. Oral Testimony

Rheinallt Llwyd

It was W. G. Hoskins, the doyen of English local history, who once claimed that:

> To the true local historian no human record, whatever its form –a hedge-bank, a wall, a street, a headstone, a farmhouse, an old man's gossip, wills and tax assessments and the thousands of other written things, a memorial tablet on a church wall – a multitude of evidences in every shape or form – no human record fails to tell him something about the past. All these evidences, whatever form they take, are interrelated.[1]

In this chapter we will consider the significance and value of oral evidence, what Hoskins referred to as 'an old man's gossip', for both community and family historians. At times it may indeed be nothing more than gossip and may have little historical significance. More often that not, however, oral testimony obtained from the minds and memories of older men and women within the community, and from those who are not so old, will provide information that is unique and invaluable.

The term that is often used to describe the process of obtaining oral evidence is 'oral history', although not everyone is happy with it. It is a fairly recent term and can be defined as: 'an account of first-hand experience recalled retrospectively, communicated to an interviewer for historical purposes and preserved on a system of reproducible sound.'[2] There is, however, a tendency to use the term in a collective sense to encompass a wide range of oral information gathered on tape or film, and many oral history collections consist not only of individual interviews and reminiscences but also of recordings of local events, folksongs and folklore and a range of other materials.

Although the term 'oral history' is a modern one, the use of oral sources in history is a very old practice. Paul Thompson in his book, *The Voice of the Past: Oral History* gives a comprehensive account of the uses made throughout the centuries of oral evidences. Thompson maintains that 'In fact, oral history is as old as history itself. It was the *first* kind of history. And it is only quite recently that skill in handling oral evidence has ceased to be one of the marks of the great historian'.[3] Even to this day in certain parts of the world where pre-literate societies are found, the only history available for those societies is the oral traditions which have been handed down from generation to generation, and in less literate times, in Europe and elsewhere, the main method of transmitting information was orally. This was particularly true in Wales, where we have numerous examples of mediaeval literary texts that are based on earlier oral versions.

The term 'oral history', nonetheless, is associated with the work initiated by Professor Allan Nevins of Columbia University. He is regarded as the founder of the subject. In 1938 Nevins maintained in the preface to *The Gateway to History* that there was an urgent need for an organisation that would make 'a systematic attempt to obtain from the lips of living Americans who have led significant lives, a fuller record of their participation in the political, economic and cultural life of the last sixty years'.[4] It was ten years later before Nevins actually began recording the memoirs of his 'signficant' Americans and he concentrated almost entirely on the reminiscences of the famous and influential, those who had changed in some way or other the course of American history. This was the beginning of élite oral history, and in the USA elaborate projects were soon set up to record in as complete a detail as possible the careers of leading public figures. Nevins argued that it was necessary to develop this new, modern technique for historical documentation because 'oral history is an essential defence against oblivion in history, against the absolute loss of historical fact that would otherwise occur'.[5] He claimed that he was seeing 'in the daily obituary columns proof that knowledge valuable to the historian, novelist, sociologist and economist was daily perishing without yielding any part of their riches'.[6] Because of developments in modern communications systems some long established methods of recording information were being replaced. Letter-writing, for example, was being replaced by telephone calls, and recording devices were replacing written reports. Nevins argued that something drastic had to be done, and he rightly claimed that 'oral history was born of modern invention and technology'.[7]

It was the history of the 'significant' and the eminent that Nevins was concerned with, the 'great men' of America, and for almost two decades oral history in the USA concentrated mainly on this area. However, with the establishment of the American Oral History Association in 1967 the frontiers of oral history expanded dramatically, outwards and downwards. It expanded into spheres of interests such as Indian history, aspects of American women's history, and the history of black communities. The emphasis also moved from individuals to themes and specific subjects, and from 'significant' men to 'insignificant' persons, those who had really little choice in the way their country or their own lives had been run.

The origin and development of oral history in Europe and the UK differed from the North American scene since some of the earliest examples of using sound recording equipment to collect oral evidence are found, not amongst the work of political historians, but rather in establishments specialising in the study of folklife and linguistics. In Scandinavian countries, particularly Sweden, Denmark, Norway and Finland the value of collecting and recording oral testimony had been an established practice since the 1830s. This led to the establishment of notable centres in Sweden such as the Institute for Folk Life Research, Nordiska Museet, at Stockholm in 1873, and the Institute for Dialects and Folklore Research, at Uppsala in 1914. The emphasis had been mainly on collecting linguistic phenomena, provincial words and expressions and the terminology associated with various crafts and customs that were rapidly disappearing. In Ireland, on the other hand, the realisation that a wealth of evidence was vanishing forever as older members of communities were dying out was the main reason for setting up the Irish Folklore Commission in Dublin in 1935. The old way of life that had existed for centuries, particularly in rural Ireland,

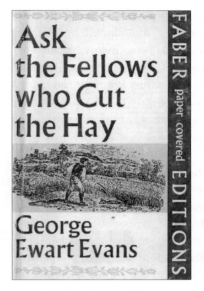

The first and last volumes by George Ewart Evans,
based upon the oral evidence collected by him

was gradually changing with the advent of new communications systems and the advancement of technology. During the 1940s and 1950s other centres were established in the UK which again were primarily concerned with collecting data for folklife scholars and linguistic specialists, notably the Institute of Dialect and Folk Life Studies at the University of Leeds (1948), the Welsh Folk Museum (now St Fagans: National History Museum) at St Fagans, Cardiff (1948), and the School of Folklife Studies at Edinburgh (1951). Before considering in greater detail the significant work undertaken at St Fagans let us briefly discuss the pioneering work of one individual in relation to the development of oral history in the UK.

'Tomorrow may be too late'

George Ewart Evans (1909–88),[8] a native of Aberpennar (Mountain Ash) spent much of his working life as a teacher and writer in East Anglia. Shortly after the end of the Second World War, he and his family moved to the small village of Blaxhall in East Suffolk, and he soon realised that he had moved to an area which still had evidence of a prior culture. Some of his elderly neighbours, such as the shepherd Robert

Savage and his wife Priscilla, were using words commonly found in the works of Chaucer and Spencer but long abandoned by younger members of the community. During the 1950s, Evans began tape-recording the reminiscences of some of the older inhabitants of Blaxhall. In 1956 he published *Ask the Fellows Who Cut the Hay*, a book based on those recordings. George Ewart Evans was painfully aware that he was witnessing the final break-up of the old community – its customs, beliefs, vocabulary, and above all its way of life:

> The book has taken this particular shape from the writer's conviction that the oral tradition is at this time of the greatest historical importance … At present, old people in this countryside are survivors from another era. They belong essentially to a culture that has extended in unbroken line since at least the early Middle Ages. They are in some respects the last repositories of this culture; and for this reason should have some of the respect given to any source of valuable historical information. Their knowledge of dialect, folk tales and songs, old customs and usages, and craft vocabularies, and their ability to identify and describe the use of farm implements that are now going into limbo after being used for centuries, are sufficient reasons why they should have the local historian's greatest attention.[9]

This meant meticulously recording their reminiscences, an exacting task, but one of prime importance. Unexcavated sites can wait to be dug up, even the collecting of printed local material can be postponed for another day, but not the recording of oral evidence:

> While the sort of knowledge that is waiting to be taken down from old people is always on the brink of extinction. Tomorrow may be too late; and once this knowledge is under the soil no amount of digging will ever again recover it.[10]

As a result of his total commitment to safeguarding oral testimony Evans went on to produce other notable volumes on the social and cultural history of Suffolk such as *The Horse in the Furrow* (1960), *The Pattern under the Plough* (1966), *The Farm and the Village* (1969), and *Where Beards Wag All* (1970). Later on he used oral history techniques to study aspects of urban history, and sections of his volume entitled *From Mouths of Men* (1976) relate to community life in the south Wales mining valley where he was brought up. His last volume, *Spoken History* (1987), which appeared a few months before his death in 1988, provides an excellent overview of his pioneering work as an oral historian. Like Allan Nevins in the USA, Evans realised that collecting oral testimony was indeed 'an essential defence against oblivion in history'.

While George Ewart Evans was recording the reminiscences of some of his neighbours in Blaxhall, working entirely on his own, and without any institutional support, a relatively new establishment in Wales was also about to start collecting oral testimony on a large scale. The Welsh Folk Museum, as it was then known, had been established in 1948, and its first Curator, Iorwerth C. Peate, was fully aware of the value of oral testimony. From the outset he realised that collecting and conserving examples of Wales' material culture was not enough; it was equally important that the oral traditions of Wales should be preserved since:

Questionnaire on Welsh Folk Culture prepared by Iorwerth C. Peate in 1937

> the principal element in conveying tradition from one generation to generation is language, and the study of language is part of folk-life studies ... recording speakers of the oldest generation is an urgent task; with them will disappear a wealth of knowledge and of words'.[11]

By 1957 a Department of Oral Traditions and Dialects had been established under Vincent H. Phillips, and it embarked on a comprehensive programme of recordings and initially concentrated on three major areas of study, namely:

1. **The pattern of livelihood and everyday life** throughout Wales. This involved recording in detail agricultural customs and practices;

customs relating to country crafts and rural and urban industries and all manner of customs relating to the household and everyday life.

2. **The lore of everyday life**, which included subjects such as seasonal customs and customs relating to birth, marriage and death, children's games and pastimes, and a whole range of evidences available in folk songs and traditions.

3. **The language of everyday life**, which dealt with the recording of dialects, investigation into phonological and grammatical features, and the collecting of the vocabularies of agriculture and industry, of domestic life and cultural activities.

As a result there are more than 11,000 audio recordings in the Oral Traditions and Archival collections at St Fagans: National History Museum 'of which 9,000 contain original fieldwork recordings' as well as other forms of oral testimony in the form of recorded radio programmes and tapes and cassettes produced commercially over a number of years. The establishment, therefore, contains invaluable sources for community historians and, occasionally, for family historians too. Any researcher should, therefore, begin by consulting the St Fagans website (*www.museumwales.ac.uk*).

By the mid 1960s oral history had also become an acceptable academic discipline, through the extensive use made of oral evidences by social historians and sociologists. Paul Thompson and Thea Vigne at the University of Essex's Department of Sociology, Bill Williams at the Manchester Studies Unit and Raphael Samuel at Ruskin College, Oxford, instigated a number of impressive projects. At Essex they undertook a major survey of family life, work and community before 1918, and the Manchester Unit was involved in subjects such as Jewish studies, the cotton industry and pawnbroking. One result of the activities of these academics was the establishment in 1973 of the Oral History Society, 'to further the practice of oral history in all appropriate fields'. The journal *Oral History*, established in 1969, became a forum for monitoring developments in oral history studies. Substantial academic volumes also began to appear which were based on the techniques of collecting oral testimony, such as Paul Thompson's *The*

Llewelyn Evans, Ystumgwadnaeth, Llanfachreth, near Dolgellau,
being interviewed by Vincent H. Phillips in the early 1960s
With the permission of St Fagans: National History Museum

Edwardians: the Remaking of British Society (1975); Elizabeth
Roberts' *A Woman's Place: an Oral History of Working Class Women,*
1880–1940 (1984) and Alun Howkins' *Poor Labouring Men: Rural*
Radicalism in Norfolk, 1870–1923 (1985).

The bibliography of oral history is an extensive one and some of the
more important items are listed on The Oral History Society website
(*www.ohs.org.uk*).

The significance of oral testimony

Despite the increased recognition of the value of oral history during the
last forty years it is still viewed with suspicion by a number of the more
orthodox traditionalist historians, who are mainly used to, and would
rather rely on, documentary sources of historical evidence. They would
claim that histories based entirely on non-documentary sources tend be
less satisfactory than those drawn from documents. Their motto seems
to be: 'There is no substitute for documents – no documents, no
history'. And their main objection concerns the validity of oral
testimony. The human memory, it will be argued, is notoriously

unreliable and an informant can, quite unintentionally, provide evidence that is entirely false. It is maintained that oral testimony is often no more than superfluous gossip, and not only unreliable but also over-simplified and distorted. It is also claimed that the personal nature of a recorded interview makes the evidence less reliable and far less objective than evidence to be found in documentary sources. A. J. P. Taylor was entirely dismissive when asked about the value of oral evidence: 'In this matter [the interview method] I am an almost total sceptic ... Old men drooling about their youth – No.'[12]

Another criticism, and sometimes a valid one, concerns the role of the interviewer. The type of questions asked and the manner of their asking can be crucial. Biased questioning can produce the sort of answers the interviewer wishes to hear:

> One serious danger does exist for the oral historian. When he is himself conducting the interview ... he may be tempted into moulding the evidence he receives; the barriers against doing this are less formidable with oral than with documentary material. By asking leading questions ... or by approaching only those informants who will give him the answers he wants, he may halfconsciously use the interview to distort the truth.[13]

The third major area of criticism concerns the actual process of interviewing. Certain informants may dislike the prospect of speaking into a tape recorder or appear before a camera and will therefore refuse or fail to be frank and forthright. Others may feel inhibited and nervous when faced with the interview situation and may not always provide the real evidence they possess: 'This is the drawback of interviews ... the final product is a wholly accurate record of what has been on the speaker's tongue but rarely in his mind or heart'.[14]

The above criticisms must be carefully considered by oral historians. No oral history project should be instigated and no interview undertaken unless clear objectives are laid down and detailed guidelines observed. However, the basic question that must be returned to is whether oral testimony is less objective and less reliable than evidence obtained from various documentary sources. Are documentary sources always objective and entirely reliable? The words of Richard Crossman on this subject are interesting:

I've discovered, having read all the Cabinet papers about the meetings I attended, that the documents often bear virtually no relation to what actually happened. I know now that the Cabinet Minutes are written by Burke Trend (secretary to the Cabinet), not to say what did happen in the Cabinet, but what the Civil Service wishes it to be believed happened, so that a clear directive can be given.[15]

George Ewart Evans held a similar view. Having been a parish councillor for many years he was intrigued with what he found in the official minutes:

Not that there was any blatant inaccuracy ... but since the time of the meeting so recorded, a selective intelligence had been at work, omitting almost everything that did not contribute to fortifying the main decisions reached.[16]

Throughout the centuries has there not been 'a selective intelligence' at work, ensuring that the official establishment view of events is recorded, whether it be on a national or local level? Some of the major criticisms of oral history are equally applicable to the more respectable traditional sources. Had George Ewart Evans taken the view of A. J. P. Taylor and rejected the evidences of 'old men drooling' we would not have his remarkable volumes on folklife in East Anglia and elsewhere. Evans, however, makes no apology for his reliance on oral testimony:

Can oral tradition be relied upon? From my own experience in one particular field – the recording of old skills and craft of the old prior society in East Anglia – I can say unequivocally that in this field I would much prefer to trust the craftsmen, the farmer, or the farmworker who had done the job probably for his lifetime, rather than any printed sources dealing with the details and nature of his work ... To a man who had spent his life at a certain work or craft it is a point of honour to describe its details fully and without distortion.[17]

Oral testimony, like all other historical evidences, must be used with the greatest of care and subjected to the rigorous standards of scholarship. Having applied these standards, it will be found that the advantages of oral history in areas of study where other documentary evidence already exists can provide useful supplementary material to reinforce or possibly correct that evidence. It enhances the task of historical interpretation. In areas of study and subjects where documentary evidence is non-existent or under-documented, the use of oral history can be unique and unsurpassable. And in the context of community history there are often subjects which are totally undocumented. Raphael Samuel, another notable practitioner of the use of oral evidence, advocated the case forcefully:

> Oral evidence makes it possible to escape from some of the deficiencies of the documentary record, at least so far as recent times are concerned ... There are matters of fact which are recorded in the memories of older people and nowhere else, events of the past which they alone can elucidate for us, vanished sights which they alone can recall. Documents can't answer back, nor, beyond a point, can they be asked to explain in greater detail what they mean, to give more examples, to account for negative instances, or to explain apparent discrepancies in the record which survives. Yet there are certain kinds of inquiry which can only be undertaken with the aid of living testimony, and whole areas of life in which its credentials are beyond question.[18]

It seems, therefore, that oral history makes two major contributions to the history of any community, and indeed occasionally, to family history, by:

(i) providing access to whole areas of the past which may be entirely undocumented.

(ii) providing community and family historians with an entirely different kind of document.

Examples from Wales

In addition to the pioneering work undertaken at St Fagans from the middle of 1950s onwards there are other interesting examples of the collecting of oral testimony in Wales. During the early 1970s the Social Service Research Council began funding a number of oral history projects such as the South Wales Coalfield Project, established in 1971.

Robin Gwyndaf, St Fagans National History Museum,
interviewing T. W. Thomas, Pentyrch and Gwaelod-y-garth.
Extracts from the interview were published in the series of
Welsh Folk Museum cassettes, 1994
With the permission of St Fagans: National History Museum

Although the coalfield's history largely goes back to the beginning of the nineteenth century, there were, a century and a half later, surprisingly few documentary sources available to record its growth and subsequent decline. Before nationalisation was finally achieved in 1947, many of the coal-owners had systematically destroyed colliery records. What remained was soon sold off to second-hand book dealers. It was obvious, however, that a wealth of information relating to various aspects of the coalfield's history was available in the reminiscences of former miners and lodge officials, and indeed a great many other inhabitants who had experienced life in the south Wales industrial communities.This project was essentially a salvage operation, 'an essential defence against oblivion', as Allan Nevins had maintained. One of the researchers, Hywel Francis, provided a comprehensive account of the experience of collecting and analysing oral testimony on that project and claims that:

For the historian of the twentieth century to ignore oral evidence is tantamount to taking a decision to write off whole areas of human experience. Indeed there are human activities which can only satisafactorily be uncovered by collecting oral testimony.[19]

Francis goes even further at the end of his account and says that 'it needs an oral historian to ask the first question and often to get the first answer.'[20] All the recorded tapes compiled during the First South Wales Coalfield Project, 1972–74, and a second project undertaken during 1979–82, are now safely located at the South Wales Miners' Library at Swansea University and, along with a variety of other archival media, form an invaluable source of materials for both national and local historians in Wales. Fuller details can be viewed on the website (*www.swan.ac.uk/swcc/*). The relevance of an oral historian asking 'the first question' is also important in the context of family history. Crucial information about family issues can often only be garnered through talking to older members of the family since they alone possess such information.

Another equally interesting example of the use of oral evidence is to be found in a case study of abandoned dwellings in some of the valleys of the eastern Black Mountains of Wales between 1840–1983. By the middle of the twentieth century these valleys had witnessed enormous depopulation, a decrease from 1,277 in 1841 to 529 in 1983, and many of the farmsteads had become derelict, were unoccupied or had become holiday homes. The aim of the project, undertaken by a group of historical geographers, was 'to provide a complete occupancy profile of all the dwellings in the area since 1840' by tracing the history of each individual dwelling, 435 in all, using a range of historical sources. These consisted of tithe maps and schedules, estate maps of the Landor, Glanusk, Duffryn and Beaufort estates, and in some instances sale catalogues relating to some of those estates. Other documentary sources used included church registers, land-tax returns, school log books, electoral registers, trade directories and census returns (1841–81). But the sum total of information obtained from all these various documentary sources could still not provide all the answers needed. It was only by interviewing six local octogenarians that the outstanding information was acquired. According to Robert Grant, one of the researchers involved, the project proved that:

The completeness of the record could only be attained using oral history methods to supplement traditional sources ... The study in the Black Mountains, however, shows how an effective marriage between oral testimony and archival material can be used to determine the period of abandonment and the location of individual dwellings. It is clear, however, that documentary sources alone are not equal to identifying the specific circumstances leading to the dereliction of individual homes. Yet explanations can often be teased from human memory'.[21]

Numerous other oral history projects could be listed with many undertaken by libraries, archive services, local history societies and individuals from the 1970s onwards, all testimony to the significance and value of the subject. Some thousands of recorded interviews were completed under Manpower Services Commission schemes which sponsored local authorities and academic institutions to set up oral history projects. One such project was undertaken at Coleg Harlech under the direction of the librarian, Martin Eckley, and George Ewart Evans was often a guest participant at some of their training days for prospective interviewers. The Coleg Harlech tapes are now safeguarded at Gwynedd Archives at Dolgellau. However, one problem with this invaluable collection, as with many others in Wales, is that without the appropriate equipment it is impossible to listen to 'open reel' tapes that have not been digitised.

As the twenty-first century approached it became the occasion to look back on the course of the previous 100 years and a number of interesting projects were undertaken involving collecting oral testimony. BBC Radio Cymru, for example undertook a project entitled *Cynllun Hanes Llafar y Mileniwm* (The Millennium Oral History Project) and some 6,000 people throughout Wales were involved. The historian, R. Merfyn Jones also made extensive use of oral evidence by interviewing some 300 individuals when preparing a series of television programmes for S4C to mark the end of the twentieth century. His popular book *Cymru 2000: Hanes Cymru yn yr Ugeinfed Ganrif* (Wales 2000: The History of Wales in the Twentieth Century) (1999) was published to accompany the television programmes. And *Merched y Wawr* (Daughters of the Dawn), the Welsh medium women's movement decided to celebrate the new millennium by launching an oral history project in conjunction with Trinity College, Carmarthen (as it then was) and the Welsh Folk Museum at St Fagans. Some 1,000 taped interviews were produced recording the experiences of women in Wales between 1920 and 1960, on a variety of topics.[22]

More recent examples of oral history projects in Wales includes the 'Italian Memories in Wales' project which was awarded some £50,000 of National Lottery Funding 'to record and preserve the memories of Italians who migrated to Wales after the Second World War and second generation Italians living here'.[23] There was also a successful attempt in late 2006 and early 2007 to produce An Oral History of Performance Art in Wales by recording publicly staged conversations with a number of key artists who had shaped the development of performance art in Wales since 1968, a scheme that was funded by the Arts Council of Wales.[24] Among many other projects that are currently gathering oral testimony are the following. The Snowdonia Society (*Cymdeithas Eryri*) aims 'to collect memories and stories about Tŷ Hyll (near Capel Curig) and the natural heritage of the area[25] and the society eventually aims to make the interviews available on its website. The Centre for Alternative Technology, near Machynlleth, which, in 2013, celebrated forty years since its establishment, has also created the CAT Oral History project, with the aim of recording interviews with some eighty individuals; those taped interviews will be later deposited at the National Library of Wales, Aberystwyth.[26] It is also worth noting that oral history has become an acceptable subject in certain academic establishments in Wales. The Ceredigion Oral History Project is part of a skills training module (entitled Oral History: The Past in the Present) run by the Department of History and Welsh History at Aberystwyth University, and the School of History at Bangor University is prominent in encouraging research students to make extensive use of oral testimony in their studies. Bangor University also 'provides local volunteers with the training and skills to conduct interviews'.

In addition to the substantial collections of oral history materials held at St Fagans: National History Museum and at The South Wales Miners' Library, reference must also be made to the National Screen and Sound Archive of Wales based at The National Library of Wales.[27] The aim of the archive is 'to preserve, promote and celebrate the sound and moving image heritage of Wales' and consists of more than 250,000 hours worth of recordings. In addition to radio and television broadcasts, sound recordings and films, cassettes and CDs and the latest digital media there are numerous examples of oral history collections which are an invaluable source for those researching community history in Wales. Also developing into a comprehensive national archive is the People's Collection Wales, where the Oral History group highlights and discusses various oral history projects in Wales.[28]

A different kind of document

When an interview is recorded, whether it be in the context of community or family history, it is obvious that an entirely new and unique document is created, and that an original document, whatever its format, should be preserved, if at all possible. For the document will contain characteristics that will be unique to the informant (interviewee)

Emrys Evans, Manod, Blaenau Ffestiniog, whose Hiwmor y Chwarelwr [Humour of the Quarryman] was another Welsh Folk Museum cassette, 1990

and the interviewer, in terms of vocabulary, dialect, phonetics, etc, apart from the actual information it contains. Indeed some oral historians would claim that oral history should be, above all else, oral and audible. However, most taped interviews, in order to make their content available to a wider public should be transcribed although this is often a time consuming and expensive process. Since this chapter is meant as a general introduction to the value and importance of oral testimony for community historians we will not discuss the purely technical processes involved. Technical guidance on how to undertake oral history projects are provided by both the Oral History Society (*www.ohs.org.uk*) and the British Library (*www.bl.uk*). What is without doubt is that the value of oral testimony and using interviewing techniques can be of immense value to both the community and family historian from time to time.

APPENDIX
Some basic guidelines in the process of collecting
oral testimony

1. **What subjects/topics need to be investigates and recorded?**
   What obvious gaps exist in the history of a particular community or family?
   What evidence already exists and in what format – written/ published?
   What 'new' information can be acquired through collecting oral testimony?
   The need to list clear objectives before any oral history project is commenced.

2. **The importance of preliminary and background research**
   It is crucially important that the interviewer is already aware of what already exists on the topic to be investigated in various primary and secondary sources.
   It would be a waste of time to merely record information that is already available in various other formats. Oral testimony, however, can be rightly used to supplement or possibly to disprove information that already exists in other sources.
   At times oral testimony can contribute entirely new and unique information that is not to be found anywhere else.

3. **Use of questionnaire**
   Devising a detailed questionnaire on the topic to be investigated is always advisable so that the interviewer knows what her/his objectives are.
   The questionnaire should provide guidelines for the interviewer but need not be followed rigidly.

4. **Choice of appropriate informant(s)**
   The old and the highly talkative are not always the most appropriate!
   Informants which have special and unique knowledge on account of their experiences in various fields should be sought.
   If the informant is aware of the unique information which she/he has, then all the better.

The testimony of ONE individual on a specific topic or a range of topics can be recorded.

The testimony of SEVERAL individuals on a specific topic or range of topics can be recorded.

It is vital that the interview is recorded only with the full consent of the informant to safeguard her/his copyright.

5. The use of adequate equipment

It is crucial to ensure that the recording is of the highest technical standard – and recording technology is developing rapidly these days!

The interviewer should be totally familiar with any recording equipment and competent in its use.

The equipment should not be allowed to inhibit the informant or affect the interview process.

An appropriate setting should be used to conduct the interview so that background noise, etc, should be eliminated.

What equipment should be used? This will depend on what is available but any format acceptable to the informant can be used e.g. oral recording, video, digital, etc.

6. The interview

A preliminary meeting with the informant should be arranged although not too many questions should be asked at this stage in case it affects the actual interview.

Arrange a time that is convenient for the informant.

Ensure that the location for the interview is adequate and comfortable – with a homely atmosphere if possible.

The main virtue of the interviewer should be empathy and her/his challenge will be to penetrate the world of the informant.

The informant should not be left exhausted and neither should the interview be rushed.

The confidence of the informant should be won over and her/his special knowledge respected.

The main aim of the interviewer will be to prod the memory of the informant.

Detailed information should be acquired wherever possible. It is the added detail that makes an ordinary interview into an exceptional one, possibly unique.

The informant should not be allowed to digress too much.

The interviewer, not the informant, should be in control of the interview.

7. **Recording details of the interview**

   (i) Details relating to the interview

   At the beginning of each recording there should be information relating to the interviewer, the informant, date of the interview.

   Each physical tape/video, etc, should be clearly identified with the above information.

   The format used should be clearly identified e.g. cassette, CD, digital recording, etc.

   Place, time and date of interview need to be meticulously noted.

   Relevant technical details need to be noted e.g. speed, length, etc.

   Unique accession number of interview.

   Language of interview.

   Whether a transcript is available.

   (ii) Details relating to the informant

   Full name, address, occupation.

   Date and place of birth.

   Education, career, marital status.

   Details of parents – and other ancestors, if possible.

   Photograph of informant and her/his home, if relevant.

   Any other relevant background information.

   (iii) Content of interview

   Summary of the interview.

   Main topics/themes discussed and their location.

   Significant other persons and locations mentioned in the interview.

8. **Final format of interview**

   What is the final format?

   Has it been edited?

   Has it been transcribed – fully without editing or part/fully edited?

Conservation and access

Ensure adequate and appropriate conservation – to avoid damage by heat and humidity, etc.

Ensure copyright status – for informant and interviewer.

Any restrictions on use e.g for research purpose only?

Creation of index/indexes to persons, topics, places, mentioned in the interview to enhance the access process.

Further Reading

In addition to Paul Thompson, *The Voice of the Past: Oral History* (2000), which is an excellent introduction to both the theory and practice of collecting oral testimony, the following texts are also worth consulting: Stephen Caunce, *Oral History and the Local Librarian* (1994); Valerie Raleigh Yow, *Recording Oral History: a Guide for the Humanities and Social Sciences* (2005); Robert Perks and Alistair Thompson, *The Oral History Reader* (2006); Don Ritchie (ed), *Oxford Handbook of Oral History* (2010).

In Welsh, David Jenkins, *Ar Lafar, ar goedd* (2007) is extremely valuable, and his *The Agricultural Community in South-west Wales at the turn of the Twentieth Century* (1971) is a prime example of the use made of oral testimony by an anthropologist.

NOTES

[1] W. G. Hoskins, *English Local History: The Past and the Future* (1966), 20
[2] Trevor Lummis, *Listening to History: the Authenticity of Oral Evidence* (1987)
[3] Paul Thompson, *The Voice of the Past: Oral History* (3rd edn., 2000), 25
[4] Allan Nevins, *The Gateway to History* (1938), iv
[5] Allan Nevins, *Proceedings of the first National Colloquium on Oral History* (1966), 31
[6] Allan Nevins, 'Oral History: how and why it was born', *Wilson Library Bulletin* 40 (7), 1966, 600
[7] Ibid., 600
[8] See Gareth Williams, *George Ewart Evans* (1991); Vincent H. Phillips, 'The Historian of England's "gwerin"', *Book News from Wales*, spring 1984
[9] George Ewart Evans, *Ask the Fellows Who Cut the Hay* (1956), 13–14
[10] *Ibid.*, 14
[11] Iorwerth C. Peate, *Tradition and Folk Life: A Welsh View* (1972), 134
[12] Quoted in *Oral History* 1 (3), 1972, 46
[13] B. Harrison, 'Oral History and recent Political History', *Oral History* 1 (3), 1972, 36
[14] F. King, *Sunday Telegraph*, 3 January 1982, 12
[15] Richard Crossman, *The Listener*, 1 February 1973, 148
[16] George Ewart Evans, *From Mouths of Men* (1976), 18

17 George Ewart Evans, 'Aspects of Oral Tradition', *Folk Life* 7, 1969, 9
18 Raphael Samuel, 'Local History and Oral History', *History Workshop* 1, spring 1976, 199
19 Hywel Francis, 'The Secret World of the South Wales Miner: the Relevance of Oral History', in David Smith (ed.), *A People and a Proletariat: Essays in the History of Wales 1780–1980* (1980), 166–80 (167)
20 *Ibid.*, 178
21 Robert Grant, 'Oral History and Settlement Change: a Case Study of Abandoned Dwellings in the Black Mountains of Wales, 1840–1983', *Cambria*, 12 (1), 1985, 108–9
22 *www.hanesmerchedcymru.merchedywawr.com*
23 *www.enaip.org.uk/index.php?page=italian-memories-in-wales*
24 *www.performance-wales.org*
25 *www.theuglyhouse.co.uk*
26 *http://blog.cat.org.uk*
27 *www.archif.com*
28 *www.peoplescollectionwales.co.uk*

20. Location of and Access to Sources

Rheinallt Llwyd

Before any community or family historian begins to investigate a topic in earnest she or he must answer two basic questions: firstly, what sources do I need to look at? and secondly, where are such sources to be found? In the not too distant past any researcher would have to travel to a library or record office or similar institution to consult primary and secondary sources and possibly make copies of relevant sections. Nowadays, it is increasingly possible to locate sources and even download some of their contents from a personal computer in the comfort of one's own home. The advent of the internet and digital technologies have radically transformed the situation and made it so much easier for community and family historians alike to locate sources and have access to their contents. This brief chapter provides an overview of some of the main institutions and services that safeguard our archives and enable us to make use of them.

Figure 1 shows that there are numerous establishments which offer services for Welsh community and family historians and most of them are located in Wales. However, there are also numerous establishments outside Wales, mostly in other parts of the United Kingdom, where documents of Welsh interest are safeguarded and which offer invaluable services to those researching Welsh topics. All these establishments have well developed websites where details of holdings

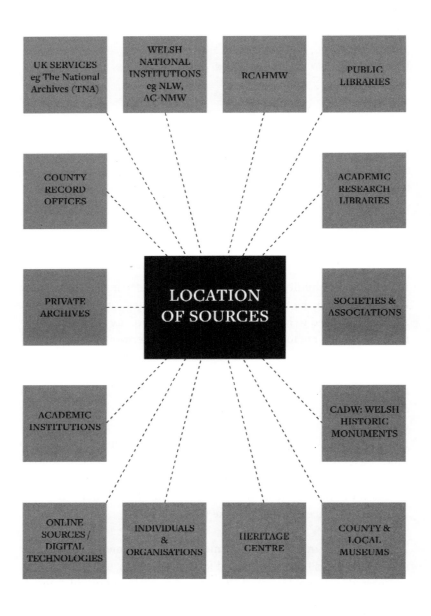

Figure 1: Location of sources

can be consulted and copies of various documents sometimes downloaded.

Establishments outside Wales

For various historical reasons there are many sources, especially primary ones, which are located in institutions and organisations outside Wales and the most important by far are those to be found at The National Archives (TNA) at Kew (*www.nationalarchives.gov.uk*).

Since 2003 the Historical Manuscripts Commission (HMC) has been part of TNA and has a long tradition of publishing information on the location and nature of records. By searching its National Register of Archives, Manorial Documents Register, and Religious Archives Survey, for example, it is possible to identify innumerable records of value to community historians in Wales. The General Register Office (GRO) (*www.gro.gov.uk*), on the other hand, is particularly valuable to those researching family history, and from the GRO it is also possible to obtain purchased copies of certificates of births, marriages and deaths.

Various Parliamentary Archives throughout the centuries can be accessed through the website of the House of Lords Record Office (*www.parliament.uk/parliamentary_publications_and_ archives*), where often legislation of direct relevance to local communities in Wales can be located.

For family historians indispensable services are offered by the Family Records Centre (FRC) (*www.familyrecords.gov.uk/frc*) and much valuable information and guidance is also provided through the website of the Federation of Family History Societies (FFHS) (*www.ffhs.org.uk/General/Help*). This is an international organisation with links to over 200 genealogical societies throughout the world. The Society of Genealogists (SoG) (*www.sog.org.uk/*), with its vast collections, is particularly useful for those seeking pre-1837 information. It also offers a number of helpful pamphlets which are available online and arranges training courses on genealogy and publishes the quarterly journal, *Genealogists' Magazine*.

Cyndis' list of genealogy sites on the Internet (*www.cyndilist.com/*) is USA-based and contains indexes to international websites on a number of relevant topics for family historians and includes a number of links to valuable collections worldwide. For a long time the *International Genealogical Index* (IGI) has also been valued since it is an index to some millions of names world-wide copied by members of the Church of Jesus Christ of Latter-Day Saints based at Salt Lake City, Utah, USA, from the entries of births, baptisms and marriages in parish and Nonconformists registers, and in wills and other documents from 1538 until circa 1885. The Mormons were refused permission to copy and index parish registers in Wales but managed to film and index the Bishops' Transcripts. This index is freely available online and can be searched (*www.familysearch.org*). It must, however, be used with care since not all parishes are included and the transcription is not always entirely accurate. Neither do the entries cover details of deaths and burials. It is, nonetheless, valuable, especially for the pre-1837 period.

One of the best collection of sources online for the study of family history in the UK is offered by Genuki (Genealogy in the UK and Ireland) (*www.genuki.org.uk*), which is a free, non-commercial website. It has been designed as a 'virtual reference library' with comprehensive information on each county within the UK and Ireland and links to other online materials. The BBC Family History website (*bbc.co.uk/familyhistory*) is another useful site to investigate, especially since it includes links to a large number of relevant organisations.

Again, for historical reasons it is known that a great deal of sources of relevance to Wales are located in European countries and in other parts of the world, where they are safeguarded in libraries and record offices, although it is unlikely that they will ever be returned to Wales! But with developments in digital technology it has become easier to locate and access them and even to download copies, occasionally. A prime example of a valuable Welsh document that is preserved in the Centre Historique des Archives Nationales in Paris is the famous letter written by Owain Glyndŵr to Charles VI of France on 31 March 1406. Although the Pennal Letter was returned to the National Library of Wales on loan for a few months in 2000 it is unlikely ever to be returned here permanently. Still it forms an integral part of the history of the remote community of Pennal in Merioneth.

Establishments in Wales

We have already seen in Chapter 3 that the National Library of Wales offers extensive services to both community and family historians in Wales, and that its resources are unsurpassed. Increasingly many of those services are being offered electronically and it is possible to investigate a large number of NLW catalogues online and a special section deals with the specific needs of family historians.

The website of Amgueddfa Cymru-National Museum of Wales (*www.museumwales.ac.uk*) provides information on all the various branches of the establishment. In addition to the main National Museum at Cardiff these include:

St Fagans: National History Museum
Big Pit: National Coal Museum (Blaenafon)
National Wool Museum (Dre-fach Felindre)
National Roman Legion Museum (Caerleon)
National Slate Museum (Llanberis)
National Waterfront Museum (Swansea).

The Royal Commission on the Ancient and Historical Monuments of Wales (*www.rcahmw.gov.uk*) is another body which has invaluable holdings and well developed databases that are totally unique for all manner of historical researchers and these have been discussed in considerable detail in Chapter 16. Also important are the services of Cadw – Welsh Historic Monuments (*www.cadw.wales.gov.uk*) which has special responsibilities for the built heritage of Wales. In addition to producing printed guides to prominent historical locations it also has an impressive collection of visual images of such locations. Another establishment that holds an extensive collection of visual images relating to landscape and buildings in Wales is the National Trust and its website (*www.nationaltrust.org.uk*) is a useful point of reference for those researching particular communities.

Libraries

One of the aims and objectives of public libraries in the UK from their establishment in the 1850s was 'to preserve the community's documentary record' and for most researchers they will be the first point of contact. Public libraries have a long and honourable tradition of collecting local material in a wide range of formats from printed sources of all kinds to maps, newspapers and ephemera, to visual materials in the form of photographs, prints and drawings, and audio-visual items such as sound and video-recordings to the most advanced digital versions of documents. The easiest way to find and locate the nearest public library for your use is to consult the website (*www.library.cymru.org*). In addition to offering traditional bibliographical services it is also possible to gain free access to the internet in all Welsh public libraries and some of the major libraries, such as Cardiff Central Library, have unique archival collections of primary sources. You will also find in almost all public libraries that there will be members of staff who are specially trained to deal with enquiries relating to family and community history.

The body that has overall responsibilities for promoting and protecting libraries in Wales is CyMAL: Museums Archives and Libraries Wales and a great deal of information about developments and services in this sector can be found through the Welsh Government website (*www.wales.gov.uk*).

Academic libraries

Most Higher Education and Further Education libraries and learning resources centres in Wales will offer suitable bibliographic and electronic services for students wanting sources relating to social history and community history. At University of Wales Trinity Saint David (*www.tsd.ac.uk*) a long established MA Local History programme is available focussing on South West Wales since 1800 . It gives students the opportunity to develop research skills and techniques and to undertake detailed analysis of primary sources.

Research libraries

Reference has already been made in Chapter 19 to the unique collections available at the South Wales Miners' Library at Swansea University. Another example of a notable research library is St Deiniol's Library at Hawarden (*www.st-deiniols.com*), northern Wales, established by William Ewart Gladstone in 1889 and one of the most spectacular residential libraries in the UK with its unique collections of materials relating to Victorian Studies and Theology.

County Record Offices

For many community and family historians their local record office will be just as important as their local public library for it is the duty of record offices to collect, store safely and make available for potential users all manner of records which form the administrative and social history of a particular area. Many of the records discussed in Chapter 9 will be found in county record offices and their branches. For further details on local authority archive services in Wales consult the Archives Wales website (*www.archiveswalews.org.uk*) where you will find answers to questions such as Where can I find Archives? How do I use Archives? and special sections on Archives for Family History, Archives for Local History, etc. There are also a list of useful links which provide information on collections held by many other establishments apart from local authorities.

Special and private archives
Very often a great deal of materials of value and significance to community historians will be found in private collections such as those of local companies and businesses, architects and lawyers, estate agents and societies of various kinds. Many such materials might eventually end up in official public record offices but there is always a danger that they might be lost forever. In almost every community, therefore, there will be important archival materials in private hands. By checking the website of Communal Archives Wales (*www.ourwales.org.uk*) it is possible to locate collections of materials in private possession that have been digitised and interpreted by community groups.

Archaeological trusts
There are four regional Archaeological Trusts in Wales namely, Clwyd-Powys (*www.cpat.org.uk*), Glamorgan-Gwent (*www.ggat.org.uk*), Dyfed (*www.cambria.org.uk*), and Gwynedd (*www.heneb.co.uk*), and each have extensive databases of important information that could be of enormous value to community historians. For example, the Glamorgan-Gwent Archaelogical Trust holds 'about 25,000 records of archaeological and historical interest' and one of the main aims of this trust 'is to advance the education of the public in archaeology'.

County and local museums
The last decades of the twentieth century saw a considerable growth in the number of museums in Wales at both county and more local levels. A comprehensive list of such museums will be found on the website of The Federation of Museums and Galleries in Wales (*www.welshmuseumsfederation.org*).

These museums will often vary in terms of their size, holdings, and range of services but will invariably hold materials of interest to those investigating their community history. Ceredigion Museum at Aberystwyth (*www.ceredigion.gov.uk*) has an extensive collection of photographs, illustrations, and documents in addition to a wide range of artefacts, as expected at such an establishment.

Local history societies
As a result of the explosion in local studies during the last few decades it is no wonder that there has been a proliferation also in the number of local history societies that have been established. For example, there are some twenty-five civic societies in Wales which aim to protect and preserve the architectural heritage of their respective towns and areas and it is worth consulting their website (*www.civicsocieties.org.uk*). Similarly there are a large number of village societies whose aim is to safeguard the history and heritage of their communities with most of these having developed websites.

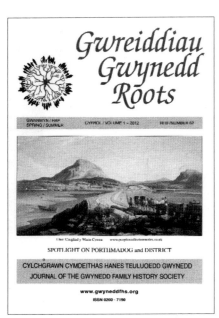

Gwreiddiau Gwynedd Roots

GWANWYN / HAF SPRING / SUMMER   CYFROL / VOLUME 1 – 2012   RHIF/NUMBER 62

I low Cnghiad y Waie Cymru   www.peopleacollectommmce.co.uk
SPOTLIGHT ON PORTHMADOG and DISTRICT

CYLCHGRAWN CYMDEITHAS HANES TEULUOEDD GWYNEDD
JOURNAL OF THE GWYNEDD FAMILY HISTORY SOCIETY

www.gwyneddfhs.org
ISSN 0260 - 7190

Gwynedd Roots: Journal of the Gwynedd Family History Society

Family history societies
Since the beginning of the 1980s there has been a substantial growth in the number of family history societies established in the UK and the same phenomenon is true in Wales. A comprehensive list of such societies will be found on the website of the Federation of Family History Societies (FFHS) (*ffhs.org.uk*), where information and news is updated regularly. Equally valuable is the website of the Association of Family History Societies of Wales (*www.fhswales.info*). The voluntary work undertaken by members of these societies in collecting and recording relevant data and creating databases of different types of sources has been invaluable.

Using online services

Nowadays, no community or family historian can ignore the increasing amount of data and information that is available electronically and since family and community history are often inextricably linked no researcher can fail to benefit from using resources available on the internet. Indeed, as Peter H. Reid claims in *The Digital Age and Local Studies* (2003, 142): 'E-genealogy has proved to be one of the enduring success stories of the Internet' since it is possible to transmit and disseminate information globally in a matter of minutes. Essential and comprehensive guidance to this fundamentally important topic is given in Peter Christian's *The Genealogist's Internet* (5th edn, 2012).

Similarly, in the sphere of community history, greater use is being made than ever before of electronic and digital technologies to gather, store and disseminate information of a local nature and some pioneering work has been undertaken in Wales. The Powys Digital History Project (*www.history.powys.org.uk*), instigated at the end of the 1990s, was highly innovative and involved gathering the local history of 'six communities in the large mid-Wales county of Powys' and was created by Powys County Archives with 'the help of the county museum, libraries, and local people' and covers a number of topics or themes which can be investigated in considerable detail. Another highly successful project was Knowing Ardudwy (*www.adnabodardudwy.org*) which was funded by the Heritage Lottery Fund and sponsored by the Merioneth Historical and Record Society with the support of four major partners: The Royal Commission on the Ancient and Historical Monuments of Wales, Gwynedd Archaeological Trust, The National Trust and Gwynedd Council. The aim of the project was to raise the awareness of present-day Ardudwy residents, and indeed people world-wide, of the immense richness of the archaeological, historical and cultural heritage of the area. One of the most notable features of the website are the sections which allow users to see various maps of the area including tithe maps, OS maps and 3D landscape maps and to use them interactively to demonstrate how the history of Ardudwy has developed over the centuries. It is an extremely valuable website for users of all ages from primary school children to older users interested in topics such as field and place names.

There are also by now excellent examples, throughout Wales, of community websites, that are based on much smaller geographical

Plwyf Llangynfelyn

Hanes plwyf

Codnodir y safle hwn hanes un plwy, sef Llangynfelyn yng Ngheredigion, drwy drawsgrifiadau dogfennau hanesyddol, gwreiddiol. Cynigir mynediad hawdd ac am ddim i wybodaeth am yr ardal neulltiol hwn, ac mae'n gwasanaethu hefyd fel enghraifft o'r ystod eang o ffynhonnau sydd ar gael mewn ardaloedd eraill. Gobeithio gall y safle fod yn fodel o'r fath wefan hanes lleol sy'n bosibl.

Mae'r safle'n un mawr, dros 400 tudalen, felly sawl dull llywio sydd. Gallwch ddefnyddio'r dewislen tynnu-lawr isod, neu fynd at fap llawn y safle. Hefyd, mae rhestr o eitemau yn nhrefn amseryddol. I ddechrau, beth am edrych ar ein arweiniad byr i'r plwyf a'n dewis o uchafbwyntiau'r safle.

Llywio'r safle: ewch i.....

Mae'r adran hanes a dogfennau yn cynnwys copïau o amrywiaeth eang o gofnodion, cyhoeddwyd a heb eu cyhoeddi, yn gynnwys:

♦ Cyfrifiadau
♦ Cofrestrau'r plwyf
♦ Cofnodion y capeli
♦ Cofnodion y Degwm
♦ Mapiau'r plwyf a'r sir
♦ Lluniau hen a chyfoesol

Gobeithio bydd y wefan o ddiddordeb ac yn ddefnyddiol i chi. Gallwch rhoi eich sylwadau am y safle ar ein llyfr ymwelwyr.

Cylchlythyr: Ychwanegir defnydd newydd i'r safle yn aml; pe hoffech chi'n cael gwybod pan ddigwydda newidiadau, cysylltwch â ni, os gwelwch yn dda.

Gwerthfawrogi'r ymwelwyr Ynglŷn â'r awduron Diolchiadau Nodiadau technegol Cysylltu â ni Hawlfraint

A parish history

This site records the history of a single parish, Llangynfelyn, in mid-Wales, through transcripts of original historical documents. It gives free and easy access to information about this particular area, but also serves as an example of the wide range of sources that are generally available for other areas. Hopefully the site can be a model of the sort of local history website that is possible.

The site is a large one, over 400 pages, so there are several ways to get around. You can navigate with the pull-down menu (below), or go to the full site map. There is also a list of items in chronological order. To start with, try looking at the brief guide to the parish and our selection of highlights of the site.

Site navigation: go to.....

The history and documents section contains copies of a wide range of published and unpublished records, including the following:

♦ Census records
♦ Parish registers
♦ Chapel records
♦ Tithe Records
♦ Maps of the parish and county
♦ Old and contemporary photographs

We hope you find the site interesting and useful. Please tell us what you think about it in our visitors book.

Newsletter: new material is added to the site quite frequently; if you would like to be notified of updates as and when they happen, please contact us

Information for visitors About the authors Thanks Technical notes Contact us Copyright

Newyddiadau diweddaraf:
Latest changes
22 Mawrth/March 2009

Google
Chwilio – Search

Cors Fochno

Ads by Google Family History Records Genealogy Family Pictures Surname History

[Brig y dudalen/Top of page][Hawlfraint/Copyright]

Cwestiynau? Sylwadau? Beth ydych chi'n meddwl am y tudalen hwn a gweddill y wefan? Dywedwch wrth y llyfr ymwelwyr:
Questions? Comments? What do you think about this page and the rest of the site? Tell us in the guest book.

Home page of the website Llangynfelyn Parish, Ceredigion

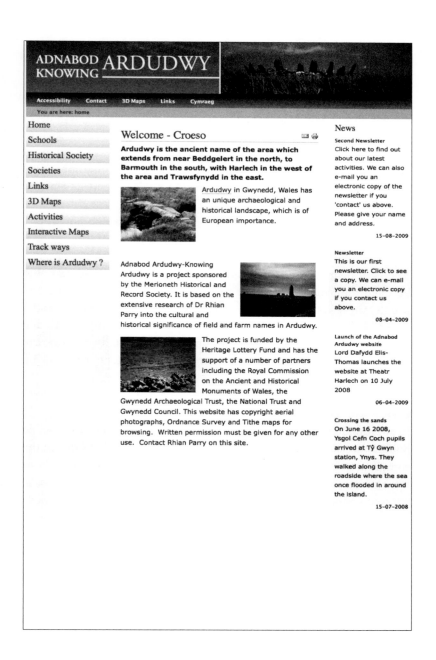

Home page of the website Adnabod/Knowing Ardudwy

areas than Powys or Ardudwy, usually based on a single village or parish. One such example is the website produced for the parish of Llangynfelyn in north Ceredigion (*www.llangynfelyn.org*). It consists of over 4000 pages and in addition to detailed current information on the parish it contains a 'history and documents' section where users can view 'a wide range of published and unpublished records' such as census records, parish registers, chapel records, tithe records, maps of the parish and county and old and contemporary photographs. This entirely bilingual site is extremely easy to navigate and its content regularly revised and updated.

Another good example of a bilingual website which contains a wealth of information is that for the small community of Rhiw in Llŷn (*www.rhiw.com*). This website 'is totally self-funded, and is run by a couple of people who are passionate about the village and its Celtic heritage' and consists of major sections on the village, Rhiw history, people, the sea, natural history, Llŷn pages, myths and legends and a 'guest book' section, which offers users the opportunity to provide feedback. Although concentrating on small geographical areas the presence of these websites and their valuable contents can now be disseminated globally.

Other sources
In addition to the main categories of sources already noted that can be publicly accessed there are also countless other sources of value to the community historian, materials which are often in the custody of establishments and private individuals, but where no public access is allowed or likely to be allowed. Amongst such sources will be those created over the years by some media organisations for radio and television programmes. Therefore, no community historian will be entirely sure that he or she has managed to locate and seen every source of interest and value – although obviously that would be the ideal.

NOTES ON THE CONTRIBUTORS

Beryl Evans

Brought up in the village of Ffair Rhos, Ceredigion, she was awarded the MA Degree in Local History at Trinity College, Carmarthen. She was appointed to her first post at the National Library of Wales in 1985 and since then has specialised in the field of family history and local history. The author of several articles on family history over the years to numerous publications, she has also contributed to television and radio programmes on the subject. At present she is the Research Services Manager at the National Library of Wales.

David W. Howell

Brought up in Stepaside, Pembrokeshire, he was educated at the University College of Wales, Aberystwyth (UCW), and the London School of Economics. He was appointed as lecturer in the Department of History, University College, Swansea in 1970, and Professor before his retirement in 2004. He is vice-president of the Pembrokeshire Historical Society. His publications deal with rural life in Wales from the eighteenth-century onwards, and include *Land and People in Nineteenth-century Wales* (1978); *Patriarchs and Parasites: The Gentry of South-West Wales in the Eighteenth-Century* (1986); *The Rural Poor in Eighteenth-Century Wales* (2000) and *Taking Stock, The Centenary History of the Royal Welsh Agricultural Show* (2003).

Evan L. James

Brought up in the Llandysul area, he was educated at the UCW, Aberystwyth. He was a lecturer at the Chelsea College and at the University of London. In 1969 he was appointed as lecturer in the Extra-Mural Department, UCW, Aberystwyth, and taught courses on local history until his retirement in 1993. With his wife Dr. M. Auronwy James he recorded and indexed graveyard inscriptions in Ceredigion, and their work has been printed in nineteen volumes. These volumes are available at the National Library of Wales, the Ceredigion Archives and the Ceredigion Library, Aberystwyth.

John Gwynfor Jones
Born in the Conwy valley and educated at the University College, Cardiff, where he lectured on Welsh History in the Department of History and Welsh History. He was promoted in 1997 to a Personal Chair, and retired in 2004. He has published a number of volumes and periodical articles on the early-modern period in both Welsh and English, especially on law and administration, the culture of the gentry and the Protestant Reformation. His publications include *The history of the Gwydir family and memoirs: Sir John Wynn* (editor) (1989); *Concepts of order and gentility in Wales, 1540-1640* (1992); *Early modern Wales, c.1525–1640* (c.1994) and *Law, order and government in Caernarvonshire, 1558–1640* (1996).

Tegwyn Jones
Brought up in Pen-y-bont Rhydybeddau, north Ceredigion, and educated at Trefeurig Primary School, Ardwyn Grammar School and the UCW, Aberystwyth. He is a former member of staff of the University of Wales Dictionary. He has published volumes on ballads and ballad composers, a volume on *Tribannau Morgannwg* and anthologies of folk poetry. His publications also include a study of Lewis Morris of Anglesey and most recently *Bro a Bywyd Hywel Teifi* (2013). He has also written numerous books for children.

Rheinallt Llwyd (Co-editor)
A native of Maengwynedd, he spent most of his childhood in Dolwyddelan and Taicynhaeaf (near Dolgellau). Educated at UCW, Aberystwyth and the College of Librarianship Wales (CLW). Worked for Ceredigion Library before joining CLW staff (later Department of Information Studies, Aberystwyth University) until his retirement in 2006. Has published numerous articles, in Welsh and English, on aspects of publishing and the book trade in Wales and edited *Llanrhystud-Llanddeiniol* (2004) and *Bro a Bywyd Islwyn Ffowc Elis* (2007).

Gerald Morgan
Brought up in Brighton and educated at Cambridge and Oxford Universities. He has been a teacher and historian. Until 1989 he was teacher, and then headteacher, at schools in Mold, Cardigan, Llangefni

and Aberystwyth. A second career saw him teaching Welsh and local history in the Extra-Mural Department of the University of Wales, Aberystwyth. He has published books and articles on a wide range of subjects such as *A Welsh House and its Family: the Vaughans of Trawsgoed* (1997), *Ceredigion: a Wealth of History* (2005), *Ceredigion Coast Path* (2008), *Castles in Wales* (2008), *A Brief History of Wales* (2008).

Richard Morgan

Brought up in Wrexham, he was educated at the UCW, Aberystwyth. He recently retired from his post as a professional archivist at the Glamorgan Archives, and previously worked with the Shropshire Archives Service (1980–84) and Powys Archives (1984-1992). He has contributed numerous academic articles and reviews to county and national historical journals, and is the author of volumes on place-names in the historic counties of Radnorshire, Brecknock, Montgomeryshire and Monmouthshire. He was the co-editor with Hywel Wyn Owen of the volume *Dictionary of the place-names of Wales* (2007).

D. Huw Owen (Co-editor)

Brought up in Cross Hands, Carmarthenshire, he was educated at the UCW Aberystwyth. A professional archivist, he was Keeper of Pictures and Maps at the National Library of Wales until his retirement in 2001. He had previously lectured at the College of Librarianship Wales and the University College, Cardiff. He contributed entries on Wales to *The Oxford Companion to Family and Local History*, ed. David Hey (1996, 2008); and other publications include *Settlement and Society in Wales* (editor and contributor) (1989); *The Gwendraeth Valley and Llanelli* (1989); *Early Printed Maps of Wales* (1996) and *The Chapels of Wales* (2012).

Helen Palmer

A native of Portsmouth, she was educated at London University (UCL), St David's University, Lampeter and UCW, Aberystwyth. Currently she is Ceredigion County Archivist. She became archivist at Aberystwyth in 1996 after previously working for Dyfed Archives, Gloucestershire Record Office and the Founders' Library, Lampeter. She has published extensively in local and family history journals such as *Ceredigion: Journal of the Ceredigion Historical Society*, and lectured on Archive Administration at Aberystwyth University.

Glyn Parry

A native of Edern, Llŷn, and educated at the University College of North Wales, Bangor. He was Head of Archival Data at The National Library of Wales until his retirement in 2012 and lectured on archival courses at Aberystwyth University. He has written a number of articles mainly on aspects of law and order and criminals in Wales and is the author of *A Guide to the Records of Great Sessions in Wales* (1995) and *Launched to Eternity* (2001).

Michael Powell Siddons

Michael Powell Siddons was born in Pontypool where he was later a family doctor. He moved to Brussels to work with the Medical Service of the European Commission. Following his retirement he settled in Merioneth. He now resides in France. He is a former Wales Herald Extraordinary and was awarded a D. Litt honorary degree (University of Wales) in 1997. He is a member of the London Antiquarian Society and the Académie Internationale d'Héraldique. His publications include *The Development of Welsh Heraldry* (4 vols. 1991–2006); *Visitations by the Heralds in Wales* (1996); *Welsh Pedigree Rolls* (1996); and the chapter 'Heraldry' in *History of Merioneth*, 11, *The Middle Ages* (2001).

Richard Suggett

Educated at Penarth Grammar School and the Universities of Durham and Oxford, he joined the staff of the Royal Commission on the Ancient and Historical Monuments of Wales in 1984 and is currently their Senior Historic Buildings Investigator. He is an Honorary Fellow of the Centre for Advanced Welsh and Celtic Studies; amongst his many publications are *John Nash: Architect in Wales* (2005), *Houses and History in the March of Wales: Radnorshire 1400–1800* (2005), *A History of Witchcraft and Magic in Wales* (2008) and *Introducing Houses of the Welsh Countryside* (2010).

William Troughton

Born and brought up in Aberystwyth, he was educated at the University of Newcastle-upon-Tyne. At present he is the Visual Image Librarian at the National Library of Wales, where he has been employed since 1992. His duties include caring for the National Collection of Welsh Photographs comprising 300,000 photographs housed at the National Library. The history of Aberystwyth, and especially its rich maritime history, represent his main interests outside his work commitments, and his publications include *Aberystwyth Harbour, an illustrated history* (1997); *Aberystwyth Voices* (2000); and *Ceredigion Shipwrecks* (2006).

Further Reading

Since most chapters in this volume have detailed references to sources, this brief bibliography lists those volumes regarded as essential background reading for family and community historians in Wales.

Gwen Awbery, *Tracing Family History in Wales: how to read the inscriptions on Welsh gravestones* (2010)

Nick Barratt, *Who Do You Think You Are? Encyclopedia of Genealogy* (2008)

John Chapman, *A Guide to Parliamentary Enclosures in Wales* (1992)

John Davies, *A History of Wales* (2007)

John Davies, *The Making of Wales* (2009)

Robert Davies, *The Tithe Maps of Wales: a Guide to the Tithe Maps in the National Library of Wales* (1997)

Hywel Francis and Dai Smith, *The Fed: A History of the South Wales Miners in the Twentieth Century* (2004)

David Hey (ed.), *The Oxford Companion to Family and Local History* (1996, 2008)

David Hey, *Journeys in Family History* (2004)

Dafydd Ifans, *Nonconformist Registers of Wales* (1994)

Geraint H. Jenkins, *A Concise History of Wales* (2007)

J. Geraint Jenkins, *Life and Traditions in Rural Wales* (2009)

Simon Jenkins, *Wales: Churches, Houses, Castles* (2008)

R. Merfyn Jones, *The North Wales Quarrymen, 1874–1922* (1981)

Thomas Lloyd, *The Lost Houses of Wales* (1986)

D. Huw Owen (ed.), *Settlement and Society in Wales* (1989)

D. Huw Owen, *Early Printed Maps of Wales* (1996)

D. Huw Owen, *The Chapels of Wales* (2012)

Hywel Wyn Owen & Richard Morgan, *Dictionary of the Place-names of Wales* (2008)

Glyn Parry, *A Guide to the Records of the Great Sessions in Wales* (1995)

John and Sheila Rowlands (eds.), *Welsh Family History: a Guide to Research* (1998)

John and Sheila Rowlands (eds.), *Second Stages in Researching Welsh Ancestry* (1999)

John and Sheila Rowlands, *The Surnames of Wales* (2013)

Peter Smith, *Houses of the Welsh Countryside* (1988)

The Welsh Academy Encyclopaedia of Wales (2008)

Peter Wakelin and Ralph A.Griffiths (eds.), *Hidden Histories: Discovering the Heritage of Wales* (2008)

C. J. Williams and J. Watts-Williams, *Parish Registers of Wales* (2000)

Index

TRACING FAMILY HISTORY IN WALES

HOW TO
READ THE
INSCRIPTIONS
ON WELSH
GRAVESTONES

GWEN
AWBERY

*Tracing Family History in Wales:
how to read the inscriptions
on Welsh gravestones*

by Gwen Awbery

www.carreg-gwalch.com